KIDNAPPED

The Abduction of
the Bongo Mission
Medical Staff
IN ANGOLA

VICTORIA DUARTE

Pacific Press®
Publishing Association
Nampa, Idaho | www.pacificpress.com

Cover design by Gerald Lee Monks
Cover design resources from iStockphoto.com | camelt (Angolan Flag Symbol)
    iStockphoto.com | DezignerAkhmeed (Soldier)
Inside design by Aaron Troia

The author assumes full responsibility for the accuracy of all facts and quotations as cited in this book.

Unless otherwise indicated, all Scripture quotations are taken from the New King James Version®. Copyright © 1982 by Thomas Nelson. Used by permission. All rights reserved.

Scripture quotations marked NIV are from THE HOLY BIBLE, NEW INTERNATIONAL VERSION®. Copyright © 1973, 1978, 1984, 2011 by Biblica, Inc.® Used by permission. All rights reserved worldwide.

Additional copies of this book are available for purchase by calling toll-free 1-800-765-6955 or by visiting AdventistBookCenter.com.

ISBN 978-0-8163-6732-0

January 2021

Contents

Chapter 1   Welcome and Farewell   5

Chapter 2   All Roads Lead to Angola   14

Chapter 3   Daily Life in Bongo   22

Chapter 4   "Put on Your Good Shoes"   31

Chapter 5   The Long March   43

Chapter 6   Through the Valley of the Shadow   49

Chapter 7   Rice and Beans, Sand and Rocks   67

Chapter 8   A Hospital in the Jungle, a Prison, and a Soccer Field   80

Chapter 9   Is It Far to Canaan's Land?   94

Chapter 10   The Jungle Is on Fire!   112

Chapter 11   Seventy People on a Truck   120

Chapter 12   Another Camp and Another Friend   137

Chapter 13   Love and War   146

Chapter 14   "The President Wants to See You"   156

Chapter 15   We Learn to Make Buns   165

Chapter 16   "Guantanamera"   173

Chapter 17   "We Were Like Those Who Dream"   190

Chapter 18   Life Goes On   205

Chapter 19   How to Be a Missionary   212

Epilogue   219

CHAPTER 1

Welcome and Farewell

It had been a day of intense activity at the Adventist mission hospital in Bongo, in southern Angola, and I was exhausted. After completing my final rounds at the hospital and leaving orders for the Angolan nurses who would be on night duty, I was finally able to go home and get some rest.

Making myself comfortable, I began working on a program for Mother's Day that we had postponed until June 13. A drama about a modern prodigal, it was well adapted for presentation by our talented African youth from the nearby seminary.

I heard a soft noise. Was that someone knocking? I opened the door; the person who had been leaning against the door shoved his way in abruptly. Recognizing a young man from the seminary who was making signs for me to be quiet, I stifled a scream.

I quickly closed the door behind him and asked in a whisper what was going on.

"Government soldiers!" he replied, with fear in his eyes. "They are coming with authorization to take all of us and force us into military service. We will have to hide until they're gone. Some of my friends have already run off into the forest; others are hiding in that abandoned house at the end of the property. Two friends and I want to hide in the empty house next door." I had the keys to the house beside mine, so I let them in through the back door, urging them to keep quiet.

The next day brought news of the capture of sixty young men in a nearby village. Among them was a student from our seminary. After a very brief training, they would be sent to the front. This raid was a hard blow for the seminary, which had to suspend classes until the threat had passed.

The officers were convinced that the young men must be hiding some-place nearby, but they were not authorized to enter private homes, so they stationed guards at strategic places around the mission to catch any who appeared.

I had to figure out a way to provide food for my young friends without being seen by the guards. At times, I would communicate with them through a series of taps on the wall. Then, after dark, they would slip over to my house, where we could eat together and exchange a few words of encouragement. I was the only one who knew about their hiding place. After a time, the soldiers must have suspected something because one of them was assigned to stand directly in front of my house.

At times, it seemed I was an actor in a police movie. Early in the morning, after taking care of my friends by the back door, I would put on my uniform and go striding out the front door with an air of great tranquility, passing right by the soldier, who would look at me with obvious suspicion. I would greet him in a friendly way and go on to the hospital, praying to God that my neighbors would not make too much noise. They peeked nervously through the curtains, admiring my courage.

The soldiers remained at the seminary for a week. We were afraid the young male nurses might also be taken. Every morning, the first thing I asked when I arrived at the hospital was whether they were all still there.

The scenes of Sabbath, April 1, were still fresh in my memory. One of our helpers brought the startling news that fourteen of our employees had been loaded onto a military truck and taken to an unknown destination.

Immediately, Dr. Sabaté went to the police to see whether he could get some sort of information. "We are at war, and these actions have a political cause" was the only explanation.

We were all deeply concerned. The mission seemed lifeless as we struggled to work under a heavy cloud of great fear and foreboding. Overwhelmed with stress, I decided to shut myself in the little library, where I wept and prayed.

Hoping to pressure the authorities, we closed the hospital and only took care of emergencies while Dr. Sabaté worked to negotiate the freedom of our employees.

Shortly after that, rumors began circulating about the prisoners. They were accused of collaborating with the government's opposition party, UNITA (The National Union for the Total Independence of Angola). It was clear that our situation could quickly become extremely dangerous.

Nevertheless, four days later, the employees were released as unexpectedly as they had been arrested. The news of their release spread rapidly, and when the truck brought them back, more than five hundred people from nearby villages came to welcome them with songs and African dances.

As June 7 dawned, the mission prepared to receive Pastor Ronaldo Oliveira, who would be arriving at any moment with his family. They were from Brazil and would live in a little house next to mine, which was very good news for me. Alexander Justino, the director of the seminary, made a special effort, with the help of the young women students, to prepare the house for its new occupants. But we wondered what the pastor would say when he learned he would not be able to teach classes because all the students were in hiding.

That morning, it was my turn to present a devotional thought to the hospital staff and patients, and I wondered how I would be able to do it. In their faces, I saw fear, suffering, and anxiety. There were young women who did not know where their husbands were and mothers whose sons had disappeared. There were the wounded. There were widows and widowers whose spouses were victims of the conflict.

What could I say to them? What did I know of the depth of their anguish?

I opened my Bible to Psalm 23. After reading it, I was able to say, "The Lord is, indeed, our Shepherd, but He has not promised that we will not suffer. As long as we live in this world, we must be prepared to deal with the consequences of evil. At times, we will even walk through the valley of the shadow of death, but we need not fear the evil things that may happen because the Lord is right there with us. He is at our side." Even as I spoke those words, I wondered whether I truly believed them.

After the morning devotions, we began our normal activities for the day.

I was especially worried about two cases: two newborn infants, children of malnourished mothers, who were struggling to survive in our old incubator. That obsolete electric box represented, in many cases, the only hope for babies. We often used bags filled with warm water to help it maintain the right temperature for the infants.

The supply of nutritional concentrate had also run out, but people continued to bring us children with severe kwashiorkor, the devastating illness caused by protein deficiency. We often saw patients with diarrhea, dermatitis, and dementia, the symptoms of pellagra caused by the lack of vitamin B3 in their diet. We began testing a new mixture of eggs and milk, to which we added vitamins. We saved the lives of some of the children, but in spite of all our efforts, we still lost many.

That fateful week, five babies died from nutritional deficiencies. We were distraught. Nevertheless, that same week, five more babies were brought in who were in the same condition.

On June 9 at three o'clock in the afternoon, the Oliveira family arrived.

We welcomed them as best we could. Since no students were present, we decided to hold a reception for them in the local church on Sabbath.

After the evening meal, I agreed to meet Rosmarie Oliveira in the morning. She planned to come to my house and prepare breakfast for her thirteen-month-old baby. When we stopped at the Oliveiras' house, we noticed that there were neither blinds nor curtains on the windows. I ran to the hospital and brought some sheets to improvise some drapes. As we sewed them together, I told them a little about the war, trying not to frighten them too much.

The Oliveiras were tired and wanted to rest. But as we were saying good night, we realized that there was no key to lock their door. Knowing that this could be dangerous, we searched diligently but could not find it. I couldn't understand how it had happened. How could a bunch of keys suddenly disappear? Finally, we decided to reverse the lock so that it could be opened only from inside. The makeshift solution seemed to work.

I said good night to the family and went back to the hospital for a final night round. Then I headed home, where I laid out provisions for the baby's breakfast. After a shower, I paused for a brief meditation. I was very happy about the arrival of the Oliveiras. Having new neighbors from the same continent was special for me. But I still felt the need for a single nursing colleague like myself—someone with whom I could talk and exchange experiences. Five months earlier, we had been told that a Portuguese nurse who was living in Germany would be coming, but since that time, we had heard no more. There was nothing to do but continue to wait. In the face of the apparent lack of answer to my prayers, I prayed once again, "Lord, send the help that I need."

It was close to midnight when, at last, I was able to retire and get some rest. As I drifted off to sleep, I recalled that the following day, June 10, would be a day of special celebration for the armed forces. A few minutes later, I fell into a deep sleep.

Suddenly, I woke up, startled. An intense exchange of gunfire could be heard coming from the direction of the military station. The full moon was spreading such brightness over the night scene that I thought it must be about six o'clock in the morning and that the soldiers were probably getting an early start on the celebration of their special day. But the boom of heavy artillery and the sound of automatic weapons and grenades soon convinced me otherwise.

I jumped out of bed and looked at the clock. "It can't be true!" I told myself, seeing the hands pointing to 1:36 A.M. Still not believing my eyes, I looked for the clock on my radio. It also said 1:36 A.M. My terror was overwhelming as I realized the war had now come to us in full force.

I have never known such fear. I began to shake uncontrollably as I stood before the window, "Lord, help us!" I cried. "We are in terrible danger. Please, take care of us: the Sabaté family, the Oliveiras who have just come. All of us who live here."

In my heart, I reproached myself for not having been more specific with the Oliveiras, for not having told them more about our situation. They needed to know that under no circumstance must they leave their house to try to get away. I wanted to run to them and tell them, but I thought that they would be greatly frightened by my sudden arrival if they were sleeping. Furthermore, I was afraid to go out with such a firefight going on. I stood at the window praying intensely but with my eyes open to see what was happening outside.

Suddenly a group of soldiers appeared at the entrance to the hospital. They pounded violently on the door. I could see the nurse allowing them to enter. *They must have some wounded*, I thought. *I should go and help.*

I imagined our current patients, so vulnerable and defenseless in the face of an attack. How frightened they must be. I thought it likely that they would try to run and hide. I wanted to go and reassure them, but I remained in front of the window, not knowing what to do.

Still shaking, I began to knock on the wall to communicate with the young people in the adjoining house. Someone responded, and I felt a bit more at ease.

I turned to look again out the window. In the hospital, something strange was happening. The frantic movements were not like those of the soldiers we knew. Furthermore, they began carrying out large bundles of things tied up in sheets, evidently loaded with hospital supplies.

Then I had a clear understanding of what was happening. *These are not the government soldiers we know; this is the opposition, the guerrilla army, UNITA, and they will come to take me.*

For a year and a half, I had been afraid, thinking of the day "they" would come for me. In my mind, I often organized my flight and thought about where I would hide. Nevertheless, now only one uninterrupted prayer came from my lips. "Lord, what should I do? What will I do and say? When they come, show me what to do, please!"

Suddenly I saw a group of soldiers running toward my house from opposite where I heard the sounds of shooting. "Here they come," I said under my breath.

As quickly as possible, I pulled the jeans I had worn the previous day over my pajamas and turned again toward the window. "Lord, show me what to do, please! Please, Lord, help me! I don't know what to do." At no time did I think of attempting to get away.

As the running soldiers turned the corner, I lost sight of them. Seconds later, I heard the thunder of heavy boots, then violent blows on a door, but it was not mine. I could see no one through the window. I ran to the back door. Nothing! Unable to understand where the pounding was coming from, I ran from window to window like a caged animal, overwhelmed by panic. It all seemed like a terrifying nightmare. That horrible shooting seemed endless. It did not occur to me that they might take anyone other than me. I never thought they could be pounding on the door of the Oliveiras.

I was beginning to calm down when I again heard voices. And then I saw them, this time, at my own door. "The time has come," I said to myself, "and there is nothing I can do."

An amazing calm overtook me. Suddenly I stopped trembling as if a mysterious hand had taken away my fear. I knew then what I had to do. *I will remain calm and try to delay them. And to discover their purpose*, I thought.

I believe the Lord allowed me to be fully awake and prepare myself mentally for the arrival of the guerrillas at my door. I had feared them so much that if they had found me sleeping, the shock would have been very hard to take.

"Nurse, get up! Nurse, get up!" they repeated.

"I am already up," I answered. "Who are you?"

But their loud pounding kept them from hearing me.

"Nurse, nurse, get up!"

"Here I am. What do you want?"

One of them heard me and came to the window. "We are messengers from UNITA, and we have come to look for you. We have a very important message for you. Open the door."

The word *UNITA* was terrifying. "A message for me?"

The soldier who spoke had in his hand a paper with a photo of his president on which could be read in large black letters the word *UNITA*.

"Yes, our president wants to talk with you, and he has sent us to take you."

"Who is your president?" I asked, trying desperately to win time.

"President Savimbi. Don't you know him? He wants to talk with you. Open the door. We are going to help you get your things ready. We will take everything you need for the journey."

"But I don't want to go with you. The mission and the patients here need me."

"No, you have to come with us. We have much better work for you."

"But I don't want to go and work for you. I want to stay here in this hospital. What will you do to me if I go?"

"Nothing. We're not going to hurt you. The president wants to talk with you. He has a car and a plane that are waiting to take you to your home."

"But I don't want to go to my home. The mission needs me."

I was surprised that the soldiers did not seem irritated by my unending questions and negative answers. I desperately wondered whether to open the door. If I went with them, what would happen to me?

They seemed like strange, shadowy figures. I could see that some wore reddish wigs. Others had their hair braided in a way that is done only by African women.

"Why do I have to go with you?"

"We are ambassadors of UNITA. It is important that you open the door. We have a message for you. Hurry up!"

I noticed they were carrying some things that belonged to the Sabatés. One had a large red flashlight that Ferrán would use when the old generator went out. Another had a curtain from the baby's room tied around his head. They had gotten into the Sabatés' house!

In a final effort to find a way out, I stammered, "I can't leave the mission without the doctor knowing."

"The doctor?" the one who seemed to be in charge asked ironically. "He left two hours ago, and so have your friends, the Brazilians."

"And what about the baby?" I asked, in great fear.

"Our men are carrying the baby. Don't worry, nurse. We are taking care of all the details."

At that instant, I understood, with great anguish, that all hope was lost. I had no choice but to go with them. My friends would need me.

Impatiently they demanded again that I open the door and renewed their pounding on it with a rifle butt.

"What are you going to do to me?" I asked fearfully.

"Nothing, don't worry! Just open the door!"

I went to the window again. In my helplessness, I told them I was a child of God, and if they did anything to me, they would have to answer to Him. Laughing, one of them replied, "We already know that. Don't worry; we are not going to hurt you." I tried to believe these men were not as bad as I had imagined them since they could laugh that way.

By now, it was two o'clock in the morning. I went over to the door and unbolted it. In an instant, the house was filled with soldiers. The leader came to me with a UNITA pamphlet showing a photograph of their guerrilla leader, General Jonas Savimbi.

"We are from UNITA, and you need to understand that . . ."

"Yes, yes, I already know that," I interrupted, "you don't need to explain anything."

Surprised by my apparent calm, the men looked at me, not knowing exactly what to say. The captives taken by UNITA usually reacted with hysteria and tears. Those who were able would attempt to flee. I thank God that at that moment, He gave me calm and, especially, self-control.

I began to observe the soldiers more closely. The leader of the group seemed friendly, but his face reflected a bitter coldness. As time went by, I discovered that these men could be simple and kind, yet at times very hard and pitiless.

"You have to pack your suitcase," said the group leader. "We are going to help you. Then you will come with us to see our president, who has a message for you. Now get dressed!" he ordered, opening my wardrobe.

"I'm ready," I replied, remembering I had put my jeans on over my pajamas.

They picked up my suitcases, laid them open on the bed, and began to empty everything from my closet into them. Why were they tearing apart my room if we were only going on a short trip? I was still in denial about the reality of what was happening.

"Listen," I insisted, "so many things! That's not necessary."

"Yes, it is; you will need them. Now just calm down. With UNITA, you won't lose a thing. We will give everything back to you when we get there."

I turned to see that a soldier was trying to reach a little box where I kept my desk supplies. I ordered him to leave them there, and he put it back in place. It irritated me to see what they were doing, and I ran behind them, telling them, "No, I will not need this. We don't have to pack that." I assumed that whatever the circumstances were, I would soon be back.

Henda, the leader, picked up my windbreaker and handed it to me. "Put this on," he said. "It's cold outside."

I obeyed and began to put on my jacket, going through the motions like an automaton. "Put on some good shoes," I heard Henda say.

Now I was watching transfixed as the men were attempting to pack up even the room decorations and personal keepsakes, things that were very precious to me. I wanted somehow to control what they were doing. Without thinking, I began taking objects from their hands and putting them back. It all seemed like some kind of horrible dream from which I would wake up at any moment.

My Bibles, one in Spanish, one in French, and another in Portuguese, were still on the nightstand. Henda asked me if I wanted to take them. I agreed, and he added them to the suitcase. He pointed to some watches and took them too. I would never see any of them again.

The soldiers continued tearing my house apart. They emptied the drawers. What the bags could not contain, they threw on the bed. They made up large bulky packs tied in sheets and carried them off. I discovered later that they had even taken my hot water bottle with the water still in it! My clothes hamper served for hauling off other things.

The soldiers in the kitchen were making everything disappear, even the food I had prepared for Rosmarie and her baby. Resignedly, I handed them a package of spaghetti, a bag with about ten pounds of rice, the beans, and other food items that were in the pantry. I picked up a freshly baked loaf of bread and handed it to them, innocently assuming this food would be for us.

The soldiers continued to work steadily until everything that could be carried off had been packed and loaded on the heads of the men who were going on ahead of us.

As my captors were carrying the last things out of my house, I saw Pastor Justino on the porch. He was watching, horrified. When our eyes met, he exclaimed, "Sister Victoria!" Terrible anguish was reflected on his face and in his voice. We looked at each other for a moment in silence.

During the previous months, the capture of civilians by the guerrillas had become the order of the day. Pastor Justino and I had spoken many times about this possibility, and I would usually say, as a chill ran over my body, "If something like that were to happen to me, I just couldn't survive. I would die of fright." And he would answer, "Don't worry. Here on campus, you'll be safe." He felt that with the men's dormitory so close to my house, the guerrillas wouldn't attempt anything. Now in his eyes, I read the question: *How are you feeling?* But I had no way to answer.

It still seemed impossible to imagine that what was happening was real and that it meant saying goodbye to the mission. "This can't be true; it can't really be happening!" I told myself again and again. There was so much suffering and need everywhere, and we were doing our best to help. How could they take us away? For years I had been preparing myself for service. From childhood, my dream had been to serve as a missionary nurse.

CHAPTER 2

All Roads Lead to Angola

I was born in the jungle-covered province of Misiones in Argentina, the seventh in a family of nine children. Our childhood was not simple or easy. My father was the eldest son of one of the first Christian families in the region, but when he was a young man, he abandoned the ways of the Lord and his faith in Him. Little by little, his behavior changed, and he became violent and aggressive. For our safety, when I was four years old, my mother left him. Not long afterward, our younger brother, who was nine months old, died of congenital heart disease. When that happened, we were living alone with our mother, and all of us were sick because of a flu epidemic. Our mother had been struggling day and night to feed and take care of us, but now she, too, was taken down with the illness.

The members of the Adventist church where we lived in Aristóbulo del Valle learned about our plight. They opened their hearts and cared for us until we all recovered. This witness of unselfish love won the heart of my mother, Rosa Duarte. She soon requested baptism, and all of us began attending church. We children started attending the Adventist school.

Once in a while, my father would visit us. Each time, we could see that his health was getting worse. My mother taught us to pray every day for him. When we were still very young, we had to leave the house and earn money to help our mother a little.

When I recall that time in my life, I am still overwhelmed with feelings of sadness. I was only seven years old when I had to leave home. I was so lonely! I missed the almost wild freedom to which I had been accustomed. I missed our mother and the noisy chatter of my brothers and sisters. Aware of how hard it was for me, my mother attempted to arrange for me to return to our humble home on some weekends.

When I was twelve years old, we learned that our father had died. We

14

were all very sad. I remember crying a lot, and I wondered why God had not answered our prayers for him. For a time, I struggled with doubt.

About that time, my sister went to study at the Juan Bautista Alberdi Adventist school, where she worked to pay for her secondary studies. I wanted to enroll under the same plan but was not accepted because I was too small. I looked very thin and weak from frequent childhood diseases. They did not think I was capable of working in a dormitory. But my goal was to become a teacher or a nurse and serve the Lord.

To help facilitate our opportunities for education, my mother moved us close to the school. My older brother obtained work as a builder at the school, and I worked afternoons in a teacher's home. We struggled hard to pay our tuition, but my mother was determined that we should all be educated so that we could have a better life than she had. God blessed us, and after many trials and miracles, I was finally able to graduate in 1971 and receive my secondary diploma.

From childhood, I had dreamed of being a missionary. The mission stories we had heard in church made a big impact on my mind. I enthusiastically read reports of physicians, teachers, and nurses on the Amazon and other faraway places on earth. It was thrilling to imagine myself among them. So when I finished my secondary studies, I enrolled in nursing school at the River Plate Sanitarium located in Puíggari, more than 800 miles from my birthplace.

I had no money to pay for my studies or for textbooks and other school supplies. But if a person was really poor and could pass the entrance exams with good grades, there was a possibility of obtaining a scholarship. There I saw my chance. That was the beginning of what would turn out to be a true adventure of faith.

The story of the long journey that took me from Misiones to Puíggari in those old trains would take up a whole separate chapter.

I finally arrived at ten o'clock at night on a Tuesday. A few pesos and one suitcase of belongings made up my entire capital to take care of myself for the next three years. I could only trust God to pay for my studies, and He did not abandon me.

After two weeks of preparation, we took exams in mathematics, biology, physics, and chemistry. I prayed that God would help me because mathematics and chemistry were never my best subjects. Thankfully, my test scores were good, and I received the full scholarship—a half scholarship would have been nearly useless because I had no way to pay the rest of the tuition.

I began my first year as a student nurse with great enthusiasm but also with great concern. I now had the scholarship, but I had no way to cover the expense for books or school supplies. At the end of three months, I had come to the end of my financial resources.

One Friday afternoon, I felt especially discouraged: My only pair of shoes was falling apart. I owed money to all my classmates. I knew that unless something happened, I would have to drop out. I would gladly have worked, but my time was filled with classwork, and I was too timid to ask for help. Alone in my room, I knelt before our heavenly Father. "Oh Lord," I prayed, "unless you do a miracle, I will have to drop out. I need work. If You help me, I will work for You. I need someone to offer me a job, but I am not brave enough to ask for it."

I continued praying this way all weekend.

On Sunday morning, even before I was out of bed, someone knocked on my door and handed me a package from my mother. In it were two pairs of shoes! How did she know what I needed?

A few minutes later, there was another knock. This time it was Dr. Tabuenca, the hospital administrator. He handed me a letter from his sister Violeta. In the envelope was money and a card that read, "Dear Victoria, I hope you're not upset because I don't write more, but you know I don't have much time. I am sending you a little money. I hope it will be useful. Violeta de Positino."

Mrs. Positino had been my advisor and one of my teachers during my last year of study in Misiones. Her wise counsel and encouragement had been a great help as I prepared to study in the school of nursing. Now, with the care and concern of a mother, she was drawing from her own limited resources to help me. I was so blessed! I received her assistance many times during the next three years. The 500 pesos (about 150 dollars) she sent me that Sunday would last a long time because I knew how to economize, but the next day, God had still another surprise for me

Monday, I began the week with a heart overflowing with joy. In the hallway, I happened to cross paths with Professor Schmidt, the biology teacher. He said he wanted to talk to me after class. I was a little worried and wondered if I had done something wrong. Because I was somewhat hyperactive, it was hard for me to be quiet and behave in the dormitory.

After class, I waited nervously for Professor Schmidt. To my surprise, he asked if I would like to work in his laboratory for two hours every evening for two weeks while one of his employees was on vacation. Deeply grateful, I praised God for answering my prayer so quickly, and I accepted the work with great enthusiasm. That temporary work turned into a steady job for the rest of my nursing program.

I slept very little during that period of my life because I had to study and work long hours. When school vacations came and the other students went home to see their families, I continued working in the lab, in physical therapy, in the hospital laundry, or doing whatever work I could find to cover my expenses.

On one occasion, I urgently needed to buy a uniform for my nursing preparation. I had begun to work not long before that, but I had not saved much money. Again, I turned to the Lord in prayer. The days passed, and my concern grew. Then, one week before the day that I needed the uniform, I met with the hospital chaplain, Pastor Mauricio Bruno, who had been my Bible teacher in the academy. He knew my circumstances were not easy. "Victoria," he said, handing me an envelope, "you know, I frequently receive donations from my patients. I thought perhaps you could use this money."

I couldn't believe it! It was twice the amount I needed to buy the uniform! Once again, I could see the hand of God guiding me in a wonderful way and answering my prayers. Whenever I recall these incidents, a feeling of deep gratitude surges in my heart for those good people God used to help me in the times of my great need. I cannot comment on them all by name, but many gave generously, and others offered me the warmth of their homes. I am sure God has prepared a special place for them in His kingdom.

These experiences caused the conviction to grow in my heart that I had been called to serve as a missionary, no matter what the impediments.

At the conclusion of my studies, I was invited to work as a nurse at the River Plate Adventist Sanitarium. I would have preferred a call to the mission field, but I had promised the Lord I would work wherever He led, so I accepted. I stayed on for four years. During that time, I received valuable technical experience and moral strength, which would prove very useful later.

My older sister had married a young man from Switzerland and gone with him to live in his native land. Alone, not knowing the language, and far from her friends, she often felt overwhelmed with homesickness. "I wish you would come to visit us. That way, you could get acquainted with a different culture and maybe learn the language," she wrote to me one day.

At first, I didn't take it seriously, but over time, I began to think that her proposal was really interesting.

Although it was hard to say goodbye to friends and family during such difficult times in Argentina, I left for Switzerland on February 2, 1979.

After taking a three-month intensive course to learn German, I began working at a state hospital near Zurich. Oh! How I cried during my time there! I was far from my native land, but I was also far from my childhood objective of always working for the Lord's cause.

A year later, having repaid the money I owed my brother-in-law, I decided to look for work in an Adventist hospital in Europe or Africa. Then, if that proved unsuccessful, I would return to Argentina.

At church the next Sabbath, I met Pastor Heinz Vogel, the Ministerial director in the Euro-Africa Division of the Seventh-day Adventist Church. Encouraged by a friend who knew my plans, I introduced myself to him and asked him about the possibility of finding a place for me in a mission field in his division. He advised me to write and offer my services. I did, and three days later, I had an answer. The division invited me to Bern for a personal conversation with the people responsible for this field.

When I arrived in Bern, I was ushered into the offices of the division Health director, Dr. Stöger. With his characteristic kindness and enthusiasm, he greeted me, saying, "You have been sent by God!" Taken aback, I asked why. "We urgently need a nurse in Angola. Would you be willing to go?" I had no idea what Angola was like or even where it was located, but of course, I was willing.

Dr. Stöger told me a little about Angola. He said a communist government was in power and a civil war was going on. But I was so excited that I paid little attention to his words and was not greatly concerned.

I soon learned it wasn't easy to get a visa to travel to that turbulent country. While I waited, I got everything ready. Our dear church pastor helped me prepare my belongings for shipment. All my things were packed and labeled "Adventist Mission, Bongo, Angola." However, my wait continued. A full year went by, and I was still working in Switzerland. My hope of being able to serve in Angola was almost gone.

The time came for me to take my vacation, and I decided to go to Argentina to visit my family. While there, I received a phone call. The Euro-Africa Division secretary asked if I would be willing to go to Chad since it seemed impossible to get a visa for Angola.

Just before I left on vacation, I had heard some terrible things about Chad. This made the decision to accept the invitation one of the most difficult I ever had to make. Furthermore, they gave me only two hours to decide! I wept while I asked God what I should do. I felt confused, and I was sad for Angola. Suddenly a thought came to mind: *you promised to go wherever you were called.* When the division called back, I told them I was willing to go to Chad.

A few days later, I returned to Switzerland, where Dr. Stöger met me with the news, "You don't need to go to Chad, Victoria. We will send you to Cameroon." We laughed about the rapidly changing plans, but I accepted.

First, I went to Brussels to study French. I had just begun the course there when I received the news that, unexpectedly, my visa for Angola had finally been approved. With considerable hesitation, the doctor asked me if I was still willing to work in that country. I couldn't believe it! Yes! Of course, I was! I had been preparing for that for a whole year! All my baggage was still marked with the address of the Bongo Mission.

I remained in Brussels for another two weeks to finish the French course. Then I returned to Switzerland to finalize my preparation. Now it was definite; I was heading for Africa.

On February 11, 1981, I boarded the plane that would take me to Lisbon, Portugal, where I picked up my visa. Then I had to wait a week for the next flight available to Luanda, the capital of Angola. During the wait, I read an article about the situation in Angola. There was a map showing the line of demarcation between the areas controlled by the two warring parties, UNITA and the MPLA (People's Movement for the Liberation of Angola). I could clearly see that the dividing line went through Huambo, the capital of the province in which the mission headquarters was located. It was frightening, but my enthusiasm was so great that I soon forgot about my concern.

My flight arrived seven hours late in Luanda, where Pastor Vasco Cubenda, an Angolan pastor, was waiting for me. It was quite an adventure finding one another in the evening shadows of the little airport. On every side, I could see the results of five years of war. Soldiers were sleeping on the ground, stretched out on benches, and walking the street. It was about four o'clock in the morning when I was finally able to get some rest in a beautiful hotel by the sea.

The next day, we stayed in Luanda to wait for Dr. Stöger, who arrived twenty-four hours later. He joined us so he could visit Angola. We flew to Huambo, where I was documented by the authorities, and in the afternoon, we, at last, went on to Bongo.

The province of Huambo is located in west-central Angola, a mountainous region with a pleasant climate. The journey to Bongo was a delight to the eyes as hills and mountain chains passed before our eyes. Atop some of the hills, we saw enormous rocks with strange shapes, standing like watchmen in the midst of the extraordinary, green, and sunbathed scenery.

The paved highway wound its way between little villages leading us toward the mission. After some thirty-five miles, we turned off the main highway to take a secondary road four miles directly into the mission. Pointing to the valley in front of us, Dr. Sabaté said, "There is our mission."

A beautiful landscape spread out before our eyes that reminded me of Switzerland with its forests and mountains. One of the peaks was even shaped somewhat like the Matterhorn, except that it was smaller and all green. As we traveled, we talked about Angola's political problems, and I soon understood that I had come to a very dangerous place.

When we came over the last hill before arriving at the hospital, I saw what looked like a military encampment with an enormous number of trucks parked along the edge of the road. Dr. Sabaté explained that the government army had set up camp there because just a few kilometers beyond the other side of the valley were enemy bases. In other words, our mission was right in the middle—directly between the two opposing forces.

The doctor assured us, however, that there had never been any problems because both sides respected the mission. This calmed my fears a little, but then he told me about an evangelical nurse who had been captured and forced to march to the border of South Africa, where she had finally been freed. At that point, I felt as if fear was beginning to close my throat. If they kidnapped an evangelical nurse, what would stop them from doing the same to me?

We arrived, and the warm welcome helped me forget my fears. The Angolan mission station director came immediately and told me that everyone wanted to welcome me. I quickly went to change my clothes, but before I could finish putting on my shoes, all the mission personnel were at the window, singing vigorously.

Overwhelmed by emotion, I thanked them with all my heart for such a kind gesture. The mission workers expressed their admiration for the courage I had shown in coming to their country to help them. They promised their help and support for every need.

On Sabbath, I was introduced to the local church and was greeted, one by one, by all who were present. I was happy for the privilege of helping these people. Dr. Sabaté read Isaiah 52:7,

> "How beautiful upon the mountains
> Are the feet of him who brings good news,
> Who proclaims peace,
> Who brings glad tidings of good things,
> Who proclaims salvation,
> Who says to Zion,
> 'Your God reigns!' "

And, paraphrasing the text, he added, "How beautiful are the hands that bring good news!"

Then I read Psalm 90:17: "And let the beauty of the LORD our God be upon us, and establish the work of our hands for us; yes, establish the work of our hands."

Those words became my daily prayer. And there was, indeed, much to do and few hands to do it. On Sunday, I made my first visit to the hospital. The Angolan nurses met me at the door, and, as I entered, they began, in their beautiful voices, to sing the hymn "God Will Take Care of You."

That hymn was to become exceedingly meaningful in my life as the first clouds of danger began to gather over our mission.

CHAPTER 3

Daily Life in Bongo

Our daily round of activities at the mission was greatly restricted due to the presence of government soldiers on our campus. They had taken over several of our houses, and there was nothing we could do about it. They were a constant presence. At any time or place, we might meet them wandering around with their weapons slung over their shoulders.

The promise of God's care that the nurses communicated to me with their songs on that first Sunday in Bongo helped me deal with a vague but ever-present sensation of fear. I tried to hold firmly to the promise that surely God *would* take care of me, whatever the circumstances. In fact, all of us who lived there put all our trust in those divine promises because no one could doubt the seriousness of the situation in which we were living.

The work was intense. There were so much misery and suffering! In addition to treating tropical and other diseases, we constantly cared for people wounded in the war.

The guerrillas had taken to burying antipersonnel mines that frequently exploded with disastrous results. It was common for civilians returning from their fields to step on them and lose their lives or be terribly maimed. Even those who managed to get to the hospital often died because we had no means of giving them transfusions.

One afternoon the army brought in a young soldier with a bullet wound to the head. He lived seven days before he died—probably from cerebral edema due to the foreign body lodged there. He was fully conscious until the last minute, but we could do nothing to save his life because we did not have the necessary instruments or medicines. His death was especially hard for me. The boy had his whole life ahead of him, and with proper supplies, it would have been easy to save him.

Some of the saddest cases were the children who would come in with hepatitis, typhoid, malaria, or malnutrition. It was not uncommon for one of them to be admitted in the afternoon, and in the morning, I would find the little bed empty. When I asked about the child, the answer would simply be, "Oh, he died." This apparent indifference was almost more than I could bear.

The lack of supplies was an ongoing problem. It took an enormous amount of time for donated medicines to reach us. The little that did arrive was hoarded and administered judiciously. It was not hard to understand why the people of Bongo had adopted a fatalistic attitude. It was a means of distancing themselves from the pain. The war had been underway five years, and since its beginning, they had been living in constant danger. Our Angolan hospital workers did not escape the effects of this reality. It was not easy to motivate them to complete surrender and dedication in service for the Master.

A month after arriving, I felt that I had nearly exhausted my reserves of courage and peace of mind. We had admitted several patients with acute abdominal infections due to intestinal perforation. Typhoid fever was rampant. We performed many surgeries, but for most of the patients, we were already too late. Often, I would spend hours at a bedside, struggling to save a patient's life. But in the end, I was forced to accept the fact that, in spite of my best efforts, the person was likely to die anyway. We simply did not have the resources to save them.

Overwhelmed by anguish and a deep sense of helplessness, I would sometimes go off by myself to cry bitterly. I could not accept so much suffering and death. It hurt me to see those young soldiers die. I was not prepared for the injustice and immorality of war. It took me a long time to admit that I was not God but merely an instrument in His hands. I recognized that the war was not His will but the result of evil and the selfishness of Godless people. As I shifted my focus, I became increasingly aware of the many miracles that the Lord was doing every day. He was working through our hands despite the overwhelming odds against us. I determined to let Him lead, and I placed my burdens on His shoulders that are so much stronger than mine.

Knowing that any day might be the last for us in Bongo, we made it a priority to open a nursing school to train our Angolan staff. The government had nationalized other hospitals, and we were afraid that the time would come when it would happen to us. The fact that we were right in the line of fire gave us a faint hope that we might be able to keep our campus. Nevertheless, both parties in the conflict claimed the area as their own, and we knew they could take it over and force us to leave at any time. Furthermore, we had heard stories of people who were kidnapped or who had disappeared. It was clear that we could also become victims at any moment.

Three months after my arrival, Dr. Sabaté began preparations for his furlough in Spain. The Euro-Africa Division had difficulty finding a replacement, but finally, a Swiss surgeon, Dr. Vergeres, accepted the call to work for two months in Angola. He arrived on a Friday, three days before the departure of the Sabatés.

That weekend there was a general meeting of the Adventist churches in the Bongo area. Nothing like it had happened for a long time, so there was great excitement. The native Angolans have their own way of organizing the meetings. The podium and seats are made of logs and straw. Each congregation was represented by a choir. For the Africans, singing is as natural as speaking is for us; they have beautiful voices and exceptional musical sense.

I accompanied Dr. Vergeres, and they seated us in a place of honor. The worship service was conducted in the characteristic style, in the open air in a wide grassy area. We didn't understand the local tribal language, but we were moved by the atmosphere of worship and joy.

With an outstanding gift for theater, the Angolans dramatize all kinds of stories or scenes with songs, most of them composed by themselves with no written music or scripts.

The young people led the afternoon meetings. They portrayed the life of an elderly man who was homeless. The beggar came wandering in from one side, singing about his misery with a beautiful tenor voice. From the front, the group of young people responded, inviting him to join them so that they could help him. The clear voice of the man, who was one of the cooks at the mission, blended beautifully with the children's voices. The quality and simplicity of the scene were deeply moving for me. Although many years have passed, I can still hear the melody in my mind.

Seated behind us was Daniel, a young teacher at the seminary. He managed the little print shop and was responsible for translating Portuguese literature into the native language for the many members who did not know any other language. Daniel had studied in Portugal, and he was one of the most promising workers at the mission. With his cheerful and willing spirit, Daniel translated the drama for us.

On Sunday, we attended the meetings only briefly because there was so much work at the hospital. Dr. Vergeres was eager to accomplish as much as possible during his brief time in Angola. Many patients had been waiting for a long time for surgery, and we had to prepare our limited resources and outdated equipment to take care of them.

On Tuesday, eight patients were scheduled for surgery. Before beginning the surgeries, we made rounds in the hospital while Dr. Sabaté made final preparations for his trip. Suddenly he burst into the room and called us urgently. He told us there was a person at the hospital entrance who was seriously wounded by a mine explosion.

"I'll try to operate," Dr. Vergeres hastily replied as he gave orders to clean up the patient as much as possible and prepare for surgery. This would be the first war victim for the new doctor.

A moment later, Dr. Sabaté was back, his face ashen: "It was the print-shop car that ran over the mine," he told us, "and everyone was killed except the young man who was just brought in." Pale and speaking with difficulty, he told us that all the shop employees, including Daniel, had been thrown into the air by the explosive device.

We ran outside, where a great number of local people had gathered and were wailing in their grief. Some soldiers who had witnessed the explosion from a distance were bringing in the remains of our friends. Just as we arrived at the scene, they were taking what was left of Daniel out of the jeep. Evidently, he had been sitting over the wheel that ran over the mine. The lower half of his body had been completely obliterated by the force of the explosion. All of the other bodies were in small pieces twisted into grotesque shapes. It was a nightmare. "Oh, God!" I cried. "Can this really be true?" I felt an overwhelming desire to flee from the horrific scene, but God placed His hand on me, and I quickly recovered my composure.

Dr. Sabaté had to leave quickly to catch the only plane to Luanda, leaving me alone to make decisions. Wasting no time, I ordered that the bodies be taken to the morgue and that security guards be placed at the door to keep people from entering.

Just then, I saw Daniel's wife rushing toward the scene. She heard about the accident and wanted to go into the morgue. I ran to meet her and took her in my arms before she could cross the threshold. I thank God I was able to keep her from viewing that ghastly image. She was in her eighth month of pregnancy.

We left the grieving people with their family members and ran back to the operating room, hoping to save the life of the only survivor. But in spite of our best efforts, the young man died a few hours later. His wife, too, was pregnant. Of the six men who lost their lives, three left widows who were expecting babies. One of them was our anesthetist.

A little later, we locked ourselves in the morgue with the doctor, and for two hours, we tried to reconstruct the faces and bodies of those young workers who had died so dreadfully. We finished the day physically and emotionally exhausted, not knowing what to think. How could we cope with the terrible doubts that oppressed our minds?

Those young men, aware of the dangers, had left early for Logonjo, planning to meet a truck bringing paper for the print shop. Since the start of the war, it had been nearly impossible to get the essential materials. Daniel and his team were willing to take the risk of traveling to get it. Their spirit of service had cost them their lives.

The traumatic images of that day haunted me. I would awake from sleep, terrified by nightmares. After the tragedy, our workload increased. That part was a blessing because we had less time to think.

We did surgeries three days a week, from morning until night, without stopping. One of the Angolan nurses administered anesthesia, and another was in charge of patient care. In eighteen days, we operated on ninety patients. We sometimes went nonstop for ten hours. The accumulated need was such that we could have worked twenty-four hours a day, and there would have still been more to do. When emergencies arose while we were in surgery, I had no choice but to leave the doctor alone and run to help the recent arrival. Or I would help one of our students deliver a difficult birth while the doctor got along as best he could. God blessed us in a special way in those days, and many were relieved of their suffering.

After the long hours, we returned to our homes very hungry. Two of us ate enough for four! I had brought some food with me from Europe. In Huambo, there was a store for foreign volunteers to get vegetables, spaghetti, rice, sugar, salt, and half a bar of soap with the ration cards. The mission gardens provided us with other vegetables and tropical fruits that helped improve our menu. We were eating heartily, but the stress and hard work kept me from gaining weight. I weighed only 103 pounds. Dr. Vergeres said that, one of these days, I would be gone with the wind.

One night while I was preparing supper, I was called urgently to the hospital to care for a young man who had just lost both legs due to a land mine. During the surgery, which was prolonged until midnight, the patient had a minimum arterial pressure. Then I noticed that his abdomen was swollen and rigid. I pointed this out to the doctor, and immediately we changed the operating field and opened his abdomen. His intestines were bloated due to an obstruction caused by the explosion, and they bulged out as soon as we made the incision. We relieved the obstruction, but it was extremely difficult to close the abdomen while we struggled to keep the patient alive.

We did not see how the young man could survive, but the next day he was better. He stayed in the hospital for a long time but was finally able to return home. He was only twenty years old and had lost both legs well above his knees. His life would not be easy.

After a month and a half of intense labor, Dr. Vergeres returned to Europe. The Sabaté family was still on furlough. Politically it was a difficult time in the country. And with the hospital full of so many patients recovering from recent operations, it was a daily test of faith to carry the heavy responsibility alone. But I placed my trust in the Lord, and things went well, despite some serious challenges.

Just before the doctor left, an elderly man had come in who needed emergency surgery. At first, the doctor refused to operate because we did not have proper supplies or equipment for the required surgery. Nevertheless, the man's condition was so heart-wrenching, we decided to run the risk. The following day, during the doctor's last visit to the wards, he realized something was wrong with the man, and we rushed him back to the operating room just a few hours before I accompanied Dr. Vergeres to Huambo to catch his plane.

When I returned and arrived at the hospital, I was immediately told that the old man was in trouble. His abdomen was swollen again, and he was vomiting continuously. It was clear that he needed emergency surgery, but what could I do alone? *I will do what I can*, I thought, and I quickly inserted a tube into his stomach. I was not very hopeful because the man's general condition was so critical. I tried to stabilize him the best I could, and then I left him in God's hands.

The next day I was surprised to find him not only alive but improving. I continued draining his stomach and providing intravenous hydration. To my surprise, he recovered completely and, one month later, happily returned to his home. As he was leaving, he came to me and said softly, "I am so happy and grateful that you didn't let me die. Thank you, thank you!"

A week after Dr. Sabaté returned, we were again shaken by tragedy. In an area some miles west of Bongo lived a group of Adventist Christians. Guerrillas often set their ambushes and attacked passersby on the road between their village and our facilities. Due to this danger, no one wanted to visit their congregation. Nevertheless, they came once a year and faithfully brought their offerings. Their feelings of isolation and their great desire for fellowship and encouragement prompted them to organize a weekend of meetings. Pastor Boaventura, his son-in-law Arturo, and Pastor Felipe, a native pastor, felt called to take a message of encouragement to those faithful believers. They left on a Friday to travel there. Friends and colleagues begged them not to go, but after much reflection, they decided to go anyway.

Fifty miles down the road, in a stretch of sharp curves and high cliffs covered with dense vegetation, they were ambushed by the guerrillas. We learned of the ambush from the army, but no one could tell us who, if any, had died or who had been kidnapped.

Sabbath came, and with it, new causes for concern. The army made raids from time to time to capture young men for military service. On these occasions, they drove through the villages in military trucks snatching every man they encountered on the streets. It was rumored they were getting ready to make one of these dramatic raids on our mission. This activity was usually carried out on weekends, so we were on high alert.

Suddenly, in the middle of the worship service, the young men in the congregation jumped up and began to run. Through the open windows, we could see that a green army truck was approaching. Those few who were not able to run remained in the chapel, waiting in silence.

I was extremely tense and nervous. The previous day, I had suffered an emotional crisis due to the bad news. And now we couldn't even worship God in peace.

The soldiers came and took up positions in front of the church. Unable to take the stress any longer, I got up and walked toward the hospital. When I arrived there, I met two courageous nurses from one of the nearby communities. They had come on a motorcycle over the deadly and dangerous road to bring Pastor Felipe to the hospital. He survived the attack, but his arm had been wounded.

The nurses told us that, in the ambush, Pastor Boaventura's son-in-law Arturo had died instantly. Pastor Boaventura, himself, was not hurt but had been kidnapped by the guerrillas. The terrible account affected me greatly. I loved Pastor Boaventura. His kindness and gentle spirit had impressed me since I first met him, and now, I was heartsick, thinking of how he must be suffering at the hands of those jungle warriors.

Fear kept me from sleeping. I would toss and turn, and if I did manage to doze off, I would be awakened by the sound of gunfire or strange noises in the darkness. At the slightest sound or movement, the soldiers would begin firing furiously as if an intense battle was going on. Many nights I slept on the floor under my bed for fear of a stray bullet.

Only 164 feet from my house was a road that came down from the mountain hideout of these guerrillas. By day, government troops used the road, but at night, the rebels would come down under cover of darkness to spy and set mines in the main roads and paths. In the stillness of the night, I could hear footsteps and voices that filled me with dread.

At times, I felt an enormous desire to flee from that place of death and suffering and return to my homeland, where I could live in peace. But then I would remember the multitudes of suffering and sick people, and I couldn't find it in my heart to abandon them. During the day, my fear was overshadowed by the heavy workload, but at night I felt crushed—asphyxiated by fear and anxiety.

During this time, I often prayed for God to give me the strength to continue and that He would free me from the overwhelming psychological pressure.

Shortly after September 1, we received a visit from Erich Amelung, treasurer of the Euro-Africa Division. He brought letters and a package that my sister Mary had sent me from Switzerland. They gave me joy and courage.

Pastor Amelung spoke to me in German as we walked to the place where we were to have lunch with the Angolan workers. I told him about my work, my fear, and the problems. "I want to remain here," I told him that afternoon, "but I urgently need a colleague to share the burden." He detailed the division's efforts to find someone and promised to do his part to make it happen. After talking with him, I felt better. The situation had not really changed, but a great weight lifted off my heart. With renewed energy and courage, I continued to fulfill my responsibilities.

Later that month, we received the news that Dr. Sabaté's wife, Conchita, was expecting a baby at the end of March. That helped me decide to go ahead with plans for a vacation in Switzerland.

The rest and relief from stress were wonderful. I returned cheerfully to Bongo with a large supply of medicine and medical equipment that I had purchased in Europe. I resumed my duties with enthusiasm, although everyone recognized that the political situation was more serious than ever.

News of attacks and kidnappings came in daily. At the mission, however, the atmosphere was strangely calm. The government troops that had been stationed close to our mission had left in September 1981. With their departure, things seemed to be much more peaceful. Shooting in the surrounding area ceased, and mine explosions were less frequent.

Early in 1982, Dr. Sabaté's parents visited Angola to be present for the birth of their grandchild. Dr. Sabaté's mother was an experienced midwife. While she awaited the arrival of her grandson, she helped us in the hospital, and we were very grateful for her assistance. On March 19, 1982, little Ferrán Sabaté Jr. was born. It was a difficult delivery, but soon, both mother and son were doing well.

Two months later, the Sabaté family accompanied the grandparents to Luanda, where they took their return flight to Spain. While alone at the hospital during that time, I admitted a two-year-old boy with a serious infection from gunshot wounds in both legs. While I examined him, his grandmother told me that the boy's family was driving when their car was ambushed, and everyone else was killed or kidnapped, including the child's mother. The boy was found two days later in a patch of tall weeds along the roadside. "At the same spot," she said, "a Red Cross convoy fell into the hands of the guerrillas, and a Swiss nurse named Marie-José was captured."

As I listened to the grandmother, I trembled. *If UNITA didn't respect even a Red Cross nurse, there's no reason to believe they will treat me any differently. At any moment, they will be coming.*

"I will be next," I told the Angolan nurse who was helping me.

The grandmother of the little boy had at one time been a prisoner of UNITA but had managed to escape. She would have been happy to tell me the details of her ordeal, but I preferred not to know. Life was already difficult enough.

We treated the child as best we could, and thankfully, the antibiotic had the desired effect. Two weeks later, he went home. The attack that had taken place just two weeks earlier made it clear that we were in UNITA's crosshairs. We were constantly aware that we were still at the mission only because God's protecting hand was over us. Our trust was in Him alone.

CHAPTER 4

"Put on Your Good Shoes"

The voice of the group leader pulled me out of my thoughts. "Put on your shoes, your good ones," he repeated. "Where are your shoes?"

I found them and handed them to Henda, who stuffed them into a bag while I put on a pair of low-cut shoes.

My greatest fear right then was that the government soldiers might arrive and start shooting at any minute. The guerrillas must have been thinking the same thing because they were shouting at me to hurry. "Quickly! Quickly! We've got to go!"

The leader was standing at my door. He looked at me and asked, "*Menina* [young lady], do you want to take anything else?"

I went back and quickly picked up my Bible, a devotional book, and a hymnal. I went out again and then remembered. "Wait! I want my album!" And I ran back to get it.

I put it in the hands of one of the soldiers, who had a surprised look. Suddenly it occurred to me that the little jar of hand cream on top of my closet might be useful. "Quick! Send a tall man to get that jar."

They seemed surprised by my request and tone of voice, but one of them stood on tiptoe to retrieve it. In the confusion of the moment, I insisted on that hand cream and didn't think of many other items that we would greatly need in the days ahead.

"Come on! Let's go!" the soldiers were shouting. We could still hear the sound of gunfire coming from the direction of the military outpost.

As we left, I saw Paulo Filisberto, the Angolan administrator of the mission. "Are you going too?" I asked him.

"No," he answered in a barely audible voice.

I hugged him and told him goodbye. The men from UNITA surrounded me, forcing me to keep moving.

Suddenly, I realized that I was carrying the keys to the whole hospital. I ran back and tossed them to Paulo, shouting that he should give them to the hospital staff. My mind still refused to accept the idea that I wouldn't return.

We passed by the Oliveiras' house. Their front door was open, and all the lights were on. I noticed that all the homes of the Angolan workers were dark and silent. As we went by the home of one of the youngest teachers at the seminary, he stood in front of his house. I spoke a few words of reassurance, knowing that he could hear what was going on. That young man had lost his parents in a kidnapping similar to what was happening to us right then, and ever since, he suffered from bouts of depression. Thinking of how it might affect him to see us taken, I tried to leave him with a few words of encouragement.

A few steps farther we passed by the hospital. I asked Henda if I could say goodbye to the nurses and patients.

"No," he responded bluntly, "if you do, they'll think you are leaving voluntarily. You are being kidnapped, and they need to know it."

As we went around the hospital, I could see the pharmacy was open and had been ransacked. I asked one of the soldiers about it. "Yes, we did that," he replied proudly.

We continued across the pasture to the edge of the mission property where the woods began. "Now, wait, menina," they ordered. They took down some wires that were stretched between two trees—a sign left by the group that had already passed that way.

Now, I thought, *we are officially prisoners of UNITA*. I began trying to get as much information as possible. I wanted to know what their intentions were. "Why are you doing this to us?" I asked the leader, who was walking close by my side.

"We don't want you working for the minority group from Luanda," he replied in a serious tone.

"We are not working for the government; we are working for the people," I replied.

We discussed this for a while until he decided to change the subject. "This is war," he said, "and we have to pursue our objective, which is to win."

As we made our way up the mountain, I looked back and could see enormous flames leaping into the sky. "Are you burning the mission?" I asked, terrified.

"No, we are burning the EMPA—the House of the People."

The House of the People was a cooperative where the villagers could bring their agricultural products and exchange them for food or clothing.

I thought of Lot and his family leaving Sodom while the city went up in flames behind them.

"Oh, and we also destroyed the police station," they told me proudly.

We walked a few yards farther. Suddenly, a large number of soldiers arose from among the weeds with their weapons aimed at us, ready to shoot. I was frightened and pulled back. Then our captors explained that these were UNITA soldiers who would go ahead of us to check the path we would be traveling. In the dangerous passes, they would set up an ambush and then remove it after we had passed.

The soldiers asked our captors, "How did it go?"

They answered: "Very well—scientific war!"

Angry, I rebuked them: "And you think it's great what you did?"

"Yes! We did everything just right."

"Only her?" asked one, pointing to me.

"No, the others are ahead, and the captain is with them."

"And the baby?" I asked. "Who is taking care of the child?" I wanted to know.

"One of our carriers will take care of the child, and the rest of us will carry all your things."

Then I saw some small boys with ammunition belts across their chests. "What are these little children doing here?" I exclaimed, horrified.

"They have come because they understand very well what we are fighting for."

We advanced at a rapid pace, going over several hills until we were almost to Kaliueke, a village I had often visited.

Beside the path, I saw another boy, even smaller than the previous ones. I touched my walking stick to his head and smiled. At that, one of the soldiers said, "It seems you are in good humor. Aren't you afraid?"

"Do you want me to cry? What good would it do? In a few minutes, you destroyed the patient labor of many years. Crying is not going to change the reality."

"Well, I think you are brave."

I've got to take advantage of this, I thought. I thanked God for giving me control over my emotions. It seemed my attitude had impressed them, and I felt that this might help us on the journey.

We arrived at a stream, and I stopped to look for some stepping stones on which I could cross. Suddenly, a big soldier picked me up and deposited me on the other side, ignoring my startled protests.

The scene was surreal. Light from the moon filtered through the trees and illuminated the soldiers moving silently along like faceless shadows.

We passed an ancient building in which huge trees had grown. We heard strange noises. Someone was hiding nearby and had left a bicycle where we could see it. The soldiers took the bicycle, and we kept walking.

Our walk soon became more difficult because the path had become rocky and wound steeply upward through the jungle. The work clogs I was wearing were too tight, and my feet were starting to hurt. Henda noticed and said, "Didn't I tell you to put on good shoes? You won't be able to walk very far like that. We picked up a good pair of shoes at your house. Why don't you put them on?" He ordered one of his soldiers to look for my bag. After changing into my "good shoes," walking was much easier.

A little later, we noticed a group of guerrillas carrying large white bundles on their heads. Thinking that they must be sheets from the hospital, I went up and touched one of the bundles. I discovered they were rolls of paper from the mission print shop.

"So, you went into the print shop?"

"Yes," they answered proudly, "we did it to cooperate with the revolution."

My thoughts went back to that sad scene a few months earlier when six young men had paid with their lives to bring that precious paper. It was painful to think that the fruits of their sacrifice were being stolen.

I asked whether they had planted the mine that killed those boys.

"Yes," they answered, "but we do not plant mines to hurt civilians. People need to be careful. They shouldn't travel on those roads. After all, we are at war."

His reply moved me to tell him about the enormous number of innocent victims that we treated at the hospital and how most of them died from their wounds. I told him about our six young workers and their wives and children.

"As I said, we can't help that. That's just how war is," he answered.

But you are the ones who cause it, I thought.

After a few minutes of silence, I asked him how far it would be until we reached the camp.

"Oh, it's close. It's not far at all," he assured me.

"How much longer will we be walking?"

"Not much farther, really. We will soon come to a place where there are trucks that will carry us the rest of the way."

We kept talking. I was determined to find out what the UNITA soldiers intended to do with us. I was too worried to feel tired. It seemed they didn't intend to hurt us, but I wanted to find out for sure.

After a while, we came to a place where a large group of UNITA soldiers was waiting for us. I was surprised to see many women among them. Later, I learned that they worked as carriers and cooks. They had also received military training, but they only participated in combat under special circumstances.

The women were carrying large bundles of cloth on their heads. Those also, evidently, had been stolen from the House of the People. With rolls, packages, boxes, and bundles on their heads, they looked like gigantic ants walking in a strange, irregular column.

A soldier covered with ammunition belts came down the trail and said, "The doctor is up ahead, and he wants to know how you are getting along."

"Please tell the doctor I am doing fine, and tell him also not to be discouraged."

It was reassuring to know that I would soon see my friends and to realize they were concerned about me.

We began walking again and about an hour later came to a clearing where I saw the Oliveira and Sabaté families. We embraced. What a relief to see each other again!

"Don't be discouraged," I said to Ferrán. It was a phrase I had often repeated while we were working at Bongo.

"I'm not discouraged," he answered with a tired voice, "but everything is lost." The expression of anguish and sorrow on his face made me want to cry.

I suddenly realized that Rosmarie Oliveira was wearing only a long nightshirt and a light cloth draped over her shoulders. Ronaldo was at her side carrying the baby. I asked if I could help him carry the child.

"No, thank you," he replied, "but could you please help my wife. She is having a very hard time walking."

Rosmarie was wearing rubber boots. She told me that she had awakened to a bedroom full of soldiers. In her shock and terror, she had not thought to put anything on her feet before leaving the house. Later, the soldiers gave her some boots to wear, but it was extremely difficult for her to walk.

I offered her my arm, and we continued walking together.

By this time, it was about five o'clock in the morning. We began to see more clearly what the soldiers were carrying: typewriters, medical supplies, even the scales from Ferrán's office.

It was very painful to watch. Those things represented years of effort, and now we saw all of it lost in a matter of minutes.

I heard Ronaldo trying to talk to one of the soldiers. Imagining his fear, I approached him and told him quietly that he would be OK, that they had no intention of hurting us. The fact that the fighters were speaking kindly to him showed it was true.

Henda, the leader of our group, said to Ronaldo, "Now I will stay with my friend the Brazilian." And he offered to carry the child. But both little André and his father refused.

Henda kept asking about Brazil: he wanted to know what life was like in that country and many other things.

The sun was beginning to rise over the mountains. On our left, we could see a small plain covered with wild banana plants. The leaves were moving gently in the morning breeze. I dropped my eyes to avoid thinking about the beauty of this scene so cruelly contrasted with our uncertain fate.

I turned and could see that Ronaldo was exhausted from carrying his son. Without asking, I took the child and put him on my shoulders. He immediately began to scream and fight desperately. I walked as fast as possible toward the front of the line. I decided to move out front a good distance and then sit down, rest, and wait for the others. The guerrillas were surprised that I could walk with so little difficulty.

After climbing the path to one of the highest elevations in the territory, we came to a cluster of very precarious huts. The thought of sleeping there was disturbing, and I was relieved to see the long column continue past the huts. I gave André back to his father, and we took turns carrying him the rest of the way.

Finally, we stopped in a small village. A group of about a hundred women and half-naked children was standing in a half-circle waiting. The soldiers completed the circle as they came in. The carriers set down their loads in an enormous heap and joined the group.

Nobody seemed concerned about us. We stood huddled against a tree, observing the scene, wondering what would happen. There was a cold breeze, and we were shivering from cold and anxiety. "Now we are in the other Angola," Conchita remarked.

The circle of people began to gather closer. One of the women began singing a slow, melancholy tune and dancing rhythmically. The rest of the group joined in, and a sort of spell took over. Then one of the men went into the center of the circle; it was the commander.

Conchita and I watched intently. We both thought we had seen this man before. His face, his figure, even the way he spoke, seemed familiar to us. Often the members of UNITA dressed as civilians and mixed with the people to gather information. We concluded that he must have been at the mission, and none of us suspected who he was.

He raised his arm and shook his fist, shouting, "Yeh, yeh, yeh!"

The people responded in chorus, "Yeh, yeh, yeh!"

"Comrades, yeh, yeh, yeh!" he shouted again.

He repeated this a number of times while moving from side to side. "Viva [long live] Africa! Viva Angola! Viva UNITA!" The multitude responded with frantic enthusiasm. At last, standing at military attention, he shouted, "Long live President Savimbi—strategist, politician, and soldier!" As a show of support for their president, the people enthusiastically shouted, repeating the commander's words in unison as they continued dancing and singing.

There was no indication that the festivities would end anytime soon, and we were hungry. I looked cautiously in the enormous pile of bundles, hoping to spot the bag in which the soldiers had put the bread they took from my refrigerator. The only things of mine I could find were a blanket and the bag with my shoes. The suitcase with my clothes had also disappeared. I wanted to change clothes because I was still wearing my pajamas under my jeans.

"Don't worry," one of the carriers had said to me, "with UNITA, nothing is ever lost. You will get it all back."

I was happy to see one of the women with the can of baby food that I had prepared for André the day before. I boldly went up and asked her for it, knowing that if I didn't, the child would have nothing to eat in the days ahead.

After a time, the captain came and led us to the center of the base. He showed us two huts in very poor condition, saying, "You can rest here. I'm sorry, but we are guerrillas, and we have nothing better to offer you." Although I was surprised at his courtesy, I couldn't help thinking, *You could have left us alone.*

As I inspected the hut assigned to the Oliveiras and me, I wondered how many fleas and ticks we would pick up. The soldiers kindly brought us a basin with water and soap, but there was still no sign of food.

Exhausted by the stress of the previous night, we went outside and sat in front of the hut. Directly in front of us, sitting on a stone, was a boy about twelve years old. Without expression, he stared at us, holding a rifle that was much too big for him.

We reasoned that he must be a recruit in training. It was hard to imagine such a small child was really assigned as our guard. We were right. A short time later, a young soldier appeared and introduced himself as our guard. He had not been present when we were captured, but he knew every detail of what had happened. He asked me if I knew about the war in the *Malvinas* (Falkland Islands). I told him I did.

"It must be hard on your family," he said. "Your country is at war, and here you are in this situation."

For an instant, I did not know what to say. Surprised at the guard's sympathy, I managed to reply, "Yes, it certainly is difficult. I'm afraid my mother will not be able to bear it. She has been sick recently."

Not long afterward, we received word that our luggage had arrived. The captain and his lieutenants were meeting in a *yango*, a small round hut used for meetings, making plans for the following day. They called me and gave me a plastic bag, in which, they said, were my belongings. My cassette tape recorder was playing familiar music. Henda, who was there as part of the officer group, commented, "You have good music; too bad so many cassettes were left at your house."

I took the bag and went back to our hut. Inside, we found some of Rosmarie's dresses and two blouses of mine. I went back to the yango and said to the captain, "Is this all you are going to give me? There is much more that was taken from my house. I don't see my suitcase anywhere."

"Yes, yes. You will soon receive everything that belongs to you," he answered.

It was at that point that I began to suspect what later proved to be true: the carriers had dumped about half of our things along the way to lighten their loads, and they had kept other things for themselves.

Around noon the next day, they brought what was left of our belongings. They dumped it all in a heap in front of the huts, and we had to dig through everything to find what was ours. Some bags and suitcases were completely empty, and others were only half full. The Oliveiras' suitcases were missing about half their contents. One of my small suitcases only had two skirts, which would be useless to me under these conditions. There was no sign of my underclothes or the bedding they had taken from my room.

I returned to the captain. "Look, most of my clothes are missing, and I don't see my sheets anywhere. I am going to need them tonight."

"Don't worry; they'll show up," he replied.

"If my sheets don't appear, you will have to give me some," I told him angrily.

"Sure, no problem," he said. "We can share. After all, I'm single too."

Pretending not to notice what he had said, I held my tongue, but I resolved to be more careful when speaking to him.

It was a very sad spectacle that lay before us. Everything that had seemed precious to us was strewn over the ground, lying in the dirt. I struggled to hold back my tears. The important thing at that point was to gather the most basic needs for the long walk, although we still had no idea how long it would be.

I began retrieving what I could find, thinking about the importance we assign to material things that we can lose in an instant. Suddenly I spied my camera at the bottom of the heap. It was brand new. I had purchased it in Europe while there on vacation. *I'm not letting them have that*, I thought to myself. I took it and quickly hid it.

The other missionaries also had lost most of their things. Dr. Sabaté had no clothing except what he was wearing. The Oliveras had arrived at the mission so recently that they hadn't fully unpacked their suitcases. More than half of their things were missing, including a new camera. Even so, they were able to rescue more clothes than we were. Fortunately, both families were able to recover enough clothing for their children.

The worst setback was that neither the Sabatés nor the Oliveiras could find any good shoes in all of that heap. They knew it would cause them a lot of trouble in the days ahead.

When we finished looking, we went into our huts and tried to gather our thoughts. We were feeling discouraged and wondered why God had allowed such a terrible thing to happen to us.

"We didn't get to work even a single day," the Oliveiras said sadly.

"We have lost everything that we loved so much," said others.

"Who knows how this is going to end?" Conchita pondered. "In a situation like this, with such tiny children, nobody knows what we're facing. Our situation looks really bleak."

I opened my daily devotional book and looked at the reading for the day—June 10. As I did, my eyes fell on the text for the previous day, Deuteronomy 33:27, "The eternal God is your refuge, and underneath are the everlasting arms. He will drive out your enemies before you" (NIV).

It seemed to me that the text was meant especially for us right then. I read and reread it to the others while tears streamed down my cheeks. The devotional reading for the day also seemed fitting. It was a lesson from Exodus 19:4, "You have seen what I did to the Egyptians, and how I bore you on eagles' wings and brought you to Myself." I was reminded that the same God who in ancient times carried His people on eagles' wings, is watching over us today. Just as the weak eaglet that is apt to fall clings to its mother for strength and protection, even so, the child of God, weak and defenseless in his own strength, trusts in the power and protection of his heavenly Father. He knows that everything that God allows to try him has as its only purpose to lead him closer to Himself and that God is very near to him.

I underlined the last part. God knew all about our situation, and surely, He had allowed it to happen, having as His only objective to draw us closer to Him. We concluded our reflection by reading the text once more, and then we prayed, asking the Lord not to allow our faith to fail.

By this time, it was two o'clock in the afternoon, and we still had not eaten anything. Dr. Sabaté went to the captain and said, "Your guests are ready to eat."

"Yes, yes, you will get something in a few minutes."

I was beginning to doubt all such words, but a few minutes later, two women arrived with clean plates, knives, and forks. They brought pans filled with fried potatoes, meat, and mashed potatoes. We were amazed at the quality of the food and how well it was prepared. As it turned out, our amazement was warranted because it was the only decent meal we would have during our entire captivity.

The captain himself came and ate with us at our hut. I sat on a straw bed behind Rosmarie. From there, I could observe him closely. With a somber expression on his face, he held his plate in his hand and ate silently, never looking up. His uniform was clean and neat. Unlike the other soldiers, he wore a white cap with military insignia. He was a small man with refined manners. In his cold eyes, I saw a dark and inquisitorial look: I could read intelligence and decisiveness but also hatred and cruelty. He avoided direct eye contact. But when he did look my direction, I could not avoid a strange sensation of fear and apprehension.

When he had finished eating, the captain courteously took his leave.

With our energy restored, we looked for a way to get some rest. I spread a large cloth on the straw, and we all lay down. The Oliveiras were especially exhausted because of the long journey from their homeland, followed almost immediately by this terrible experience. Within a few minutes, they were sleeping soundly. But I was losing my sense of serenity and found it impossible to rest.

In the prevailing silence, I understood that my worst fears had come true. We were now prisoners of UNITA. One after another, the events of the past year and a half crossed the stage of my memories. Bitterly grieved that I might never again see our beloved mission station, I began to cry. I made every attempt to stifle my sobs because I didn't want to awaken the Oliveiras or let the soldiers know my weakness.

The afternoon passed, and it began to grow dark. The Oliveiras woke up, and together we built a fire in the hut. The Sabatés joined us to talk and exchange impressions. Ronaldo was curious to know more about UNITA and what they wanted from us. We told him about individuals who had been captured and then released unharmed. He was extremely worried because that afternoon, he had been called twice and interrogated. The soldiers asked him about the position of Brazil with respect to UNITA.

He had attempted to answer as accurately as possible, but he really didn't know much about it.

Speaking as softly as possible, we agreed among ourselves on how to answer when we were interrogated. We knew that our precautions would probably not be enough, but we also knew we must do what we could to prepare. We agreed to firmly insist that as missionaries, we were politically neutral and that our only purpose was to serve others.

We received word that we would be on the trail again as soon as the moon came up. We were to have our luggage ready because we would be ordered to leave at any moment. The Oliveiras lay down again on their cot and went back to sleep while Ferrán returned to his hut with his family. A group of men seated themselves in front of our hut to keep an eye on us.

I tried to make myself comfortable on a camp chair that the guerrillas had brought from the Sabatés' house. The cold night air and the uncomfortable position of the chair, combined with my sadness and anxiety, made it impossible to sleep. A sense of anguish pressed against my chest. I started contemplating our location. We were not far from Longonjo, where the government had a strong military base. What if someone tried to rescue us? I imagined. There would certainly be a firefight. What if it happened in the middle of the night? How would they know where we were sleeping? It would be impossible for us to get away from the crossfire.

The hours passed slowly, and as they did, my anxiety increased. I heard the soldiers who were supposed to be guarding us start to snore. I stood up and silently crept outside. They were all sound asleep on the ground embracing their weapons.

We were at the top of a hill. I could see a path descending and then disappearing into the forest. I knew that if I followed the path, I would soon come to familiar territory. A fleeting idea of attempting an escape crossed my troubled mind. I shook my head as if to chase away the thought. It was clear that my colleagues needed me. I went to the outdoor toilet not far from our hut, and when I came back, I had to step over the guards who were still sleeping peacefully.

A few minutes later, I heard the footsteps of someone walking back and forth near the hut. I heard quiet voices. Fearfully, I wondered what they had in mind.

Apparently, the soldiers had started a fire. They sat down and continued to talk softly. By the flickering firelight, I could see the soldiers' silhouettes. I heard Dr. Sabaté's name mentioned repeatedly. I strained to listen. I heard them laughing softly as they recalled capturing the doctor and how terrified he had been. I continued to listen until someone came and scolded them for making noise. Then silence reigned again with only the sound of soft snoring.

After a while, I again heard whispering. The whispering frightened me more than anything else. Fear again clutched at my throat. It was very dark. If we were attacked, there would be no way to escape. I tried to pray but couldn't concentrate.

Finally, the full moon appeared and slowly began to climb higher in the sky. As the minutes passed, I was troubled, wondering what was happening. Then, unexpectedly, clouds covered the sky, and everything grew dark again. Suddenly, a figure appeared in the doorway and called, "Get up! We have to go."

We jumped up and attempted to dress adequately for the trip. Rosmarie, who had only been able to put on thongs when she was captured, had no proper footwear. The boots they lent her had caused a wound in her right leg that was so painful she could no longer stand to wear them. She put on my lightweight shoes, and we went outside. The Sabatés were putting their baby into his basket. Conchita was able to find some sweatpants, but, like Rosmarie, she had no shoes but her white nursing footwear. As we prepared for the march, we trembled with fear and worry about our uncertain future.

We wondered who would be able to carry the children. The baby was no problem because he was sleeping peacefully in his basket, and he could easily be taken by one of the carriers, but little André wanted to be with his mother. When anyone else attempted to carry him, he screamed loudly. Rosmarie was a tiny, fragile woman. It was clear that she could not carry him too long. After considering several alternatives, Ronaldo took him and tied him to his back, native style. Although André continued to cry, he did seem to accept that option better than the others.

Through the shadows, we saw soldiers falling into line silently and cautiously. It was an eerie scene with many silhouettes moving in the darkness. We wondered where so many men had come from. With a stern look, the captain gave detailed orders in a low voice, and the first group started off.

"Now what's going to happen?" Conchita whispered, worriedly. "What are they going to do to us?"

I didn't answer, but I silently told myself, "Vicky, you don't have children to worry about. It is your duty to keep calm and help the others."

Then we heard the order, "*Twendy*! [Let's go!]" And the column we were in began to move down the mountain through the dark of night.

CHAPTER 5

The Long March

The soldiers placed our group from the mission hospital about midway to the back of the line as we walked single file. The Sabaté family went first. I followed them, and Ronaldo Oliveira and his wife were behind me. The captain and some of his most important associates were behind us. One of them was a young man who asked me about Argentina.

We followed a narrow pathway that passed through the center of the village and down the mountainside. After about half a mile, the descent became extremely steep. We had to go down in the dense darkness, holding on tightly to the branches and roots, feeling carefully with our feet before each step to avoid slipping.

We tried to help one another along. The soldiers walking at our side also assisted us to ensure that no one would stumble and fall. After passing through that difficult stretch, we came to a valley covered with dense vegetation. To avoid following any established paths, the soldiers led us through grass that was over our heads. It kept slapping us in the face as we walked.

Suddenly, a young soldier covered with ammunition belts appeared directly in front of us, pointing his weapon directly at us. I jumped back, feeling like my heart nearly stopped. That scene was repeated many times during our journey. I never understood why the guards, who were supposedly there for our protection, had to suddenly bolt out of the darkness with their rifles aimed at us.

"Look at that man," whispered Ferrán, pointing at the ambusher who was now walking at our side. "He is a typical guerrilla; he is watching us even though it seems he's not."

The guerrilla led us to a stream at a spot where a fallen tree served as a bridge. We crossed it precariously and then continued to descend the hill until we came to an open plain. At that point, the soldiers went into full alert, warning us that we were in serious danger. We advanced as rapidly and silently as possible. The troops were tense and constantly surveyed the horizon.

Dawn found us crossing a high plateau covered by fields of dry grass. Now we could better see how our group was organized. There was a vanguard of armed soldiers. They were followed by the carriers, mostly women. We were next, located in the center of the column. Our guard and the captain marched by our side, watching us closely. The last group was a heavily armed guard of soldiers.

By eight o'clock, we were passing through a valley that ran between two familiar-looking mountains. *This must be the high valley that can be seen from the mission*, I thought. From where we were, we could see the hill that stood in front of the village where our nurse Lucas lived. The view made our hearts ache.

I worked my way forward and asked Conchita, "Do you recognize where we are? The mission is right down there."

"Yes, I know," she answered sadly, "but I don't want to look."

A few weeks earlier, we had visited this same region with Dr. Sabaté's parents and had joined the people there for worship in their little chapel. We never would have believed that we would see the same region under very different circumstances only a few weeks later.

Walking was becoming increasingly difficult because our legs were getting weak and cramping. Conchita had a hard time walking with her sandals, and her feet were now bleeding. We took turns carrying André, although he still cried loudly whenever he wasn't either sleeping or in his mother's arms. We were extremely tired, and our stomachs were twisted and cramped from hunger, but it seemed the soldiers had no intention of stopping.

Just then, Ronaldo saw some sugarcane growing close by the pathway. We cut several stalks and peeled them with our teeth so we could suck on them as we walked. The refreshing sweet juice gave us energy and made us feel better.

Next, it was baby Ferrán who began to cry, so our captors allowed us to stop for Conchita to nurse him.

The previous day, among the heap of things the soldiers had pillaged, I had found an empty saline bottle and filled it with water for the journey. We took advantage of our present stop to drink a small amount of the precious liquid. We had to ration it because we only had about a pint for all of us.

Our conversation turned to speculation. "Who could have thought this would be possible?" "If we had only known it was coming, we could have gone away." Conjectures came and went.

We tried to comfort ourselves with the idea that we were probably captured to protect us from the danger of firefights that were about to happen there. But then, on the other hand, what would happen to the patients, the students, and the personnel who were left behind?

We tried changing the subject. Ronaldo told us about the varieties of sugarcane in his country and suggested that we talk about the favorite foods that each of us would eat when we got back to our homelands. This turned out to be our favorite topic of conversation throughout our captivity because we were always hungry.

We wondered whether news of our disappearance had reached Europe and whether any efforts were being made to save us. We were all certain that someone from the mission staff had immediately called the division office in Switzerland to let them know. (Fortunately, we did not know how wrong we were.)

When the baby had finished nursing, we continued our march. After a while, I put André on my shoulders and walked as rapidly as possible so I could get ahead and take a rest. I made it a good distance and then sat on a rock to rest. As I entertained the child to keep him cheerful, I became concerned because the Oliveiras didn't show up.

After some time, one of the soldiers came and told me, "You need to go back. Your friend from Brazil is sitting beside a stream, crying and saying she can't walk anymore."

"I can't walk anymore either," I replied. "I carried the boy up here, and I can't carry him back. Every time he sees his mother, he cries and only wants to be with her."

"There is no time to cry. She has to get up and walk."

Immediately, I was overwhelmed with guilt, realizing how harsh my reaction was. I felt that there was no alternative but to grit our teeth and go on if we wanted to survive. A long time passed. Finally, the rest of the group caught up to where we were, and we resumed our journey.

At midday, the soldiers ordered a halt in a wooded area to prepare some food. The carriers went and got us some water. It looked pretty dirty so I asked Rosmarie if her family members were vaccinated against typhoid. She told me they weren't, which worried me because I knew it would be very easy to get sick under the circumstances.

On the afternoon of our first day of captivity, Conchita and I had nearly wept when we saw the medicine from our pharmacy carelessly strewn across the ground. Recalling how difficult it was for us to get medicine, it pained us to see it trampled as if it were worthless!

We picked up as much as we could, choosing the things we thought could be useful. There were antibiotics, boxes of chloroquine for malaria, pills for diarrhea, and a few tubes of vitamin C, along with some ointments for wounds. I later found some children's aspirin and also put that into my pocket.

Since the water at our current stop was almost undrinkable, Ferrán put some vitamin C tablets in the jar to make it less dangerous. We wondered what we would have to eat.

Our last meal had been at noon the day before. Our mouths watered as we recalled the delicious potatoes that they had served us. After a little while, a group of soldiers brought us a good quantity of oranges in bags made from their shirts. We ate the oranges eagerly. Then, they came around with the main dish: chicken with *pirão*—a thick mush made of finely ground corn flour. The menu wasn't bad, except for the absence of salt and the fact that there were still some feathers clinging to the partly raw meat! With some difficulty, we were able to get down part of the meal. André could eat almost nothing. We wondered *How much longer will we have to put up with this?*

Noticing the expression on my face, Ferrán said, "Just be thankful that at least we have pirão. In a few days, we might be eating the straw off the sides of the huts."

"Look here," said Conchita, "before we left this morning, a woman gave me this can. She said it's honey."

We lifted the lid, and the sight turned our stomachs. It was a yellowish mash of bees' heads, wings, larvae, and wax. Nauseated, we quickly put the lid back on the can. We lay down under the trees, intending to rest. Above us, we could see the sky through the branches. It was a brilliant blue, and the birds sang in the warm sunshine as they hopped cheerfully from branch to branch. It seemed nature was trying to distract us from our gloomy thoughts.

A bit later, Ferrán got up and opened the honey can again. He took a stick and pushed the mass down so that the honey rose to the surface. He licked the sweetness from the stick and invited us to try it. Before long, we all overcame our revulsion and were eating it with our fingers, tasting the honey and spitting out the leftover mass.

In the meantime, the soldiers talked by radio with their headquarters in the southern part of the country. They told us that their president was interested in knowing how we were. He wanted to know if things were going well for us.

While lying there looking at the sky, I strained to overhear what the soldiers were saying among themselves. I heard them mention my nickname: "Eh, the menina walks very well. She is even able to carry the child!"

One of them came over and asked me, "Are you accustomed to long hikes like this? Did you do this before? How can you walk so well and even carry the little boy?"

Once again, I thought it might be helpful for them to have a positive image of me. I said, "Just wait. We'll see how much more I can stand."

The extensive distances I had to walk as a child had been excellent training. Nevertheless, I'm sure that didn't explain everything. On this pilgrimage, I felt extra energy that I knew did not come from me. I am convinced that God provided an extra measure of strength, enabling me to bear the situation.

We started on our way again, through a hilly area. That afternoon, we came to a knoll where we had a beautiful view of the valley. In front of us, we could see potato plantations in carefully cultivated terraces. It was an amazing scene.

"Those plantations are yours?" we asked.

With pride, a soldier said, "The people who cultivate those fields and the people who live there belong to UNITA."

As we gazed at the scene, we thought that if this was the area where we were heading, we should at least have enough to eat. Unfortunately, it was a vain illusion. At sunset, we reached a stream with clear water splashing down over the rocks. Finally, clean water that we could drink with pleasure! We all drank until we were satisfied.

Just past the stream was a steep mountain. Ferrán carried little André for much of the way. Then I took him as we approached the mountaintop. The climb was so steep at this point that we had to grasp tree branches to avoid slipping. We had gotten a little ahead of the others, so Ferrán stopped to wait for his wife.

With an expression of anguish, little André watched the place where he expected his parents to appear. I sang to him, hoping to take his mind off his troubles. When I sang, he sang along with me, and so we slowly climbed the steep mountain. Finally, the Oliveiras came into sight, coming up with great effort. We reached the top together. But the Sabatés still had not shown up.

It was Friday, and the sun was setting on the horizon, so we decided to sing some hymns. But we were so tired we could hardly make a sound. After a long time, Conchita finally came into view. A few yards away from where we were sitting, she leaned against a tree and began to vomit. She had probably drunk too much water before climbing. The poor woman was exhausted. We were glad that, for today, we had reached our destination.

Once everyone had arrived, we were shown to the place where we were to sleep. The people's living conditions were wretched! Their huts clung precariously to the mountainside, and they lacked even the barest essentials necessary for daily living.

We asked for a pan or basin so we could wash, but they didn't have any. They didn't even have a bowl we could use to give some food to the child. André was crying from hunger. Since we had no other option, we prepared a little bit of the powdered food that we still had and fed him from our hands. Among the things I had rescued from the guerrillas that had looted my house was a small bag of granola. The bag had burst open, and most of the granola was scattered in my larger bag. We gathered what we could to supplement the food for the little one. Seeing him so miserable filled us with sorrow, and we couldn't hold back our tears.

Two soldiers brought us water of doubtful origin. The whitish color and terrible taste made it impossible for us to drink.

The hut assigned to us had two sections. In the smaller area, there was a place for a fire. The Oliveiras and I would sleep in the larger space. There was evidence of previous guests. The place was filthy, and the dirt floor was alive with fleas.

I wrapped a bedsheet around my body and attempted to make myself comfortable in one corner. As I was trying to organize my thoughts, I heard Ronaldo say, "It makes me so sad to hear our little boy crying from hunger and not be able to do anything about it." Anguish flooded my heart and added to my fatigue. In utter discouragement, I felt no desire to pray.

A slight sound made me turn. There, in the flickering light of the fire, I could see an emaciated dog drinking some of our precious supply of water, but I made no attempt to stop him. I never told the others about it. I knew that the next day we would have nothing else to drink, but I simply didn't care.

CHAPTER 6

Through the Valley of the Shadow

Our first Sabbath in captivity arrived. It was June 12. We were eager to rest and have a worship service. The previous day, I had asked our guard, "Could it be that tomorrow you would allow us to rest instead of walk? As you know, we are Adventists, and tomorrow is our day of rest." He didn't reply then, but on Sabbath morning, we were happily surprised that no one came calling us to continue walking.

We gathered in one of the huts to study the Bible, and we prayed fervently. As we were concluding, Ferrán and Conchita were called for interrogation. Almost two hours later, it was the Oliveiras' turn to go. Ronaldo was afraid because he didn't know what they wanted from him.

Conchita told me later what they had asked her. "Where are you from? What are you doing in Angola? Name? Age?" And they asked for other personal information. Her answers were carefully recorded in a notebook. After the questioning, the captain held them over for two hours of political diatribe. The longer he went, the louder he spoke. From my hut, I could hear every word. He went on and on without stopping, and I wondered where he learned to give such a formidable lecture. He talked about the objectives of UNITA and the necessity of fighting the enemy. He also attempted to explain why they had captured us. He claimed that the objective of UNITA was to remove us from the line of fire. They knew that we had no political affiliation. In other words, it was all for our own good, so we would not suffer the consequences of the war.

He attempted to make his argument as strong as possible, but we remained unconvinced. We knew all this had little or nothing to do with the political reason for our capture.

It was almost two o'clock in the afternoon when my turn came. They repeated the same interrogation, but the questioning came to a halt when the captain asked my age:

"And you are still not married?" he asked.

"No, not yet," I replied.

"And how is that? Hasn't any man discovered you?"

"Well, apparently not. At least, not as far as I can tell."

When I said that, I couldn't help laughing aloud, and they laughed with me.

Just then, a soldier came running in, "Have you finished yet?" he asked. "We have to go."

"Yes, yes, we'll be ready in a minute," the captain replied. He turned to me and asked, "What do you think of our politics?"

"Well, you know," I began, weighing each word carefully, "I haven't really thought much about that, because as a nurse in the mission, I am not related to any party. I think you have good intentions. However, I did not come to Angola for political reasons, but only to help the people."

"When you left Europe, didn't you know there was a war going on in Angola?"

"I had heard something about that, but I was really not very well informed."

"All right, well, we have to go now. We can continue our conversation on the way." It was a relief to know I would not have to listen to a third rendition of the same harangue.

Before leaving, they provided some food for us. Rosmarie and Conchita tried to find shoes that would be better for walking. The previous day, the top edge of Rosmarie's boots had worn through the skin on her leg, and she couldn't continue that way.

The soldier gave her a pair of oversize shoes that could have fit Ronaldo. She took a firm stand and said, "I'm not leaving here unless you get me some shoes I can wear." Eventually, one of the soldiers found a smaller pair. They were still three sizes too big, but she stuffed them with paper so she could continue walking without quite so much difficulty. Conchita took the boots and put them on over the pants to protect her legs from the rubbing, allowing her to walk better than she could with the clogs she had brought from her house.

Sitting in a corner, I watched as they organized for the journey. The soldiers ran back and forth, shouting orders for every carrier to take their place and carry as much as possible. They were speaking in Umbundo, so we couldn't understand, but we could see it was no easy task getting everyone organized, and it took almost two hours to get the long column ready to go.

It must have been after four o'clock in the afternoon when, at last, the column slowly began to move again. The heavily armed soldiers led the way. We missionaries followed, closely guarded by the captain and Henda. Directly behind us were the carriers, and last, the rear guard. All together we were about two hundred people.

We made our way down the side of the mountain like an immense undulating serpent trying to find its way. At the foot of the hill was a valley covered with grass that was over our heads. There was no path; we had to make our way along with our arms and elbows, but the grass fought back, resisting our advance and, as we had experienced before, slapping us across the face and the head. Little André suffered the most as the straw beat against his poor little head without mercy.

For hours, we continued up and down the low hills. At nightfall, we came to a halt so that Conchita could nurse her baby. We were all thirsty and on edge. I found my bottle of water and handed it to André. After that, his parents had a drink. Then Ferrán, thinking we had already had some, drank all that was left. He didn't leave a drop.

When I realized what had just happened, I was overcome with rage. "Why did you drink it all? Didn't you think that we might be thirsty too?" I shouted.

"But . . . I thought you already had some," Ferrán replied, surprised.

But I couldn't stop myself. "Didn't you consider that I first shared with the others? Your wife and I have not had a drop!"

Only someone who has been through such an ordeal can imagine how it feels to be so upset over a few ounces of water. I was trembling with fury and could hardly control myself. We hadn't had any water for hours, and we wouldn't have any again until the next day. The enormous physical effort had dramatically increased our thirst. Thank God, I still had a tangerine, which I shared with Conchita.

As we started to walk again, André began to cry at the top of his lungs. We couldn't calm him down. He refused to be with anyone but his mother, but Rosmarie didn't have the strength to carry his weight. Then little Ferrán joined in the chorus, and together they made an awful noise. The captain came running excitedly and said: "The children must not cry right now. We are entering enemy territory. We must keep absolute silence!" Understanding the urgency, Ronaldo put his son in his wife's arms and said, "Take the boy; we'll see how far we can go." As if by a miracle, suddenly both André and Ferrán were silent, and the baby went back to sleep.

By now, it was completely dark, and the vegetation was even thicker and higher. We couldn't see the person walking in front of us. We were afraid someone would stumble and be hurt.

In our attempt to see where we were placing our feet, the Oliveiras and I lost contact with the group, and we couldn't find the path. We didn't know where we were. Rosmarie began shouting, "Wait, wait for us!" But it seemed no one heard us. We knew we were getting farther and farther behind, but we just kept feeling our way along with no idea where we were going.

Fortunately, the captain soon appeared, making his way through the tall grass. "Someone needs to stay with us all the time," we told him. "We can't find our way in this darkness." He promised to keep track of us and repeated, "You must walk in absolute silence. There is a military outpost not far from here, and we have to get past it without being detected." We joined the group again and stayed close.

The full moon appeared over the horizon. Its light filtered through the trees in the thick woods, casting long shadows and making a spooky scene as our shadows moved along silently through the tall grass. Fear kept us on edge and made us alert to every sound. We peered anxiously among the trees, wondering whether the enemy was lying in ambush in the thick vegetation. We imagined them crouching behind every tree with their guns pointing at us, ready to shoot. The guerrillas' heavy footsteps seemed too noisy, the crackle of branches made us jump, and even the normal sounds of nature at night seemed like war cries to our disturbed imaginations. The faces of our guardians were tense and alert, further escalating our fear. It was evident that our situation was extremely serious.

A group of soldiers walked on both sides of us. Suddenly, we halted, alarmed at the sound of footsteps running in our direction. I started to ask what it was when, with great relief, I recognized a detachment of the rear guard moving rapidly toward us through the foliage. In the thick shadows, I could see the captain's serious look as he whispered precise orders. The soldiers at the head of the line moved quickly to the rear.

The hours passed as we attempted to keep up with the steady pace of the soldiers. When Rosmarie could no longer carry her little son, she handed him gently to Ronaldo without stopping. In our hearts, we were all thanking God that the child was sleeping peacefully.

We prayed unceasingly, perhaps more fervently than ever before. I remember raising my eyes to heaven and crying out to God for mercy. I remembered the words of Psalm 91. "For He shall give His angels charge over you . . . lest you dash your foot against a stone."

"Lord, please keep your promise to us now. Our feet must not stumble for any reason," I silently pleaded.

Another text came to mind. "I have been young and now am old, yet I have not seen the righteous forsaken" (Psalm 37:25).

My efforts to recall these and other promises kept me from thinking too much about our danger, bringing me a ray of hope and giving strength to my aching legs. We were all praying silently, "Lord, we know we are not righteous except by Your grace. But right now, we need You desperately. Without You, we can't take another step. We don't understand why we are in this situation, but we are placing our trust in You. We need You. Don't abandon us, please!"

Each of us wrestled with God in our own way, but no one spoke. Even the children were silent as if an angel were closing their mouths. Little Ferrán normally woke up every three hours to nurse. However, he slept peacefully through that whole night without making a sound.

Little by little, we exited the wooded area and were soon walking through fields of corn. Not far in the distance, we could see the village where the government troops were stationed.

The guerrillas kept insisting that we needed to stay silent and walk faster. However, keeping quiet was not easy because the dry corn stalks crackled when we stepped on them. We trembled with both cold and fear.

Dr. Sabaté was having trouble walking. For several hours, he had been feeling nearly unbearable pain in his left knee. In the pocket of my windbreaker, I still had a handful of children's aspirin. He took six of them and felt some relief, but not for long. He started limping again and was moving slower and slower.

The soldiers were impatient. "We must get completely through this area tonight. In daylight, we will be an easy target for the enemy. If there is an attack, you will not be able to get away." They told us angrily, "It won't be a problem for us because we can go through the territory day or night. But you are not prepared. We don't want to face an attack with you here."

I silently wondered, *So why did you kidnap us? No one invited you to do it.*

We tried to tape Ferrán's knee, but it didn't help. The captain ordered his men to carry him. "We cannot afford to keep going so slowly."

The soldiers had brought a hammock because they thought the women probably could not stand the walk. They laid Ferrán on it, and four soldiers carried it on their shoulders.

"Ferrán, I can't believe this! But, I guess, that's how men are," I said, teasing him.

Ronaldo was also having a difficult time walking. Years earlier, he had suffered from inflammation in the bones of his feet. Now, unable to rest them, he was in intense pain.

I heard someone behind me groan pitifully. I turned and saw a young soldier beside the road, a teenager who couldn't have been more than sixteen, bent over with pain. Apparently, he had severe abdominal cramps, making it impossible for him to keep walking. Sadly, no one paid any attention to him. The carriers and soldiers rushed by without hardly a glance, and the poor boy was just being left. I turned back and quickly ran to him. I put two aspirin tablets in his mouth and then hurried back to my place with the others.

Because Ronaldo was limping, barely able to continue, Rosmarie and I took turns carrying their boy. The little fellow was getting heavier and heavier in our tired arms, and, since he was sleeping, we couldn't carry him on our shoulders. Poor Rosmarie! I thought she would faint at any moment. Grasping at any solution, I asked the carriers for some rags and used them to tie him to my shoulder. That way, I was able to hold him close, lightening the load on my arms.

We eventually came to a swampy area with mudholes everywhere. The thick clay stuck to our feet and made walking difficult. We couldn't see the holes or puddles, and before long, our feet were soaking wet. I stepped in a hole and fell. I got up quickly, grateful to God that I hadn't broken a leg.

Soon, we were once again feeling our way through tall, thick grass, trying to keep up with the soldiers. The path narrowed until, suddenly, in the pitch-dark night, we found ourselves at the edge of a wide rushing river. We all looked at one another, wondering how we were going to cross.

"I'm afraid," Conchita whispered.

The guerrillas whispered softly to one another, and then, without any explanation, they began hoisting us up on their backs and marching into the water. From the bank, I watched as Ronaldo clung to a soldier with one hand and to his son with the other, fearing that at any moment, they would both be plunged into the icy water. The scene was like something from a movie: the dark figures moving silently, illuminated by the light of the moon; the broad river; the tall grass; the weapons hanging from the guerrillas' shoulders.

It was a long way across the river, and I could see that the men, with water up to their waists, struggled with their human cargo. When they came for me, I resisted being transported. Instead, I crossed by jumping on little islands formed by the water plants that grow in the river.

It was very cold, and the soldiers were wet, but there was no time to dry. We had to continue as rapidly as possible. Their cold faces reflected their concern.

A new difficulty presented itself: ditches that evidently had been dug to drain the swamp we were crossing. The guerrillas easily jumped over them, but it was not so easy in the dark with children in our arms.

I attempted to jump with little André hanging from my shoulder, but I miscalculated the distance and went in up to my knees in the icy water.

Shivering and miserable, I was jerked away from my gloomy thoughts by a scream. I turned just in time to see Conchita disappear into one of the deep holes. The soldier who was walking just ahead of her turned and, in one swift move, pulled her from the water. Poor Conchita! She traveled the rest of the night soaking wet. It's a miracle that nothing worse happened as a result.

It must have been after midnight when we crested a hill where we could see twinkling lights in the valley below. We could hear dogs barking and music playing.

"What's this?" I whispered to the guard at my side.

"It's the enemy military base."

Terrified, I could see that the front of our long column was getting dangerously close.

"We are going so close," I stammered. "What if the enemy soldiers discover us and there is a firefight?"

"Don't worry. It's the weekend, and they're all drunk," the guard answered.

"What do we have to do if there is an attack?" I asked.

"Don't worry" was the simple answer.

But the sense of dread was almost overwhelming. Cold sweat ran down my back as terrifying visions of peril flashed through my mind one after another. What would we do if there were a firefight? The situation for me was not as complicated because I was alone, but what about the others? And the children? I sent up a silent prayer. *Lord, don't allow these people to notice us, please. You know that a gun battle would be fatal for us.*

Ronaldo was walking slower and slower. The soldiers attempted to hurry him, but he could only reply, "I'm doing the best I can. I can't go any faster."

One guerrilla came up to him and said, "The people of Israel also had to walk fast to reach their destination."

"Yes, but they were considerate, and they adapted to the pace of the women and children," he responded dryly. In spite of my trepidation, I couldn't help but smile when I heard the exchange.

My stomach ached, and I wanted to get out of the area as rapidly as possible.

I estimated that we were marching about two hundred yards from the base. The dogs must have heard us because they barked wildly. We crossed a small stream and then began climbing a hill toward the nearby village, leaving the military camp behind.

As we approached a paved highway, a group of soldiers went ahead to protect us from attack while we crossed it.

"Hurry! Faster! Faster!" snapped the soldiers. "If we're still here when the sun comes up, we will surely be attacked."

"We are carrying children and haven't had any water since three o'clock this afternoon," I said softly.

Due to the exertion and sweat, we were losing a lot of water, and my legs were starting to feel numb.

A little later, we crossed another highway. I saw three civilians staring at us with startled expressions. *They are going straight to the government soldiers to tell them about us*, I thought, fearfully. Then I looked again and saw soldiers kneeling in the thick vegetation with their rifles pointing directly at us. I froze.

"They're our men," a soldier told me. They were using the same uniforms as the enemy, so they wouldn't be recognized as members of UNITA. This scene was repeated many times during that terrible night. I never got used to it. I wondered why they had to point their rifles at us if they were there to protect us. Every time they appeared, I thought my heart would stop.

I was beginning to feel faint. We needed water urgently. The previous day we had boiled a little rice for André, who had diarrhea. We placed it in a can that we gave to the carriers. But we couldn't find it because we didn't know which of them had it. With nearly two hundred people in our group, counting soldiers, carriers, women, and children, finding anything was practically impossible.

When I felt as if my legs could no longer carry me, I went to the captain and told him, "This is torture. You're pushing us beyond our strength. We can't continue any longer."

"Menina Victoria," he answered, "don't lose courage now. If you do, we will have no one to count on. We have confidence in you!"

Just then, a soldier came running up to us. "Menina Victoria, come quickly. Doctor Sabaté needs you."

I ran as fast as possible, following the soldier. Ferrán was seated beside the path. He had turned his ankle, and his walking stick had punctured his right cheek just below his eye.

I put a tightly wrapped bandage on his ankle so that he could at least limp along.

Ronaldo, also, could endure no more. His pain had become unbearable. The soldiers were extremely upset and were losing patience with him. They urged him to hurry. He could only answer, "I can't. I can't."

At last, they laid him on a hammock, and six men carried him for a while.

I had been carrying André for a long time by now. My arms were aching, and my back hurt from being bent under the weight. One of the soldiers offered to carry him, but the little fellow began to scream at the top of his lungs, so I had to give him to Rosmarie.

She was praying aloud for the Lord to give her strength. I was walking by her side to support her, and from time to time, we took turns carrying the baby. We went on hour after hour, practically dragging our feet. At one point, I felt myself getting dizzy, and I started to stagger. "Please, let me hold on to your arm," I begged a soldier who was at my side.

"Give me the boy," he said, taking André out of my arms, but again, the little one started to scream, and I had to take him back.

We continued walking, our tongues dry from thirst, like automatons putting one foot in front of the other, trying to find the strength to take one more step. Unconsciously obeying orders, we walked rapidly, not knowing where we were going. It seemed that the night would never end.

I continued begging soldiers for water. My courage was giving out. It seemed to me that without water, I couldn't live much longer. *If they leave me beside the path, it's OK with me*, I thought. Rosmarie must have been thinking the same thing. She trembled as she leaned on my arm.

Just then, the guard that was walking with us brought us a stalk of sugarcane. We accepted it with desperate eagerness and peeled it with our teeth. Whoever was not carrying the child would peel the cane and share.

We felt better for a little while, but the effect soon wore off, and we soon felt exhausted again. "Water! Water!" we begged from every person we met.

Apparently, they understood that they needed to do something because I heard them say they were looking for the carrier who had the can of water with rice. They found the girl, and at last, we received a few swallows of the vital liquid. It helped a lot. It gave me the energy to carry the child and help Rosmarie until dawn.

We kept on walking up and down the hills. Suddenly, we stopped, and the soldiers threw themselves silently to the ground while another group went off to scout. Then they took us off the path, and we made a wide circle through the brush. The next day, they told us that a group of government soldiers had been waiting for us on the path.

It must have been around five o'clock in the morning when we came to a jungle crossroads. A fine misty fog made our clothes wet, and we were getting very cold. Finally, the soldiers decided to call a halt. They stretched out on the ground and almost immediately began to snore.

We tried to huddle together to warm each other but to no avail. We were chilled to the bone and shivering uncontrollably. Our teeth chattered. We couldn't build a fire because the enemy would have spotted us at once.

I worried as I looked at my friends and saw the bluish color of their lips and cheeks. Conchita and André coughed and coughed incessantly. I got up and went to the captain. "Please, can't we go on? If we stay here, we will get pneumonia. We are turning blue from the cold."

"All right," he said and called his men. The march went on through an open field, and a new day began to dawn. We were more miserable than abandoned dogs, and we were exhausted to the point of death.

Now Ronaldo was on his feet again. I gave André to him and said, "It's your turn now. Your wife and I have carried him all night. Everyone has to take their fair share of the burden." I felt guilty saying it, but I had truly run out of strength.

Ahead of me, a boy about nine or ten years old was chewing on a stalk of sugarcane. I asked if he could give me a piece of his cane. "You only want a piece?" he asked with the innocent generosity of childhood. "No, I'll give you the whole thing. I can find another one."

I walked ahead rapidly. I could do nothing to help my companions. At that point, we were all pretty much on our own. When we were within earshot of one another, we did nothing but complain, which only made things worse.

The vanguard was walking too fast for me to keep up, and the rest of the group was far behind.

Suddenly I realized I was alone in the middle of an enormous corn-field. The stalks were bent over under their own weight. The wind made a mournful sound in the tree branches, and an uneasy feeling came over me. What if I were to meet a government soldier? He would be unable to tell if I was a prisoner or part of the enemy force.

I waited in silence. A few minutes later, I was relieved when I saw the rear guard coming toward me. I ascended a hill with them and sat down, waiting for the others to catch up. I was alarmed when I saw the Oliveiras approach. They were a picture of absolute misery, with deathly pale faces and dry, cracked lips. They came slowly, holding hands, while a soldier carried their sleeping child. It was clear to me that they wouldn't be able to stand this ordeal much longer. The Sabatés arrived shortly thereafter, and we ate some sugarcane, attempting to regain a little strength.

The cane was wet with dew and covered with a thin layer of black moss. When we peeled it with our teeth, our hands, face, hair, and clothing became covered with the black sticky mixture. Conchita looked at me and laughed.

When everyone caught up, we started walking again. Every step was painful. We kept on hearing the same promises: "We are almost there." "In a little while, you can rest." "We're about to arrive."

Slowly the sun began to rise above the horizon. Its warm rays started to dry our clothing and warmed our stiff limbs.

As we entered a large field of straw, the soldiers scattered in all directions. They soon returned with tangerines and shared them with us. I put some of the tangerines in the hood of my windbreaker that I carried tied to my waist. This was a temptation for the others, and before long, I noticed that my windbreaker hood was getting lighter and lighter.

A little farther on, the soldiers found some wild guavas. They were still green, but we ate them eagerly.

The young man who had tried to encourage Ronaldo to walk faster the night before by using the example of the children of Israel was walking by my side now, and we began to talk. He told me he was raised at an evangelical mission and later joined UNITA. The conversation took my mind off my aching feet and the feeling of total exhaustion.

The warmth of the sun and the brief rest on the hilltop had given us new courage. It also gave us hope that we would "soon arrive" at the next camp. If we had known that the march would last into the afternoon, we probably wouldn't have been able to lift our feet off the ground.

We came to another river. It wasn't very wide, but it was quite deep. The exhausted soldiers were ordered to carry us across. In the center of the river, there was a little island where I slipped off the back of my carrier and said, "Let me try it on my own. I can jump from plant to plant and cross by myself."

The water plants are like tightly bound bundles of straw that would actually hold you up. By jumping from one to the next, I was able to cross without difficulty.

A group of angry men awaited us on the other side. They were arguing about the importance of making better time. In their view, we were excessively slow. Conchita wanted to change her baby's diaper, but the soldiers were unwilling to wait. She became very angry. It had been more than twelve hours since the baby's diaper had been changed, and his skin was very irritated. Conchita became desperate.

"Why didn't you leave us where we were? Can you tell me why the children have to suffer? It's not their fault."

"Come," I told Conchita, "I'll help you. We can do it quickly."

"But how? I don't have any clean diapers or lotion for his skin."

We washed the baby with cold water and wrapped him in the diaper that we had been using to cover his head from the sun. Then Conchita sat down to nurse him.

The captain was annoyed because of the time we were taking. I went to him and said, "You have to think about the children. They have to eat and be changed."

"Right," he said dryly. Then he waited in silence. Everyone was surprised at the tone of the conversation.

Despite his youth, the captain had a dignified self-assurance and an air of authority. The men treated him with great respect. I enjoyed talking with him, and at times we even joked with one another. I determined not to be intimidated by his authoritarian air, and when I protested our treatment, I talked to him firmly and directly. The guerrillas were shocked whenever they saw it.

I believed I could speak freely because I never asked anything for myself but always spoke on behalf of my companions. No doubt, the Lord allowed me to find grace in the sight of these rough men of war.

After we had taken care of the children, we began walking again. I spoke with the young soldier who had been raised by evangelicals. He was the radio operator. He told me about the victories of UNITA and filled me in on the political situation. I asked him how he could reconcile his Christian beliefs with his active participation in the war. He answered that, for now, the most important thing was to win the war. After that, there would be time enough for religion. We exchanged ideas for a long time, and I learned about the strategies and techniques of UNITA.

With difficulty, we made our way uphill through a field of tall grass that was wet with dew. It must have been about eleven o'clock in the morning when we came to the top of the hill. We stared in awe. There in the valley below us was a beautiful plantation that appeared to be abandoned. It was a small paradise. Narrow channels of crystal-clear water along the edge of the field formed a perfect square. In the center were fragrant orange trees and tangerines whose branches were bowed under the weight of their golden fruit. Small apple trees reached for sunlight among their taller brothers, and there were even some scattered rose bushes. Along the edges of the canals grew a rich profusion of sugarcane.

For a few moments, we just stood there, unable to really believe our eyes. When the reality sunk in, we quickly reacted, following the soldiers who went bounding down the hill. We lay down and drank our fill from the water; we washed our faces and then jumped over the canal to the plantation and began to pick oranges and tangerines. The soldiers cut sugarcane, and each of them made a bundle that they hung from their backs.

We ate and picked as much fruit as possible. It seemed we had never eaten such delicious fruit. We had no backpacks to carry them, so again, I put as much as possible in the hood of my jacket. Then we pulled off some branches with the tangerines still attached. We could carry several in our hands this way.

It was hard to leave that delightful spot. We had been on the march for more than twenty hours with nothing to drink or eat except for the small amount of fruit we had eaten at dawn. This unexpected feast renewed our energy. We ate and laughed for a while, forgetting the suffering we had just endured.

Bearing our precious tangerines, we left the valley and, along with the soldiers, climbed the hill to the first wooded area where we sat down, leaning against the tree trunks to wait for the Oliveiras, who were just arriving at the plantation below, accompanied by the rearguard. A large number of soldiers were still in the valley picking as much fruit as they could carry. Those who were with us lay on the ground under the trees to rest.

"The camp where we are heading is nearby?" I asked.

"Yes, we'll be there soon."

"Oh, so we can come back here often and pick more fruit."

"Ah, well, no. It's not that close. It's still quite a ways farther."

"And how much longer will it be before we get there?"

"Not too much. Maybe another four hours."

"Four hours! We can't possibly walk another four hours."

"Yes, you can," he answered. "We'll make sure you get there."

Meanwhile, the Sabatés arrived, and we took off our shoes to rest our feet. The conversation turned to the usual topic of how our families must be coping with the news of what had happened to us and what the Adventist leadership was doing to secure our release. We felt refreshed, and our courage revived.

Suddenly, we heard a gunshot. We all flinched and asked what it was.

"It's nothing. Don't worry," the guerrillas reassured us.

We tried to settle our fears by talking about the experiences we had gone through during the night. "My constant prayer was that God would guide our footsteps so we would not stumble," I told Ferrán.

"And nevertheless, I stumbled; I twisted my ankle and jabbed my walking stick into my face," he answered.

"In spite of that, we can be very grateful to God that nothing really serious happened, considering the danger we were in."

With these words, a scene came back to my mind from the previous night. As we were going down a hill, I was terrified to see a military encampment ahead. I looked at my companions, evaluating what an attack would mean to us. There would be few alternatives. A terrible discouragement came over me, and my faith wavered. I couldn't understand why God had allowed this to happen. Couldn't He have protected us? Why hadn't He?

In my anguish, I lifted my eyes to the starry heavens and cried out, "Father, You see us from Your throne, and You know our situation. We don't understand why we are here. Nevertheless, You are more powerful than these men. Protect us if it is Your will."

As I spoke those words, it seemed as if God Himself were looking at me from beyond the stars. It felt as if the Lord came down and started walking with us. A profound peace came over me. Although I couldn't see Him, I clearly perceived the divine presence at our side. A sense of peace came over my mind, and I knew for sure that nothing bad would happen to us. I knew we would suffer a lot, but no one would take our lives. Encouraged by the revelation from heaven, I ran through the column looking for my friends to share the good news with them. "Don't be afraid. Nothing bad is going to happen to us," I whispered to them. "God is with us here."

A second gunshot brought me back to reality. Then there were several more. We jumped to our feet, but a strong guerrilla, responsible for the column, ordered us firmly, "Don't run. Stay right here."

We obeyed, but the shots continued. Conchita snatched up the basket with her baby in it and looked around wildly, trying to decide what to do. "Here, let me take him," I said to her. But she refused. Suddenly, the soldier who had carried the child during the night grabbed the basket, put it on his head, and disappeared into the tall vegetation. "Wait! My baby! My baby!" shrieked the distraught mother, trying to follow. I ran alongside, wondering what was happening to the Oliveiras who had not arrived and might be in the line of fire. I took her arm, and together we ran as fast as we could, attempting to catch up with the carrier.

The soldiers, in a flash, organized themselves into three columns that advanced in parallel order through the thick grass while we ran desperately, slipping and sliding as we went.

In the general confusion, Ferrán ran off in a different direction, and we lost sight of him. "Ferrán, Ferrán, don't leave me!" Conchita shouted in a panic.

I still had some tangerines in my hand, but I dropped them to run more freely.

I couldn't help but admire the guerrillas' ability to carry enormous bundles of sugarcane and tangerines in their hands and equipment on their heads and in their backpacks without losing a single piece.

With a slight push, I encouraged Conchita to go on. "Let Ferrán go; you follow the baby!" The huge soldier who was the leader of the column stayed at our side, and with a strange serenity, he kept repeating, "Everything is going to be all right. There is no problem. Just keep calm." But the rifle shots and grenade explosions continued.

A mortal fear motivated us to run for our lives. We ran downhill without stopping. We entered a wooded area and crossed a stream, jumping across on the rocks in a frenzy to escape the danger. Exhausted, we held on to some plants to keep our balance. "I can't do it. I can't run anymore," Conchita moaned.

"This is no time to cry," I told her sternly. "You have to go on."

At the sound of the gunfire, little Ferrán awoke and began crying. In an effort to calm his mother's nerves, I rushed to catch up with the carrier, took the baby in my arms, and held him to my chest. I tried to go on as rapidly as possible, but Conchita begged me, "No, stay behind me, please. The baby has to stay with me. I prefer to have something happen to me and not to the child."

Despite the intensity of the moment, that beautiful expression of motherly love touched my heart. She preferred to protect her child with her own body if attacked from the front while running.

I couldn't stop thinking about the Oliveiras, who had remained behind. "Lord, take care of them. Don't let them be killed!" I prayed aloud.

Before long, Ferrán rejoined us, and we continued on together.

I have no idea how long we kept running. It seemed like hours. Finally, we came to a clearing in the woods. The troops stopped and ordered us to halt. Conchita fell to the ground, exhausted. "I can't go on. I can't. I can't." Her face was red, reflecting her exhaustion.

Taking her lovingly in his arms, her husband calmly said, "Don't give up, sweetheart. You are strong. I am amazed at how strong you are and how much you can bear. Don't lose your courage now."

We sat on the ground, trying to calm ourselves. I felt faint. I trembled from head to toe, still overwhelmed by the desperate panic. After a few minutes of rest, a group of soldiers stood up to scout the area and make sure that the enemy was not nearby.

A guerrilla came up to Dr. Sabaté and said: "If the situation is critical, you must never leave the group again. We must always stay together. It's dangerous to have the Brazilian in the line of fire," he added.

A few minutes later, the big guerrilla who always seemed so calm came carrying something tied up in his shirt, and he handed it to me. It was the tangerines I had thrown down by the trail in my mad dash. What an amazing act of kindness from this man! I thanked him profusely.

Then the Oliveiras came. Their faces were red with fatigue and fear. A soldier was carrying André, who was screaming wildly. We tried to calm him, but it was impossible. Our nerves were at the exploding point. Ronaldo tried in vain to calm his child, but the little one screamed all the more. I got up and took him in my arms, but still, he screamed hysterically. His screams seemed to pierce my feverish forehead, and I thought I would lose my mind.

When everyone had arrived, we were ordered to continue walking. We passed the ruins of some cabins, probably an abandoned village. As we walked by, we saw some plants loaded with small ripe tomatoes. They were dusty, but we picked as many as possible and ate them as we went along.

André kept on crying, wailing mournfully. He wanted to be in the arms of his exhausted mother. But his crying was wearing on our nerves, making us irritable. Without thinking, I snapped, "If you planned to come to Africa as missionaries, you should have gotten the baby accustomed to being with other people and not just clinging to his mother all the time." Immediately I was overwhelmed with guilt. I'm glad I didn't hear Ronaldo's reply.

Feeling helpless, I ran to the front of the line to escape the screaming, but in my anguish, I, too, wanted to cry and scream.

When I came to where the captain was, he turned and looked toward me. He had an expression of deep worry on his face. I sensed that something was seriously wrong, but I didn't care. "We have been walking for more than twenty hours, and André has had nothing to eat," I said furiously. "He is screaming and crying in desperation. I don't know what you are thinking, but we can't go on like this. He has to get something to eat. Furthermore, the heat is terrible."

Tears welled up in my eyes, but I managed to control myself.

"Right," he answered and kept on walking. Later I learned that the carriers gave my friends some dried meat, and they were also given some wild bananas that the men found along the way.

I moved ahead rapidly to join the vanguard. The radio boy stayed with me. It was clear he had been commissioned to watch me because every time I separated from my group, he appeared as if by magic and never left my side.

We walked a long time until we came to the foot of a hill where there was a stream of cool water. I bent down to get a drink, but I got dizzy and nearly fell into the water as I did so. I felt nauseated, and my legs felt weak. A soldier caught me by the collar and lifted me up.

Nearly out of strength, I asked where we were going. "We're almost there," one of them said. I was sure he was lying to me again. "At the top of this hill is the camp. Just a little farther."

I don't know how, but I managed to climb the hill. There was nothing there but a couple of trees. Some soldiers were lying under their shade. For a second, I thought this must be the camp, but there wasn't even a hut in sight. Then my accompanying soldier admitted to me that we were lost and they couldn't find the path.

It was too much. It seemed as though a dark pit were opening under my feet. Losing control of my emotions, I began to cry uncontrollably. "I can't take any more. We have been marching for more than twenty hours with almost nothing to eat or drink. And now you tell me we're lost!" I shouted hysterically. I was at the end of my rope and couldn't help expressing myself.

The soldier tried to reason with me, "Look, menina, don't talk like that," he said. "If the captain hears you, he might lose patience with you."

"I don't care if it's the captain, or the major, or the president," I snapped. "Put yourselves in our place. Can't you see how we are suffering? . . . And the children? We were perfectly OK. Why did you have to take us?" I moaned as my body shook with sobs.

Others nearby looked on in surprise. One of them came over and offered me a piece of dried meat and a tangerine, but in the state of mind I was in, I couldn't eat. I sat on the grass and sobbed uncontrollably, trying in vain to calm myself while large tears continued down my cheeks and onto the tangerine I was attempting to peel.

At last, I managed to calm down a little. The men who were with me explained that the soldiers who normally camped there had moved unexpectedly, and while some in our group tried to find which way they had gone, it was better to wait there together.

I tried again to make myself comfortable on the grass, still sobbing. I fell asleep for a few minutes and then awoke. I realized that we had been there for more than an hour, and there was still no sign of the rest of our group.

I was worried about the Sabatés and the Oliveiras. *I hope nothing has happened to them*, I thought. *Maybe they need my help and don't know where I am*. As the minutes passed, my concern grew. Seeing that everyone was asleep, I got up quietly and started back the way we had come.

Suddenly, I realized I was alone on an enormous plain. There was not a living being in sight. As I heard the breeze whispering in the branches of the few trees, I was overwhelmed by the feeling of utter aloneness. I recalled the words of the captain. "If we get into a critical situation, never leave the group. Everyone must stay together."

A chill ran down my back. Only a short time before, we were running for our lives, and now I was exposing myself unnecessarily to danger. I quickly made my way back to the soldiers.

I woke up the radio operator and asked him to go with me to look for the others. I had to know what was happening. Together, we went back down the pathway. We had not gone far when he pointed in the distance. "Look, there is the group." The long column was slowly approaching the stream where I had gotten dizzy.

Once they reached me, I could see that the Sabatés and the Oliveiras were nearly unable to stand upright. They dragged their feet and stared at the ground, moaning at every step. "We can't go on. This is beyond what is humanly possible," Ferrán said.

Attempting to encourage them, I told them how I had broken down emotionally. But I insisted there was no stopping. We must go on.

We crossed the flat land and came to a spot where there were a few trees and a small stream that was cool and clear. It was refreshing to wade across the creek and cool our burning feet. "If we're not far from camp, I'll come back here and take a bath," Ferrán said, showing signs of encouragement.

As we continued our journey, we heard a bomb explode in the distance. The captain explained: "That is probably the government soldiers who were pursuing us this morning. They want us to know that they are still there, but we are too far away for them to harm us."

We continued uphill through the woods. Late that afternoon, we came to another abandoned camp, and we stopped for the night.

What a joy to finally be able to rest! At last, we could take off our shoes. After a short prayer of thanks to God for His care, we ate the last of our oranges. We had walked for twenty-seven hours straight.

The captain reassured us, "We'll spend the night here, and tomorrow we will march only three hours."

CHAPTER 7

Rice and Beans, Sand and Rocks

The camp where we would spend the night was empty and the huts abandoned—abandoned, but not uninhabited. The whole place swarmed with vermin of every kind: fleas, ticks, lice, and spiders; crawling, hopping, and flying.

Nightfall came quickly. We longed for a bath! We were all filthy, but we had only a very small amount of water. We gave André a drink and washed him a bit with what was left.

The soldiers cooked the rice they had taken from my house, adding the tomatoes we had gathered along the way and a few beans. The resulting meal was actually quite good, except for the dirt that the rice had picked up during the journey. But it didn't matter. We were so hungry; we didn't hesitate.

Only André refused to eat. Acting out the frustration we all felt, he would throw himself on the ground and then take off running and screaming as if he had gone mad. We tried running after him and speaking softly, but nothing we did seemed to calm him. He ignored his parents and wouldn't allow anyone else to touch him. Rosmarie burst out crying: "My child! What's happening to my child? I never saw him act like this before!" André would stare at us with wild eyes and struggle as if fighting some invisible force.

Dr. Sabaté watched his antics for a while and then said, "The child is going through a crisis. Leave him alone, and it will soon be over." I knelt down and slowly approached the boy, showing him a tangerine. For a moment, he seemed to calm down and began to play nervously with the collar of my pullover. Then suddenly, he struck me with his fist, and, twisting out of my arms, he ran off again. But Ferrán was right. When we ignored him, he eventually calmed down, and finally, around ten o'clock that night, he fell asleep.

We adults were also incredibly tired. The previous night we hadn't slept at all, and now we were falling over with fatigue. There wasn't a bed for me, and I didn't want to lie down on the floor because of the insects scurrying around. The worst were the chiggers. They burrowed under the skin and caused nearly unbearable itching.

I made myself as comfortable as possible on a folding chair. I slept miserably and woke up early. My whole body was sore because of the poor sleeping position and ached from the extensive workout of the previous day.

Now for a good bath in the river, I thought. We weren't allowed to go far from camp, but the exhausted soldiers were sound asleep. A young native girl was awake, so I asked her to go with me. After about a ten-minute walk, we found a stream. It was icy cold. The air temperature must have been below freezing because there was frost on the vegetation along the edges and a thin layer of ice on the water. Nevertheless, I desperately wanted to get cleaned up and wash my clothes.

Fortunately, on our first day away from the mission, I had found a small piece of soap that I kept among my things as a precious treasure. I slipped into the icy water and bathed quickly, finishing with my tangled hair. I washed my clothes and spread them in the sun to dry. After the icy bath, I felt as if I had been reborn.

The young girl and I quietly made our way back to camp, where most of the group were still sleeping. The captain was so tired that he was completely unaware of our escapade. Later, when he learned about it, he said nothing.

Little by little, the camp started to come to life. The Oliveiras and Sabatés wanted to go to the creek too. The captain sent guards with them, and soon we all enjoyed feeling clean once again.

We remained at the encampment until noon, and then we started walking once more. Two men from another village joined us as guides. We soon learned that one of them was an Adventist. Ronaldo and Rosmarie decided to carry André themselves this time, to avoid the stress of the previous day. Ronaldo carried his son on his back like the native women, a practice he would continue for the next twelve days.

At nightfall, we came to a small village. Long before we arrived, we could see the glow of the village campfire and heard the drums announcing our approach. As we entered the village, the drumming ceased, and the base commander came out to greet our captain.

They assigned us two huts: one for the Sabatés and the other for the Oliveiras and me. But Ferrán and Conchita had to move outside because their hut was so small they couldn't even lie down.

The darkness was intense. We couldn't even see a hand in front of our faces, so Conchita asked for a light she could use when she needed to take care of her baby. After quite some time, they brought her a kerosene lantern—the old type that could be hung on a hook. It looked like something from the nineteenth century.

"What a curious thing!" I said to the captain. "Where did you get that great lamp? Can you get me one too?"

A wry smile crossed his tense face. "Unfortunately, no. It is the only one in the village," he replied.

They brought us a supper of boiled potatoes, and after that, we prepared for bed.

The Oliveiras used the platform of rough-hewn boards as a bed for themselves and their child. I pushed our bags and suitcases together and attempted to find a comfortable position to pass the night.

Next to our hut was the shelter where the captain met with the commander. We could hear them talking in quiet tones.

Suddenly, the drums started throbbing again. Curious, the Sabatés and I decided to follow the sound. We stumbled through the darkness, trying not to get lost until someone offered to lead us. We could barely see our guide's face in the darkness, but we followed anyway. We came to a place where a boy of about nine was playing the drums with amazing skill. His hands tapped the complicated instrument with speed and precision while a group of natives sang and danced to the sound. We watched for a few minutes and then returned to our hut to try to get a little sleep.

Next door to our hut, the conversation of the commander and the captain continued. We could clearly hear the voice of the captain getting louder and louder. Something serious must have happened. I strained to hear what they were saying, and it soon became clear: For security reasons, the guerrillas do not usually stay in the same village for more than a month. So, the previous inhabitants of the village had moved to another place.

According to their protocol, before undertaking the move, they sent a group of scouts to check the trail and find a place to set up the next camp. While on their mission, they unexpectedly encountered another group of guerrillas whom they didn't recognize. In the confusion of the next few moments, they fired at each other and then discovered they had killed one of their own. The captain continued to lecture until midnight.

"Keep alert! Vigilance is the most important rule for a guerrilla!" he repeated again and again.

The next day, we rose early and prepared to leave. We hoped to get an early start and take advantage of the cool morning. But no one came for us. We waited for a long time. Becoming impatient, I decided to look around the camp and see what was going on. I hadn't gotten far when I found the captain standing in front of his troops and lecturing them energetically: "Our leader will not be happy when he finds out what has happened," he declared. "He knows that our president won't tolerate accidents like this. He will certainly want to know if his people are really capable of carrying on this war."

While listening to him, I thought, *The captain has missed his calling. He's a great preacher!*

Before returning to our hut, I went around the backside of the village, where I met up with a little boy who was leading a cow with a rope around her neck. When I stopped to visit with him, a group of naked children quickly gathered around us, staring at me curiously. Nearby were some women preparing food for the soldiers. They were stirring some kanjika in an old gasoline tank they used as a kettle. Kanjika is made from corn that is cooked for hours until it is soft. Animal fat, pieces of meat, and vegetables are then added. As a child, I had eaten kanjika often. It's a common food in northern Argentina. But the way these women were fixing it didn't make it look one bit appetizing. It had a horrific odor, and just the sight of it made me lose my appetite.

As I was returning to my hut, I met three men carrying large banana stalks on their shoulders. I was delighted to see the fruit and asked if we could have some. "Yes, of course, no problem!" they promised, but they continued on their way, and we never saw the bananas.

A chigger had burrowed under a toenail on my left foot and was tormenting me, so I went to Henda, our guard, for a needle to remove the critter. While digging under my toenail, I listened to him tell me about the UNITA's struggles and victories.

"These guys," he said cynically, referring to the government soldiers, "are so poorly trained that we have no trouble finishing them off. Every blast of our guns means one less of them."

"And you smile when telling me this?" I asked. "These 'guys' are your brothers."

"Only as long as they don't have a gun in their hands," he answered.

While we talked, I learned that we would soon cross the Cunene River. "We need a picture of this," Conchita said. "Do they actually intend to get all of us across this broad and deep river without a boat?" I was never without my camera, either in my hands or hanging from a shoulder strap.

And in my camera bag, I had eight rolls of film that I had brought from Switzerland just two months earlier.

So far, I hadn't attempted to take any pictures because I was sure it would be forbidden. Nevertheless, I went ahead and asked Henda to get permission from the captain for me to take some.

To my surprise, he replied: "Yes, of course. Take all the pictures you want."

His authorization came so easily that I began to wonder: *Why would they let me take pictures? Are they planning to confiscate them before we leave? What do they have in mind?*

Those questions didn't stop me, however. I immediately went looking for things to photograph. The first "victim" was Ferrán, who was seated on the ground behind the hut trying to eat his pirão.

When the day came for us to cross the river, they allowed me to go last so that I could take photos of the crossing. The captain stood right in front of the camera so that he would be plainly visible.

For the crossing, only one small canoe was available. It wouldn't hold more than four or five people at a time, so we spent most of the day in the process. When, at last, we were all on the other shore, it was late afternoon. It was very cold, and the entire river bank was muddy and wet. The area was covered with tall grasses and a thick canopy of trees—an ideal hiding place for serpents and vermin that we were certain would be waiting for us.

We had walked only a short distance when we came to a narrow stream. It was not very deep or wide, but someone had built a "bridge" across it. The bridge was made of a line of sticks driven into the mud one after another all the way across. Then, two rows of thinner branches were firmly tied to the first horizontally, forming a kind of fence. The soldiers held on to the upper branches and laboriously placed one foot after the other on the lower ones to traverse the stream.

As I watched the people slowly crossing one by one, I wondered, why go to all this effort when the stream clearly was not very deep or wide? The reason, I learned, was that the waters were infested with crocodiles. I was still thinking about that when one of the carriers unexpectedly came, and before I could protest, he picked me up, jumped into the water, carried me across, and set me down on the opposite side.

With everyone safely on the other side, we walked for a few more minutes until we came to solid ground where we could set up camp for the night. The area was covered with dry grass, but the soil was quite damp. To protect ourselves from the penetrating cold, we spread out a sheet to lie on and pressed together to stay warm. Thus, we passed the night. Early the next morning, before sunup, we were up and on our way again, continuing our forced march.

In the following days, we walked on average between six and ten hours a day. We slept wherever night found us. Although we knew we were heading south, we didn't know where we were. We could only follow orders: "Twendy!"

On June 16, a week after our capture, we met the major that the captain had been telling us about. He was an exceptionally handsome fellow, sharply dressed in his uniform.

The captain introduced us and took us to a circle of seats under the trees' thick foliage. The captain and the major took their seats solemnly before us. Standing directly behind the major were four soldiers who comprised his personal bodyguard.

"The two women walk fairly well," said the captain, pointing to Conchita and me. Then he gave detailed information about the events that had taken place thus far.

"Very well!" the major said when he had heard the account. "We brought a little food. As soon as we eat, we'll be on our way again."

The two leaders talked about different matters among themselves, including the accident in which the soldier had lost his life. Then they called the radio operator, whom they planned to raise to the rank of sergeant. The young man stood at attention and gave the major a sharp military salute.

The major stood to his feet and ordered: "Remove your coat!" The soldier obeyed. The major raised his arms and brought them down forcefully on the shoulders of the radio operator, and with that, the young man was officially promoted to sergeant. The major congratulated him, saying, "Now you are a sergeant!" He wished him success and gave him his charge, "Carry on, always looking forward!" Then all his companions shook his hand and congratulated him.

I often conversed with that young soldier. He had a small radio with him that morning, and he asked me if I had heard any news about the war between Britain and Argentina in the Falkland Islands. Since our capture, I hadn't heard anything.

Late that night, when we were seated around the fire attempting to dry some of our freshly washed clothing, the major called to me: "Menina, come quickly!" I hurriedly stumbled through the darkness to where he was. He told me he had just heard on the radio that Argentina had surrendered and the war was over. While suffering the burden of my own circumstance, I had been concerned and saddened, knowing that my own country—home to all my loved ones—was at war. The news that it was over brought great relief.

That night, we again slept in the open, and early in the morning, after a meager breakfast, we were ready to resume our walk. We had all caught colds from the combination of cold weather and physical exhaustion. Little Ferrán had red eyes and a runny nose. It was frustrating that the children had to suffer for no good reason, but there was nothing we could do.

We began to walk through a densely wooded area. We had gone only a few minutes when we came across some women seated in a circle in a clearing, singing revolutionary songs and swaying to the rhythm of the music.

One of them stood up and recited a poem entitled "Angola." It recounted their nation's sad history and told of the tears shed for the victims who were the price of the longed-for freedom. It described how the guerrillas of UNITA fought with all their strength to achieve a noble objective. The poem ended with an exchange of military salutes. The women returned to their base, and we continued on our way.

That day we were especially tired. We hadn't adjusted to the food, which consisted mainly of pirão with rice with beans, and most of the time included sand and grit that crunched between our teeth when we chewed it. We tried not to think about how the food had been prepared on the ground. We tried not to think about the total absence of hygiene. Furthermore, the mixture was prepared without salt or oil, making a sticky paste that was hard to swallow. That night, when at last we stopped to make camp, I felt so weak I could hardly stand. I didn't even have the strength to get ready for bed.

I wondered how much weight I had lost in those few days. I was very thin, even before being captured. The stress and privation at the mission had already brought my weight down to 103 pounds. Now I couldn't even guess how little I might weigh. I only knew I felt very weak and that my legs were about to give way. As I leaned against the wall of the hut, it became clear to me that I needed to take action to survive. Eating was now a matter of life or death. We must eat anything and everything they gave us if we were to make it to the end.

Later, while the Oliveras and I were lying on the ground in our little hut with no roof, I asked them what they had expected when they arrived at the mission. I told them, "I was happy knowing we would be neighbors and that I would share the backyard with people from my own continent."

"Now, just a week later, we're so well acquainted that we share the same bed," quipped Ronaldo. Our hut was so tiny there was hardly room for the four of us to lie down. We were, in fact, sharing the same "bed," lying side by side on the floor and staying close to keep each other warm.

"The sky is the limit!" Ronaldo said as he contemplated the beauty of the heavens spread out in splendid array over our heads. Ever after that awful night passed in the midst of untold dangers, the brilliant stars were a symbol of hope for me. Every time I saw them, I sensed that God was watching us from His throne.

June 18 was a Friday. We walked all day, and that night we again made camp on top of a hill with no roof over our heads. We tried to make ourselves as comfortable as possible for our Sabbath devotions. Gathering all our strength, we sang with heartfelt enthusiasm: "We have this hope that burns within our hearts, hope in the coming of the Lord." We read a devotion and closed with prayer.

"Why are you singing today?" asked a soldier who had been observing us.

"Because tomorrow is the Sabbath, the holy day of rest," we answered.

While we scouted for a place to make our beds, I saw something that made me laugh. The recently promoted sergeant was talking with another guerrilla about his footgear. I looked at his feet and saw that his boots' soles were completely torn loose in the front. Like two great mouths, they opened and closed at every step, revealing his toes.

When the soldier saw me laughing, he began to laugh too. I went over and asked him, "Is this how you do things? The major comes with a great ceremony. He puts his hands on your shoulders and says, 'Good job! Carry on! Keep up the good work,' but he doesn't even give you a good pair of boots. How can you 'carry on' *that* way?"

The soldier heartily laughed as he stared at his feet.

I personally did not care for the major. He was arrogant. He promised us food that never came. And on top of that, he had no concern about the condition we were in when we went through his base. Not a thing improved.

The captain heard us as he passed by and turned back to ask what we were talking about. "I was saying that UNITA promises a lot and claims to offer even more," I replied. "Everyone is going to be better off. They say, 'Onward! Forward!' but no one thinks about new shoes for a recently promoted sergeant."

"But Menina, it's just that no one knew that shoes could tear like this," said the young sergeant, in defense of the major.

The captain just laughed and walked away. The next day the radio operator tied some twine around his boots to hold them together and continued as if nothing were wrong with them.

While we waited for our food, we prepared a large bed where we could all sleep together in the open air. André protested because he wasn't ready for sleep yet. He wanted to play a little longer in the sand. It began to get cold, and his mother said seriously, "André, I'm going to shut the door right now, so you don't run off!" We all laughed.

Later, as we were conversing, Ronaldo said, "You know what's the first thing I'm going to buy when we get back to Brazil?"

"A door?" I said, interrupting him. We all enjoyed another laugh at that.

While I was going through my things, I found a lemon that I had picked up when we first began our journey. It had been a long time since we had eaten any fruit, and there was great rejoicing over this rediscovered lemon. "Let's make some lemonade," someone suggested.

A few days earlier, Ferrán had found a little plastic jar that the soldiers had taken from him, and he had taken it back. Among the things the men took from my house, I had carefully hoarded a tablespoon of sugar in a small package. Wasting no time, I headed out into the darkness to find the cook and asked him for a little water. We squeezed the lemon, added the sugar, and soon the precious lemonade was ready. It was wonderful!

Forgetting for a few moments how tired we were, we all sat on our beds and passed the jar. Since Conchita was nursing, we allowed her two sips. Never before was lemonade so delicious.

After we finished the lemonade, I found the cook again and asked if he could make a light soup for André, who had diarrhea and couldn't tolerate the mixture of rice and beans—and sand.

On my way back, I saw the captain working with some young men who were setting up his camp. They had carefully bent down a tree branch and tied it in place. Beneath it, they set up his bed. From where I stood, it looked like a greenhouse. Remembering the earlier conversation about doors, I couldn't resist the temptation to say to him as I went by, "Captain, don't forget to close the door before you go to sleep."

"I have no need to close the door of my house," he replied, "but maybe the door of my soul." He went on to tell me that for several days he hadn't been feeling well. He tired easily and felt weak. He asked if we had any type of medication that might help.

"I can't offer much," I answered. "What you need to do is change your lifestyle. You are always sleeping out in the open—rain or shine. You are always going, crossing freezing rivers at night, and eating whatever you find. It's no wonder you're sick."

"But I feel weak! I've never felt like this before."

"It's no wonder, with the type of life you live," I repeated. "You don't get proper food—no vitamins or necessary nutrients to keep you healthy. It's really hard for me to understand how you can keep up this life. To get back your strength, you need a less stressful life and proper nutrition," I explained, although I imagined a negative response.

As expected, he did react. His demeanor quickly changed, and with a serious expression on his face and an authoritative tone, he said: "I can't even think about a comfortable life as long as my country and my people are not free."

I shrugged my shoulders. "I understand, but in that case, there is not much I can do."

Later, I took him some vitamins I had saved the day they captured us.

The next day was Sabbath. On our day of rest, we walked all day without stopping. We were exhausted, and we were disheartened because we had not been allowed to worship the Lord on His holy day.

Every morning, before setting out, we took a few minutes to pray. The soldier who guarded us quickly became familiar with our routine and would wait for us to finish before starting the march. We were grateful for the kindness. Those short devotions were a precious source of strength and courage. On that particular Sabbath, we weren't even allowed that privilege. Long before dawn, we were ordered to march, and we didn't stop until late that night.

On our journey that day, the captain announced that we would be arriving at the next military outpost. "It is likely that we will separate, and you will continue with another group. We have to go back," he told us. UNITA had divided the country into military regions, with each one designated by a number. We were captured in region number 71, and now we would be arriving in number 19.

"Why do you have to go back?" I asked him.

"To continue other services."

You call it "services" when you kidnap people and make them walk like the condemned, I thought.

The next day we arrived at a camp that, according to them, was at the center of the region. It was around midday, and we were seated together, waiting for them to bring us something to eat or tell us where we would spend the night.

After what seemed like an eternity, some carriers arrived with the dreaded rice and beans with sand. We were very hungry, so we courageously tried to swallow the mix without thinking too much about the dirt.

Suddenly, a beautiful woman appeared before us. She seemed almost like a vision. Her head was covered by a beautifully colored cloth, and her ears were adorned with large gold rings. In one hand, she held a clean plate filled with what looked like buns baked in an oven, and in the other, she held a teapot filled with what appeared to be hot coffee. A girl who was with her brought a jar of clean, filtered honey. The beautiful woman greeted us courteously and set the food before us. She told us to help ourselves to as much as we wanted. Incredulous, we looked at one another, too amazed to respond. It was hard to believe she was real.

"Go ahead," she encouraged us. The food looked appetizing, and when we tasted it, it was exquisite. At last, we could eat something delicious and hot. And, at last, we could eat until we were satisfied!

The woman told us that she made the buns from corn and sweet-potato flour and the coffee from roasted and ground corn. "Before, when we were in the city, we had everything," she explained. "But out here in the jungle, we have to use our wits to find whatever we can." She stared at the ground sadly.

She told us that before the war, she had been a teacher in the port city of Benguela. But because she had been active in supporting UNITA, she and her family had to flee and hide in the jungle when the communists took over. We could see she was a refined and educated woman. We asked if we could take a little of the bread with us. Without saying anything, she turned and left. She soon returned with a large stack of the same bread. We received it with deep gratitude.

We gave the horrible mixture of rice, beans, and sand, leftover from lunch, to some soldiers who took it eagerly.

With our hunger satisfied, we felt a tremendous need to bathe. Our last bath had been in the little icy stream several days before. Just before entering this camp, we had crossed a small stream. Rosmarie and I went to look for the captain and ask his permission to go wash. We found him resting in the tent of the base commander. He sent a messenger with his authorization, and they organized an escort of twelve men to keep custody of us.

They went with us to the stream, and they stood there on the bank. What should we do? We had intended to take off our clothes. "Ah, could you excuse us? We need to bathe; could you go away a little?" we asked them.

The men thought it was funny and began to laugh. After teasing us about it a bit, they did go far enough away for us to feel comfortable. We could no longer see the soldiers, but we could hear them laughing loudly and talking among themselves in their native dialect. Ronaldo and Ferrán found a quiet corner for themselves. It felt wonderful to wash our bodies, our hair, and our clothes. When we had finished, we returned to the base.

Back at the base, we were assigned a small hut where we could all sleep. Since there were no bunks, we tried to make ourselves comfortable on the straw-covered floor. We were happy to at least have a roof over our heads because the nights were very cold. For supper, they brought us some fried potatoes in the bottom of a kettle, hardly enough for one person. What a blessing that we still had some bread from the midday meal!

It was getting dark, and before the light of day disappeared completely, we wanted to have our devotions. We were in the middle of it when two men came, wanting to talk with us.

The first one said he was *Senhor* (Mister) Rodrigues, an Adventist who had been trapped in that part of the country at the start of the war. He knew many people from the mission, but he had heard no news from them since. His joy was visible when we told him about them. At this base camp, there was a small hospital (if you could call it that), and Mr. Rodrigues was in charge of it. His brother was a pastor in Cameroon.

The man who was with him that night had previously worked at an evangelical mission and now helped him care for patients here at this base. Comforted and encouraged by our friendly encounter, we read the Bible together and prayed.

Ronaldo spoke to them about the importance of standing firm for the commandments of God, even if it was difficult and dangerous. This chance meeting was, no doubt, as deeply meaningful for Mr. Rodrigues as it was for us. We talked late into the night.

He told us the story of an old, well-worn Bible that he carried with him everywhere he went. One time, when a firefight broke out, he dropped to the ground. A moment later, there was a lull in the shooting, and Mr. Rodrigues leaped to his feet and ran for his life. His beloved Bible was lost in the chaos.

It was some days later before he was able to return. With no real hope, he went to see if there might be some scattered pages of his Bible left. To his immense joy, he found first one part of the Bible, and then another, and another. They were scattered in different places. Some of the pages were flapping in the wind, but he continued his search, picking up the parts one by one. To his astonishment, he found his entire Bible except for the cover. He crafted another cover for it and once again was carrying the precious book next to his heart.

Before saying goodnight, we prayed together, and he asked us to take greetings to his brother.

It was very cold that night by the time we were able to lie down. The wind howled in the trees and came right in through the thin straw walls of the hut. We were half asleep when we again heard the voice of Mr. Rodrigues: "Sorry to disturb you," he said. "I brought you some bananas. They are still a little green, but in a few days, they'll be ripe, and you can enjoy them."

It had been days since we had any fruit. We were overjoyed and expressed our gratitude.

He left, and soon everyone but I was sound asleep. I lay awake, going over the day's events in my mind. Unexpectedly, I heard the sound of soft footsteps approaching our hut. I went to the door, and there was the lovely lady who had given us the bread. She whispered: "When I saw that they gave you such a meager supper, I decided to bring you some more. You shouldn't have to go to bed hungry."

"I am so grateful," I told her, deeply touched, "but as you can see, all the others are already asleep. I guess they won't be able to eat it right now."

"What a pity!" she exclaimed in a soft voice. "It's so sad to go to bed hungry!"

My eyes filled with tears. I was moved by this woman's compassion for people who were complete strangers to her. Her thoughtfulness and her cultured, gentle manner were like a ray of sunshine in the midst of our perplexity. The next day she again provided us with bread, honey, and hot corn coffee. To us, these simple foods were a rich banquet, and we will not easily forget her kindness.

CHAPTER 8

A Hospital in the Jungle, a Prison, and a Soccer Field

After breakfast and morning worship, I decided to look around the village. On the way, I met Mr. Rodrigues, who invited me to visit the hospital. I couldn't help but admire how they were able to care for the patients without any standard medicines or equipment. I didn't see a single syringe for giving injections; nevertheless, there were several people with amputated limbs, and they appeared to be well cared for. There was a young man who had broken his leg a few days earlier. His limb was immobilized. I noticed a woman whose leg was terribly swollen because of a snakebite lying on a cot in the corner. "What do you do in these cases?" I asked Mr. Rodriguez. "Do you have some type of antivenom?"

"No, the only thing we have is what we can get from the jungle," was his reply.

He showed me leaves and roots gathered from the forest. They used them to prepare different medicines and antivenom. Then he took me to a hut where they had a collection of powders they had prepared from different plants, each one for a specific illness. He showed me one of the powders they used for treating malaria.

"We only have a problem when treating the children," he explained. "We still haven't found the right dosage for the youngest ones."

Suddenly, we heard loud voices and shouting. We ran in the direction of the commotion, and there, beside one of the huts, were some people holding a stick from which hung a large snake.

A woman had picked up the straw mat on which she slept, and there was the serpent coiled up, ready for action. It was not very long, but it was thick and covered with gray spots. It had an enormous head. Just looking at it was enough to turn my stomach. Our hut was not far from hers, and from then on, I was constantly worried about the snake. At night, I would

80

get up and carefully search our sleeping quarters. I would lie back down, still unable to sleep, haunted by visions of serpents slithering under little Ferrán as he slept peacefully in his basket. So I would get up again in the darkness and make sure the baby was all right. Often, I would lie awake for hours, unable to relax. I was afraid of the serpents, the soldiers, and the uncertain future. The last vivid scenes of our capture at the mission continued to play in my head like a never-ending nightmare. The darkness and its unfamiliar sounds increased my restlessness and anxiety. Constantly on alert, I could find no peace, even in prayer.

And as if all this wasn't enough, Conchita found lice in her hair. That was all we needed! "Why does this have to happen now?" she complained bitterly as she combed and washed, checked, and rechecked her hair and clothing. The rest of us tried to console her, thankful that we had not yet been attacked by the intruders.

The following days were exhausting. The food was always the same, and there was always sand grinding between our teeth.

André cried continuously because of his hunger and frustration. We adults grew weaker. Our legs, like cotton rags, refused to work. One day while trying to swallow our small servings of rice, beans, and sand, we saw some women and children in the distance. They had baskets on their heads and moved slowly toward us. They were bringing shelled corn, honey, and sweet potatoes to sell. When they arrived, we asked them how much they wanted for the sweet potatoes. One of them asked for a pair of shoes for her little boy. Of course, we didn't even have shoes for ourselves. Nevertheless, we were able to barter one of my blouses (I still had two) for about eleven pounds of sweet potatoes. The Oliveiras traded a pair of André's pants for some honey.

The rest of the day, we entertained ourselves by talking about the food we would eat when we got back to civilization and about what might be happening in the world.

That evening, after our huts were assigned, we put two sweet potatoes per person in the coals around the fire, and we went to prepare our beds before dark. A little while later, we gathered around the fire with eager anticipation, imagining the rich flavor of our sweet potatoes. To our disappointment, we discovered that half of them had been stolen. When we returned to our huts a little while later, we discovered that more sweet potatoes had been taken from our bags. From then on, I used the bag of sweet potatoes as a pillow. More than once, I was awakened by fingers attempting to pull the precious food right from under my head!

The captain was ill and steadily growing weaker, but that didn't stop him from slowly walking by my side, engaging me in conversation. He constantly probed in an attempt to learn my political views.

"As a nurse," I explained, again, "my mission is to serve God in the person of my neighbor. Any engagement in the war is incompatible with that view. In war, people kill each other. That is against God's will and opposed to my ministry of saving lives. Since the beginning, God's enemy has provoked people to make war with each other, but it was never God's plan."

"So, you think we are devils?"

I sighed, knowing I needed to carefully measure every word. Fortunately, the captain was walking a little behind me and couldn't see the expression on my face.

"If your country fell into a civil war," the captain insisted, "wouldn't you make every effort to defend your land and your property?"

"I would try to take care of the wounded and sick, but I would not make political commitments," I responded. "I am here for everyone who needs care. I could not commit myself to a party."

I wanted him to understand that I had no intention of joining UNITA or any type of political organization, no matter how noble it seemed to him.

The captain was not satisfied with my answers. He wanted me to admit that he and his men were fighting for a just cause. Attempting to bring our discussion to a close, I assured him, "I greatly admire the commitment and dedication you and the others bring to your cause. Surely you have reasons for what you do. But, I cannot say that all that UNITA does is right."

On another occasion, he got me involved in a long discussion about marriage between blacks and whites. "The problem is not the color of the skin but the great difference of mindset," I told him.

"What do you mean by difference of mindset?" he insisted.

"Well, for example, to a European, the way that an Angolan practices hospitality is difficult to accept. The European places great importance on privacy and cannot imagine having people around constantly getting into the intimacy of the family relationships." He couldn't fathom it. Africans blend hospitality and community life as essential to their lifestyle.

In his conversations with Dr. Sabaté, the cunning captain also tried repeatedly to stir up political discussions. Once I overheard Ferrán say to him, "Those involved in political matters have a very different viewpoint than we missionaries. Nevertheless, we can talk because we each have the freedom to do as we see best."

It must have been around the twenty-first or twenty-second of June that we met up with the new commander—a lieutenant colonel who would be in charge of us from then on. We worried about how things would go under this new leader. Considering the circumstances, Captain Chimuco had treated us reasonably well. He kept us to a strict discipline of at least eight hours on the trail every day, but he was considerate when the situation demanded it.

Our introduction to the new commander took place in an almost festive air. As we drew close to the village where we were to meet the new group, they carefully organized the column with us in the middle and soldiers ahead and behind. We entered through a wide gateway made of sticks and grass. No one spoke a word. The captain and his team went ahead to greet the lieutenant colonel.

After a few minutes, they sent for us, and we, too, were welcomed with a military salute. The commander apologized for not being better prepared. He explained that they were not expecting us until the next day. Nevertheless, a fire had been built in each of the huts where we were to spend the night.

Up to that time, I had always been afraid to sleep alone in a hut. So, I stepped forward and said, "I prefer to sleep with the Oliveiras in their hut."

"But why?" asked the commander, surprised. "We have started a good fire for you in your hut so that you will not be cold during the night. Furthermore, you will sleep in your own straw bed, and you will be much more comfortable."

"Maybe, but I don't know . . ." I answered, unsure of what I should do.

"Come," said the captain. "I will accompany you to your house. Or are you afraid that UNITA will kidnap you?"

"No, I'm not worried about that. UNITA kidnapped me once, and I doubt very much that they'll want to do it again." Everyone laughed, and then the captain escorted me to my hut. I asked if he could send one of the young women carriers to spend the night with me because I did not feel safe being alone in the dark hut. I quickly made my bed and then left before it got completely dark. Our guard was coming down the path with a tray of little loaves of bread that one of the women had prepared for us. I accepted them gratefully and continued on to the Oliveiras' and Sabatés' houses to share with them. When I returned in the dark, I could recognize the figure of the captain escorted by his aides, leaving my house. He had come to visit me and found I wasn't at home. *I hope they don't get the idea of coming during the night*, I worried. But, I thank God, nothing like that ever happened. In fact, during our entire captivity, the soldiers were completely respectful in dealing with us women. The young woman carrier sent by the commander came and made her bed close to mine, and other than a few hours of insomnia, I had a peaceful night.

Very early the next morning, we said goodbye to the group that had captured us and with whom we had been traveling for so long. The soldiers seemed genuinely sad and assured us that they had never before escorted people like us. "With the other captives, we had all kinds of problems, but you were always calm. You are different," they told us.

Dr. Sabaté spoke on behalf of the whole group, "We will always remember you," he said. "Of course, in times of war, things are different, but who knows? Maybe we will meet again after the war."

The men came to attention, clicked their heels, and then, with a final salute, they turned and marched off. It was with a strange mixture of sadness and uncertainty that we watched them disappear into the jungle. The captain lingered a few minutes longer to ensure a smooth transition and introduce us to the new group who would now escort us.

"Now, look," we told him. "When you captured us, you promised to take us to your president, and instead, you are abandoning us out here in the middle of nowhere. That was not our agreement."

The captain seemed genuinely troubled and uncomfortable. "What I promised," he said, "was that I would do everything possible to see that you arrived safe and sound at the base." Then he shook our hands and marched off. We were officially in the hands of the new group.

We soon discovered that this group had a hard time getting organized. Often they told us we would leave early in the morning, but then they would spend the morning scurrying back and forth, and it would be nine o'clock before we were actually on our way. Because of the late start, we had to rush to get to our next stop. Again and again we told them, "We want to leave early in the morning so we can rest at midday rather than walking in the scorching sun." But it was no use; they simply couldn't get organized.

Fortunately, this group had a very kind cook who went to great lengths to prepare the best meals possible under the difficult circumstances.

She was a refined and pleasant woman—a nurse who had been brought up in the city. I asked her how she came to be involved with UNITA. She told me that she belonged to the party before the war. Her husband was an important leader. They had three small children and enjoyed a comfortable life. One night her husband ran into the house saying, "Hurry, hurry, bring the children! We have to go! The communists are bringing the Cubans to our country. We've got to get away!"

So, with nothing more than the clothes on their backs, they jumped into their car with their children and sped away under cover of the night until they came to this forest, where they were still hiding. That was the experience of thousands of families in Angola during those tragic days.

This woman had given birth only three months before, so she sympathized deeply with our plight, especially the situation of Conchita and Rosmarie with their little children. As often as possible, she prepared warm water to bathe the babies. When she saw how difficult it was to get André to eat, she even gave us a little of the precious condensed milk that she had obtained for her own baby. She came every morning, bringing a glass of it for the child until her own supply was gone. I was amazed by her sacrifice, given how difficult it was to obtain milk under those circumstances. In the days ahead, when we didn't have enough to eat, it felt as though she was suffering with us.

On our second day of marching with the new group, I started feeling poorly. The troop commander approached me and said: "The captain informed me that the menina walks very well and is always at the front of the column."

"That's right," I replied weakly. "I just hope I can continue like this."

Over the next few days, we crossed three deep rivers. The soldiers had inflatable rubber boats, so we were able to cross without getting wet. Between the rivers, we traveled broad plains covered with nothing but tall, dry grass. This type of terrain offered an ideal hiding place for snipers. So we would wait in the shade of the trees reaching the river while a scouting group went ahead and checked out the area. Next, a vanguard of troops crossed, and then we were allowed to cross. The operation took a long time, but it gave us an opportunity to rest our aching legs.

By the time we reached each river, we felt tired and discouraged. We walked for hours and had to run at times to keep up with the soldiers, so when we came to the rivers, we dropped to the ground, exhausted. We only wanted to stretch our legs and rest our exhausted bodies.

Sometimes the soldiers used the breaks to offer us some food. This group prepared food at night and carried it in kettles on their heads. This allowed us to eat without wasting time. However, the food was cold and solidified, and, of course, filled with gravel.

When we left our camp on the morning of June 24, I felt a strange pain in my legs. I felt sick in general and was experiencing abdominal cramps and diarrhea. We came to a river, and after we crossed, I felt even worse. By afternoon the problem was worse yet. My whole body ached. It got dark before we came to our stop for the night. The walk was made more difficult because we were climbing a mountain on a narrow path that was like a ditch that had been washed out by the rain. My cramps kept getting worse, and in the dark, I stumbled and fell several times. I felt like crying.

It was extremely difficult for me to keep up with the group, but I didn't want to complain. But, as my pain continued to increase, it became harder for me to disguise my misery. I took advantage of every opportunity to rest. I just collapsed and stretched full length on the ground. I felt as if I could not take another step. I was writhing with cramps in my calf muscles, in my thighs, and in my abdomen. My chest hurt so much I could hardly breathe. It was horrible.

The commander said to me, "Menina, I'm a little disappointed in you. They told me you were a fast walker and that you were always at the head of the group. But that isn't what I'm seeing."

If you only knew how I feel, I thought, but I did not answer him.

It was quite late when we arrived at camp that night. I immediately lay down on my mat and went to sleep without eating a bite.

Early the next morning, the commander came and asked how I was doing. The women who had brought our breakfast told him I wasn't well. The Sabatés were also concerned. But, thank God, I was much better.

It seems that the water we had drunk the previous day was contaminated, and apparently, I was the one most affected by it.

That Friday, as we walked, the commander announced: "Tomorrow we will have to walk all day, and we'll rest Sunday, or we can rest tomorrow and walk at least eight hours on Sunday."

"If it's OK with you, we would much prefer to rest tomorrow and walk on Sunday," we told him. "We really would like to be able to rest on God's holy day."

"Oh, of course! You are the people who don't work on Saturday, aren't you," he answered. We learned later that he was the son of an evangelical pastor. All his brothers were fighting for UNITA; only his parents were living in the city.

That Sabbath, while everyone else was resting, we were very happy that we could study our Bibles and worship peacefully. We were grateful for the opportunity, even though the uncertainty in which we lived filled us with sadness and worry. In every prayer, we poured out our souls to the Lord, pleading for His help and mercy.

In the afternoon, I took my Bible and went to read and meditate alone in my hut. I needed time alone. I often contemplated the mission at Bongo. Just before we were captured, I had been appointed as Sabbath School superintendent, and we were busy preparing a special program for the following Sabbath. It was the end of the quarter, and we were making cards to congratulate those who had birthdays in the previous three months. That was our birthday custom, and we also took up a special offering. People brought their best produce from their gardens—potatoes and corn, vegetables, and fruit. Conchita prepared a special song and was practicing it with some of our musically talented workers. But when that Sabbath arrived, we weren't there. We had no idea what was happening to our brothers and sisters at the mission. A deep melancholy feeling filled my heart. Tears ran down my cheeks as I cried silently. I wrote in my diary, "Today, it has been sixteen days since we were captured. Today they allowed us a day of rest. I feel sad when I think about Bongo. Lord, why are we here? Why would You let something like that happen to Your children? Why do we have to weep in captivity?"

I had just finished writing that line when I heard footsteps outside. The commander was there with his aides, and they asked if they could come in. They greeted me courteously and asked how I felt. Then the commander told me, "I just heard that the leaders of the Adventist Church in Europe recently learned about your capture, and they are taking the first steps toward your liberation."

Seated on my cot, I lifted my head and stared at him, dumbfounded. From the beginning, we had assumed that the Euro-Africa Division was informed about our disappearance the same day it happened. We were certain that many prayers were ascending to heaven on our behalf. The thought gave us strength in our exhaustion. When discouragement nearly plunged us into a dungeon of despair and depression, we imagined the Euro-Africa Division leaders and our families interceding for us, and our hearts were filled with fresh hope. We were able to go forward, trusting that we would soon be delivered. We often talked about it. We imagined how they might have reacted when they first heard the news of our kidnapping. But now the commander was telling me, "They recently learned . . ." What had happened during the past two weeks? Why hadn't the mission staff informed them at once?

The voice of the commander brought me back to reality. He assured me we would be released soon. We talked for a few moments. I told him that remembering all that we had left behind made me sad, and I felt the tears about to start.

"Menina, don't cry," he said as he turned to leave.

When he had gone, I let the tears fall freely while I prayed for my brothers and sisters at the mission and for ourselves. When I recovered, I ran to share the news with my colleagues.

That evening, the commander came and invited us to visit the village. He wanted us "to have something to tell when you return to your homeland."

One of the carrier girls went with us. They had assigned her the task of winning André's friendship so that she could carry him. Up to this point, we had taken turns carrying him. But as the days went by, we were getting weaker, and the child seemed heavier and heavier. None of us could carry him for more than half an hour and keep up the pace of the march. It was hard on the little boy and on us. Several times I had asked the captain to send someone to help us, but every time an unfamiliar person touched him, André became hysterical and broke into frantic screaming, clinging to his mother with all his strength. Nevertheless, it was getting to be more than we could take; something had to give. Thank God this cheerful young woman was able to win his heart, and soon André was sleeping comfortably on her shoulders without protesting. She carried him from that day forward to the end of the journey.

The commander pointed out that the houses in this village were different from those in other places. Here, only the roof showed aboveground. The living quarters were dug into the earth. From a distance, only the roof was visible. When we got up close, we could see the living area underground. They were built this way to be less visible and better protected in case of attack.

At this village, we also saw another remarkable field hospital. Among the patients were both children and adults. And, just as in the other villages, they were lodged in miserable huts. A nurse explained each case to us. We saw some who had lost their limbs in combat. We saw a young man who had been shot in both legs. The nurse had operated and mended the fracture very well. The wound was completely healed, and the man had recovered the use of both legs. These people were amazing! How did they do it? They operated under the open sky, and they didn't even have a pair of gloves, not to mention antibiotics and similar luxuries. Nevertheless, infections were rare. We were also shown a young woman who had been shot in the shoulder and was perfectly recovered.

As we neared the end of our village tour, we saw something in the distance that looked like a large cage. "What is that?" we asked.

"That is a prison," was the answer.

We went over to look and saw that someone was seated inside the cage. The cage was made of thick wooden bars, and it was only about three feet wide.

"Why is that man in there? What did he do?" we asked.

"You know that guerrillas are not allowed to get drunk," explained the commander. "This fellow went to a nearby village and bought some native liquor. He came back drunk. Tomorrow when he gets out, he'll receive two hundred fifty lashes."

Oh, the poor man! we thought. Two hundred fifty lashes seemed excessive for what he had done. The commander must have realized what we were thinking. After a brief hesitation, he said to the guard, "OK, let him out. Today we have visitors. We are going to give him amnesty."

With his head down and totally humiliated, the prisoner stumbled out of the cage. "Thank these people for your liberation," the commander told him. "If they weren't here, you would stay right there until tomorrow, and then you would get your two hundred fifty lashes. Is that clear?"

"Yes, sir, it is clear," the man responded weakly.

"Are you going to get drunk again?"

"No, sir! I will never do it again."

"You know what will happen to you if you do?"

"Yes, sir!"

"All right, use better judgment next time and be thankful that you were saved."

"And think, young man, about the damage that alcohol can do to your health," added Ferrán.

At that, the young soldier hung his head still further.

"OK, go now, and make sure it doesn't happen again!" the lieutenant ordered severely.

I would imagine that soldier is still thankful that we were captured.

As we continued our tour, some long lines of fiber drying in the sun caught our attention. "Those are the fibers we use to make cloth," they explained.

As we had traveled along the jungle trails, we often saw trees from which all the bark had been removed. They explained that the bark would be submerged in water until the pulp decomposed, revealing very strong fibers. Next, they were beaten until all the soft tissue was gone, and only the cellulose fibers remained. The fibers, woven naturally between themselves, formed the long ribbons, or bands, that we now saw laid out to dry.

Once they were dry, they could be colored with a natural dye, giving them a beautiful appearance. The fiber was even stronger when woven into a fabric. When the colored cloth was completely dry, what was once tree bark had been transformed into a soft, warm cloth.

Necessity is the mother of invention, we thought. Necessity had awakened their ingenuity, and with only what nature offers, somehow, they discovered that it could satisfy a basic need.

Finally, our tour took us to a vantage point where we could observe their military exercises, songs, and dances. We had seen similar displays every time we arrived at an inhabited village. It was a mystery to us how these people, after interminable hours on the trail through the jungle or across the burning desert, found the energy to jump and shout for hours in a wild frenzy.

As the column entered the village, the participants in the exercises formed two concentric circles facing each other, one of women and the other of men. One person gave the pitch, and soon the whole group was singing and moving their bodies in rhythm.

Most of the songs expressed anguish over their loss of freedom and a firm resolve to get it back. Other songs praised their president. The native language, which lends itself to pathos, was not strong enough to express the depths of their tragedy, so they complemented the words by dramatizing them as they sang.

It was almost dark when we first arrived to observe this latest ceremony. The commander gave the order, and everyone stood and sang the national anthem. Next, a designated officer led out in military exercises. This officer was the only guerrilla we had seen who was overweight. His belly seemed even more prominent as he swelled his chest while shouting orders. He had to lean back quite a bit to keep his balance. "Attennnn-SHUN! Present arms!" he yelled. The man's unusual appearance, his hoarse voice, and his awkward gestures struck me as hilarious. I was in a serious predicament because I was standing right next to the commander. Suddenly, the man was standing directly in front of us to present his troops: "Commander, sir, at your orders, sir!"

The only thing that saved me was the darkness. The commander couldn't see me shaking or the tears running down my cheeks from holding in my laughter. "That man could be used as an advertisement for cough drops." Ferrán said later.

We rested well that night in preparation for our return to the exhausting rhythm of the next day's march.

We were nearing the great Kalahari Desert, and the terrain we were crossing was growing steadily sandier. Some stretches still ran through the jungle, however, and the tall trees protected us from the burning sun. At first, the sand was firm beneath our feet, but as we continued, it became drier and looser, making it much more difficult to walk. Before long, the trail sloped steeply upward, and we could climb only with our feet placed far apart. This seemed to help us avoid slipping backward. As hard as we tried, we couldn't advance rapidly in the loose, hot sand. Even the soldiers complained.

We climbed endlessly, again following a small channel apparently caused by rain. After more than eleven hours on the trail, we were exhausted, and our legs were cramping, yet we struggled on. We slipped back at every step as we climbed. As my strength faded, I started grasping at stones and roots. At times, I advanced on my elbows and knees. No one seemed to notice or have any concern over my difficulty. The soldiers were climbing as best they could with their heavy knapsacks, and my friends were far behind.

"Lord, help me!" I whimpered, forcing my exhausted body to take one more step. Several times I slipped back a few feet until some roots stopped my slide.

Even today, when I close my eyes, I can still see those tangled roots. I don't know how I finally managed to get to the top, but when I did, I fell to the ground, exhausted. I remained there until my friends arrived a long time later.

After everyone had rested a little, we continued a short distance to the village. It was June 28. At first, we could only see a single small hut at the entrance where everyone had to register, and beside it another one that served as an administrative office. The smell of fresh-cut straw was in the air. Apparently, the huts had been built just before we arrived. In front of the cabins was a cleared field with some poles at either end. When we asked about the strange sight, they explained that it was a soccer field for the soldiers. "If you have time, come back later, and we'll have a match," one of them said with a twinkle in his eye.

"And what if the enemy shows up while we're at it?" I asked.

It was already quite late, so there was no dance or military display that night. We all went directly to our huts where we were to pass the night.

We noticed that the huts at each base were different. Evidently, the design was up to the local base commander. The ones here were like small bungalows. Each had two rooms joined by a hallway. Each room had a window with straw thickly woven to look like jail bars. The beds looked like sofas, and they were large enough to easily sleep two to a bed.

We were pleased to learn that we would be so comfortably housed at least once on our long pilgrimage. When the leader announced that we would be there for two days, we felt like royalty. At last, we could rest! We had been walking now for eighteen days. The Sabatés and Oliveiras were especially grateful for the two-day rest. Their feet were covered with sores, making every step painful. We all knew it was useless to complain. My shoes had split and were coming apart on both sides. I gave them to our guard, and he brought them back repaired. Conchita's shoes were also in very bad shape. They had large holes that were growing larger, making it very difficult to walk. She was irritated that the soldiers didn't seem to care about her plight.

In front of our hut was a log bench where we would sit and talk to take our minds off our sad memories. The soldiers from the first group had told us that we would eventually come to a place where trucks would take us to the border. We were hoping that we would be back in our own countries by the first week in July.

June 29 was a rest day, so I got up late. Bombasa came to say hello. While we were waiting for our food, Ronaldo and I entertained ourselves by writing advertising copy for a new company called UNITA TOURS. We decided that UNITA stands for Unión Nacional e Internacional de Turismo Angolano [National and International Tourist Union of Angola]. Here is our ad:

> The only qualification you need to participate in one of our tours is that you are a foreigner working in cooperation with MPLA (People's Movement for the Liberation of Angola). Due to our company's extensive activity, you will be picked up directly from your own home at a time of day or night that cannot be determined ahead of time. If you enjoy astronomy, traveling with our company will allow you to study the stars directly above your own bed. Authentic cuisine will be prepared by our local cooks and served on rustic plates during your extended tour. To ensure that you experience all the beauties of our country, you will occasionally travel at night led by our expert tour guides. When you travel with us, avoid the bothersome reminders of civilization and leave your shaving products at home. During your entire safari, you will be guarded by the experienced tour guides of UNITA Tours so that nothing will happen to you.

We were glad to find a humorous diversion, but when darkness fell, sorrow seemed like a crushing weight on my chest. I wrote in my journal, "I am oppressed by my memories. I think about the mission and all that has happened. I'm sad, and I don't want to spend another day without walking. When Bombasa came and told us that tomorrow we will remain here, I started to cry."

After a meager supper, when everyone else had gone to bed. Ferrán and I remained for some time, sitting in silence and staring into the fire. The guard noticed that we seemed sad, and felt sorry for us so he asked if we would like to attend the political party celebration. After asking permission from the commander, he took us to watch the scene.

There was a huge bonfire in the center of a large circle. The heat was welcome because it was very cold.

First, the women sang the revolutionary song. This was followed by other songs and dances. One song was a tribute to the fallen soldiers that we had heard before. Their soft singing made the atmosphere melancholy, and everyone lowered their heads reverently.

A group of soldiers had guitars and some ancient instruments that they played enthusiastically. To close the program, they sang a song dedicated to a major who had died a year earlier on the battlefield: "How sad that Kayuquito died so young! Killed by the enemy, and we must avenge it."

Suddenly, one of the musicians jumped into the middle of the circle and, with his fist in the air, shouted, "Yeh! Yeh! Yeh! Down with the Cubans!"

To which the group responded, "Long live UNITA! Long live President Savimbi!"

Then a large, fierce-looking soldier, who was always the most active in the celebrations, began to run and dance around the edge of the circle. Everyone repeated a phrase he was singing. At first, I could not understand; I leaned forward and listened carefully until I could make out that they were singing "Our guide! Our guide!" They repeated the words harmoniously, and as the dancer continued his movement, their voices grew louder and louder while their bodies swayed rhythmically. It was another song honoring the president.

When it was finished, one of them came over and said, "The cultural part of the program is over now. We will continue talking about other things. The guard will go with you."

We could tell that they didn't want us to hear what was going to follow, so we returned to our cabins. Late into the night, we could still hear the shouts and songs of the soldiers.

CHAPTER 9

Is It Far to Canaan's Land?

The next day, the colonel invited us to visit the base. Gradually, the realization that we had been captured to provide publicity for UNITA became clear to us. They wanted us to share a positive message about them when we were released. Accompanied by the colonel and the base commander, we once again were to be shown their way of life.

As we passed by a grove of trees, we saw a group of young women listening as a soldier dictated some lessons from an old, worn-out book. They had no way of taking notes, but they were there listening, seated on a tree trunk or on the ground. The colonel explained to us that this was a nurses' training program. When their course was completed, the young women would accompany the soldiers to the battlefront. He told us that at all their bases, they offered classes in literacy, hygiene, and political science, which all were required to attend.

When we returned, we came to one of the underground cabins. It was much larger than the ones we had seen before, and it was long and narrow. It had six beds carefully lined up. Everything was orderly and clean. "This is the hospital," they told us. The patients had been removed because they were cleaning the interior. While we listened and observed, the nurses began bringing back the patients. The majority had amputations or fractures, and they seemed well cared for.

On July 1, at last, we were on our way once again. We left quite late in the day because our leaders were waiting for orders before starting. We knew that we had come to military region number 63. We had been told that when we came to this region, we would find trucks waiting to carry us to freedom.

At noon, when we had finished lunch, we asked the colonel whether it was true that we would soon come to a place where vehicles would be waiting for us. He frowned and asked, "Who told you we would be meeting trucks? We still have fifteen days of walking ahead of us."

His answer struck us like a thunderbolt. Dumbstruck, we slowly sank to the ground. We were overwhelmed at the thought, convinced that we had no more strength to continue. We had been through all kinds of suffering and troubles. We were weak and tired. In the past few days, we had gotten back some of our strength. Our spirits were buoyed by the hope of arriving soon. Now we saw nothing but a long journey in front of us. We had been dragged through sand and swamps, thirsty and hungry, constantly plagued by the fear of enemy attacks and sickness. Now we were totally discouraged. We couldn't believe what we had just heard. The colonel noticed our dejected looks and said to me, "But, I don't want the menina to be sad."

I turned and stared at him for a moment. He was a short, very thin man, always dressed in black. He held a cane in his right hand and wore a little felt hat on his head. His small face and narrow nose, uncommon among the Africans, bore a kind expression. His large black eyes with long eyelashes gave a strange beauty to his face. He seemed to take things less seriously than Captain Chimuco. He sat in silence in front of his hut. He looked at us with a thoughtful expression while he puffed on his long pipe. When the column was ready to march, he stood up and came over to us while a servant picked up his folding chair and followed behind him.

The colonel was an enigma to me. How could a man who seemed so refined be a guerrilla? The soldiers told us that despite appearances, he could be cold-blooded and seldom missed when he fired his gun. One time as he and I talked about the war, his eyes suddenly flashed like fire, and his voice became bitter with hatred and contempt for his enemy. Nevertheless, when I went to him with a request or to ask about something, his eyes would sparkle, and he appeared meek and generous. He never missed an opportunity to invite me into his cabin to converse. But occasionally, he would tell me something with a slight sense of double entendre that led me to be cautious and keep my distance.

After our latest stop, we marched in resigned silence, struggling to keep up our courage. Because we left late, the soldiers tried to make up time by hurrying us. We were nearly sick with depression and fatigue, and we longed to stop anywhere we could and rest. The last rays of the sun illuminated the landscape when we arrived at an abandoned village. Three beautiful huts, lined up side by side, were assigned to us, and we hurried to prepare our beds before dark.

Suddenly, someone pointed to the sky. As the sun slowly sank over the horizon, it painted the heavens with hues of purple and scarlet. The long shadows of the trees and bushes reached out toward us, while on the opposite side of the sky, the moon silently rose with indescribable splendor over the landscape. The stillness of the night came and wrapped us in peace, calming our anguished spirits. "The Lord has not abandoned us," we whispered as we admired the serene beauty.

Early the next morning, a Friday, we were underway. By observing the sun during the day and the Southern Cross at night, we knew we were heading steadily southward. That morning, however, the sound of Ronaldo's voice behind me interrupted my pondering. "We are going in a circle," he whispered. "The sun has changed its position."

He was right; the sun was on our left, not ahead of us as usual. It appeared we were walking southwest. "Where are they taking us?" was the question on our minds, but we didn't dare ask.

Late in the day, we descended into a valley. In my imagination, I told myself we might be coming to a place with more food and water than what we had been receiving. A small, comfortable-looking village soon appeared among the trees, and our lieutenant ordered a halt. In my diary, I recorded, "July 2, we came to a beautiful village. They have given us water to wash. Argentina lost to Brazil in Barcelona."

We found this last bit of information interesting because we captives were from Argentina, Brazil, and Barcelona. Our guard always carried a radio along with his rifle, and he let us listen to the game. With our backs against a large tree in the middle of the jungle, we sat and listened to the announcer's excited chatter. When I realized that my country's team was losing, I lost interest and left. I imagined how much worse were the feelings of my countrymen who had just lost the absurd war in the Falkland Islands.

The next day was Sabbath. We were sad that we had to walk nearly all day. At sunset, we reached an old abandoned village. The straw huts were filled with termites and other vermin. The termites build their nests by making tunnels of earth and sand through the straw. That night, every time we moved, sand and dirt fell in our faces. On top of that, rats of all sizes ran in and out among our things, and the air was filled with every species of insect. The straw walls were so thin we could easily see through them. As we sat in front of our huts, we tried to console André, who was hungry and crying. We impatiently waited for them to bring us something to eat. Finally, they brought us a plate of boiled sorghum. André ate his portion and his mother's as well.

There was very little water, and someone had stolen our last scrap of soap two weeks earlier. So, hungry, tired, and dirty, we lay down to sleep. In spite of the nice fire, we were cold all night.

On Sunday, we weren't given any food until midday. Ronaldo wouldn't touch it. The previous day's sorghum had given him severe stomach cramps. "Don't say anything," I whispered to him. "Let them bring your food, and the rest of us will eat it." As it turned out, when the sorghum with cooked beans arrived, just the sight of it turned Ronaldo's stomach. But the rest of us lost no time devouring his food to the last morsel. I didn't like the horrible mixture either, but, at that point, I ate whatever was available.

Nothing is harder than being hungry and knowing that there is no way to satisfy it. It makes me tense and jittery, and in this case, I could hardly walk. I only weighed 103 pounds when we left the mission, so I didn't have much reserve to carry me through. Once, I said to the colonel, "You can ask me to walk for hours, and I will do it, but don't ask me to go hungry because that will be the end of me." The women who handed out the food knew it, and whenever they could, they would give me extra.

That Sunday was difficult. In the afternoon, after we had eaten, we began walking, but we moved along slowly. Every few miles, we passed by groups of soldiers with their rifles at the ready. They went ahead to spy out the countryside while the rest of us stopped and waited in total silence. We didn't move ahead until we heard the words, "All right, go on." We continued walking and waiting, walking and waiting.

Around three o'clock in the afternoon, we halted again. "We must have absolute silence," came the order. We trembled with cold and fear. We sensed we were in danger, and we were troubled by the uncertainty. Conchita's lips were turning blue. We tried to warm ourselves by jumping around and walking back and forth, but the cold penetrated to the bone. We couldn't build a fire because of the risk of being seen by the enemy, who must have been very close. By the end of the day, our legs were swollen from standing for so many hours, and we were shivering severely from the cold.

The colonel explained that we were going to cross some railroad tracks and that the enemy often planted land mines at the crossings. He told us he had sent two groups of soldiers ahead to clear the area we would be passing through. As darkness was falling, the spies returned and spoke quietly to the colonel. A few minutes later, we were ordered to proceed, "Keep close together and move in absolute silence!"

Fear made it hard to breathe, and it was very difficult to stay silent. A group of soldiers was just ahead of us and one behind us. Our guard guided us through the darkness, "Watch out! There is a hole here." "Here are some low branches, be careful!" "Step over the fallen tree." I was in front, so I would immediately turn and pass the word to whoever was walking behind me.

At one point, we had to cross a small stream. I don't know how we did it in the pitch black. Our fear-filled walk worked up a sweat, and the moisture on our faces and backs gave us a chill. The tension was unbearable. It was clear that we were in grave danger, and there was nothing we could do to defend ourselves. We were totally dependent on the soldiers. A firefight with enemy forces would likely be the end of us. And when we looked in the faces of our guards, even they seemed terrified. They marched in two columns, one on each side of us, with firearms ready for action. Their demeanor, alert and constantly peering into the dark jungle, told us that the enemy was very near. It was as if I could feel the cold breath of evil on my neck. I stifled my urge to bolt in an attempt to flee the phantoms that it seemed were pursuing me.

The colonel's face also reflected the tension of the moment. Earlier that day, he had declined his lunch, and in the evening, while we waited, he kept his distance. We could see he was deep in thought.

We now made our way through a thick jungle. The trees were close together, and it was very dark. We couldn't see the low branches, and they hit us in the face or on the head as we passed. We felt sorry for little André when the branches hit him from time to time. I am convinced the angels hushed him. He only complained softly and continued sleeping without crying all night. On the other hand, I felt like crying every time I saw a branch hit him in the face.

Suddenly, we came to the edge of a steep drop-off. The soldiers that were ahead of us jumped, dropping into the darkness. Then they ordered us to jump. We couldn't see them. It was terrifying to jump into the empty darkness, but, with no other option, we jumped. The soldiers caught us in their strong, uplifted arms, stood us upright, and ordered us to run as rapidly as possible to the other side of the tracks. When we reached the other side, men were waiting to lift us up the embankment.

I was so frightened that I didn't wait for help. I dashed across the rails and started scrambling up the other side on my hands and knees, holding on to roots and branches as I went.

It all happened so fast. There was no time to think; we operated solely on the impulse to get away from the danger. It was very difficult for the carriers. The heavy burdens on their shoulders made it impossible for them to cross in complete silence. Once we were all on the other side, we were directed to run for the cover of the trees. I saw the Sabatés following me, breathing hard. We hurried on, terrified by every noise, including the sound of our own beating hearts. I was worried about the Oliveiras. When we jumped, I lost sight of them. I kept looking back to see whether I could make out their silhouettes in the darkness. The soldier at my side was irritated and insisted that I hurry. Attempting to calm my nerves, he assured me that they were coming along and everything would be fine.

As I looked up into the starry heavens, I remembered the experience we had come through on that terrible night when we had walked for so many hours. *The Lord was with us then*, I thought, *and I am sure He will not abandon us now.* The same assurance of divine protection came over me again. I remembered His promises.

After about half an hour of running and fast-paced walking, we came to a paved road that evidently had not been used for a long time. Again, soldiers formed columns on both sides of us, and we crossed rapidly. The colonel stood off to one side and observed calmly. His demeanor made us believe that we were safer now. Once we had all crossed the road, he said, "We made it!"

Our sense of assurance was fleeting because we discovered a long line of soldiers lying in the woods, ready for an ambush. It was a sight I could never get used to. We continued our walk another two hours through the woods. We traveled rapidly but as carefully as possible. We couldn't afford to have someone get hurt. The guard, who was walking just ahead of me, turned to warn me that there was a fallen tree on the road. Then, just as I stepped forward, he took a step backward and came down hard on my foot. I screamed and pushed him forward. We didn't have time to stop, and I suffered from pain in my foot for the rest of the journey.

We came to a broad open field. We continued with a strong impression that we were being pursued. Baby Ferrán began to cry. We couldn't stop for long, but Conchita knelt quickly on the ground to nurse him. The scene couldn't help but awaken a sense of compassion. As I watched this mother kneeling on the cold ground with a child at her breast, the words of Matthew 24:19: came to mind. "How dreadful it will be in those days for pregnant women and nursing mothers!" (NIV). At that moment, I was grateful to be single and without children.

We learned later that just five hundred yards in each direction from the point where we had crossed, government soldiers guarded the railroad tracks. I don't know how they failed to notice us. Either they let us pass on purpose, or the angels closed their ears so they could not hear us. We could only thank God for His care in that critical situation.

Just after midnight, we came to a sparse grove, and they told us we would spend the rest of the night there. The soldiers built a fire and gave us leftovers from the noon meal. The food was cold and tasted awful. What we really needed was water, but there was none. Soon after, we were all asleep.

It must have been about four o'clock in the morning when they awakened us, and we started hiking again—with no water and no breakfast. We marched on through wooded and sandy areas, then more woods and more sand. The terrain was so difficult that I thought we would never get anywhere, at that rate. The soldiers kept such a fast pace that we often had to run to keep up. I went on as best I could, attempting to place my feet in the footprints left by the soldier ahead of me. The locals had learned a special way of planting their feet to help keep them from sliding backward on the unstable surface. I was weak from lack of water and food, and it was hard for me to keep up.

At noon we came to an abandoned village on the top of the hill. There, again, we were given neither water nor food. We knew that the soldiers also had no reserve of food. Weak and exhausted, we lay down on the ground. Ferrán had a fever and felt miserable all over. He quickly fell asleep. The rest of us waited, eagerly hoping that someone would bring us a little water and something to eat. As we lay on the ground, hungry, thirsty, and totally exhausted, our wait seemed endless. Finally, after what seemed like an eternity, they brought us a plate of rice slightly sweetened with honey. The rice was actually more like a flavorless rice powder cooked to a sticky paste. André, Ferrán, and Ronaldo could choke down only a few bites, but we women ate as much as possible. I was afraid that if I didn't, I wouldn't be able to take another step.

When we finished eating, they brought us a little water. It was undrinkable because of its terrible smell. Conchita used it to wash her baby. The rest of us waited, hoping we would get some drinkable water from somewhere.

Not long afterward, we heard the colonel's voice, "Let's go!" Desperately, we ran to find the carriers who sometimes had a little water, but they were already far down the trail. I have no idea how we continued, having had nothing to drink since the previous day and after experiencing so much stress. No doubt God was holding us up with his powerful right arm. Three hours later, as if in answer to our fervent prayers, we came to a river with crystal-clear water. At last, we could drink until we were satisfied.

We couldn't help but worry, wondering where our next meal might come from. For days, our food had consisted mainly of brown sorghum, and now, we had seen the last trace of rice disappear. Due to our poor food rations, we were considerably weakened. It was now the constant subject of our conversation. We talked about nothing else for hours as we walked along; we all imagined our favorite foods from home.

As we journeyed across the desert, I could think of nothing but food and water. For hours, those two words went around and around in my mind. I seemingly had no control over my thoughts. Unable to move them in a different direction, I thought I was losing my mind. I was like a caged animal, pacing back and forth, back and forth in the same place. I didn't dare tell the others what I was experiencing but wondered whether they felt the same thing.

Due to my state of mind, I cannot recall long stretches of the journey. We walked along with our heads down, watching the path and feeling the pain in our feet. We moved like robots, unaware of our surroundings. At times, when we had been crossing a plain for a long time, the voice of our guardian would suddenly bring us back to reality, "*Twendy! Kowaso! Twendy kowaso!* We need to go faster, you up ahead, hurry!" Then, everyone would run.

Sometimes as if awakened from a dream, I would ask, "When did we leave the woods?"

"Oh, a long time ago. Didn't you notice?"

Our lack of water was becoming severe. My water bottle had been broken for a long time. We had hoped to replace it with a plastic bottle that we had found among the things the soldiers took from Dr. Sabaté's house. But we had to give up carrying the water when we could hardly carry ourselves. As time passed, we became apathetic. It seemed we were no longer thirsty. Only when we saw water did we realize our thirst, and we would all be eager to drink.

Little by little, our circumstances were changing our personalities. In the beginning, we tried to help one another, but as time went on, we each became concerned only with our own problems. We were aware that God was with us and that He was protecting us; nevertheless, we were becoming hard and selfish. If there was only a little food, each of us tried to get as much as possible. The same thing happened with the water. It was getting harder and harder to control our feelings, even when we were aware of them.

Sometimes we talked about the problem among ourselves. Who knows why God allows such things to happen to us? Maybe the Lord is preparing us for worse things to come in the future. Who knows if someday we will be grateful for all we have learned about survival? In that sense, we were eager to learn everything we could from the guerrillas.

The day we ate the last of the rice, we saw some fruit that looked like cucumbers growing along the path on ground-cover plants. The soldiers began to pick as many as they could, and the column became completely disorganized. It irritated the colonel, who yelled at his men to get back in place and get moving, but, an hour later, we all appreciated it enormously. When we stopped at the village for the night, the cook served everyone a large plate of the fresh fruit. They were slightly bitter, like pickles, but to us, they were delicious.

The previous day, in my concern over the scarcity of food, I pleaded with God, "Lord, please, give us enough to eat. If you don't, I don't know how we can stand it much longer!" When someone has never been hungry, they often don't even know why they are praying when they say the blessing. But when we were aware that our food was becoming more and more scarce, our prayers became vivid and earnest.

The cook also was disappointed about not being able to serve better meals. With a mother's heart, she was truly kind to us. She sympathized with us, even though she had no solution to the problem. But on this night, after serving us the bitter cucumbers, she brought us some steaming squash and pumpkin soup. When she saw how excited we were, she told us that the people who lived nearby sold her the produce that afternoon. The food was delightful, and we felt like we were having a party in a five-star hotel. We even had sweet potatoes! We were so impressed; I recorded it in my devotional book.

The next day, the soldiers told us, "Today, we have a surprise for you. We will not walk as far as on other days." For quite some time now, we had noticed that the word "soon" seemed to have a very different meaning to the guerrillas than it did to us. If they said, "Soon, we will be arriving," that meant we would be walking another four or five hours. Or if they said, "We're almost to the base," that could mean another twenty miles! When they told us we were going to have to walk all day, we assumed that meant half of the night also. Up and down the hills, we would continue across the sandy desert. In my journal, I wrote, "July 6: I'm always hungry, even though last night we ate better. Life is nothing but walking. Today we walked through cultivated fields and jungle." Having been disappointed so often, we no longer believed anything they told us.

We could hardly believe our eyes when, in fact, a village suddenly appeared in front of us. "Look!" our guide said triumphantly. "This is our surprise. We really meant it. We will stop now and spend the night here."

We were truly happy. Our legs seemed less and less capable of supporting our weight. We had so much muscle pain that we could hardly remember feeling any other way. We often experienced muscle spasms that made us writhe in pain. When we stopped, for any reason, it was very painful. We wondered if we would ever be able to walk again. Our taut muscles seemed like dry, inflexible cords. Groaning and complaining, we would slowly take our first steps. Then, as we started walking, our muscles would begin to feel better. Because of it, we tried to go along as steadily as possible and stop only when it was absolutely necessary.

We often thought about Bongo. One Tuesday, I turned to Ferrán. "Do you know where we would be today?" I asked.

"Yes, today we would be in surgery," he answered without hesitation.

On another occasion, he asked, "Do you know the story of the Brazilian pastor who was a prisoner in Mozambique?"

"Yes," I replied, "but Ronaldo probably knows the story better."

When Ronaldo caught up with us, he told us the story of Henry Berg, a missionary in Mozambique who was taken prisoner during that country's war for independence. Berg was freed after several months through God's power and mercy. During his time as a prisoner, he had to endure many hardships. I was interested to learn that before going to Angola, each of us had heard of Pastor Berg's experience.

Before I went to the Bongo mission, I had gone on vacation in Argentina. While there, I learned that a few weeks earlier, Pastor Berg had visited some churches there and shared his story. When they found out I was going to Africa, people asked me, "Have you heard what happened to Pastor Berg?"

"Yes, I have heard about some of his experiences."

"And you are still willing to go?"

"Yes, I will go!"

Ferrán and the Oliveiras had heard the same questions. "Now we're on that list," Ferrán said bitterly. "And who knows how much longer we will have to exist in this situation?"

We had naïvely expected to be back in our home countries by July 15 at the latest. Now it was July 6, and we were growing increasingly pessimistic.

Every day, the guerrillas received their marching orders from general headquarters via radio. When we arrived, they told us that the following day we would stay at the base. This was not especially good news because we knew that every day of delay meant another day before we would be free. Furthermore, we suspected that the enemy was nearby and that the guerrillas were hoping to avoid an encounter.

Before going to bed, we read 1 Samuel 14:6 from a devotional book. "Nothing restrains the LORD from saving by many or by few." After we read, Ronaldo prayed, asking the Lord to free us one way or another. Clinging to that promise kept us from being unnecessarily worried. That devotional book was very precious in our eyes. Often, it seemed that what we read was written with our situation in mind. How grateful we were to have it along.

I had been carefully carrying the little bag of bananas that Mr. Rodriguez had given us fifteen days earlier. Every day I took them out of the bag and inspected them to see if they were ripe yet. It seemed to me I had never seen any bananas take so long to ripen. That evening, I checked them and noticed that they were beginning to get a yellow tint. I put them back, planning to hand them out the following day to my travel companions.

In the early morning hours, I awoke suddenly. I heard a strange noise coming from the bag of bananas. I got up just in time to see a little mouse running out of a hole that it had chewed in the side of the bag. I opened the bag to see what he had left and found that the little rascal had eaten a whole banana and half of two others. Grumbling with anger, I picked up my precious bag and put it under my head.

The next morning, we decided it would be better to eat them half green than to let the mice eat them fully ripened.

"Ladies, come and see," the colonel called us early one morning. We went to his hut, just across from ours. There we saw a woman lying on a straw bed covered only with a stiff black cloth. Sleeping beside her was a baby that had just been born. It was cold, and the child had no more than a tiny scrap of the same stiff material between its legs. Conchita felt so sorry for the poor little thing that she took one of her own baby's few shirts and put it on the little one. The face of the young mother was radiant as she thanked us again and again.

"July 7: Obligatory rest," I wrote in my journal. We spent the day talking together, trying to keep ourselves entertained. Before we went to bed, we again asked the colonel if we could leave in the cool early morning hours and rest at midday when the sun would be beating down on our heads and burning our feet on the hot sand.

Long before sunrise, we were up and ready, seated on our luggage, waiting impatiently. The guerrillas wandered back and forth, but the column was not being organized. As the cool hours passed, our stress level increased. Ronaldo complained about an enormous blister on the sole of his foot. It was getting worse because of a hole in his only pair of shoes. Conchita could no longer find a way to tie her worn-out shoes together, and she complained bitterly that the guerrillas had no interest in helping solve the problem. The Sabatés stewed over how to keep André calm.

From my makeshift seat, I wondered what I could do to help them.

Helplessly, I realized that I no longer had the reserve of calm and strength that I had at the beginning.

When, at last, we continued our way, the path turned out to be incredibly difficult. We felt that this was the worst of our entire journey. Of course, we had no idea what lay ahead.

The whole day we walked through thick woods with no trail. The soil was sandy, and we were climbing uphill. The colonel had warned us, "Today, we will be walking at least six hours. We need to reach a river that is about twenty-five miles from here."

The soldiers marched faster than usual. Sometimes they simply ran, and we did the same to keep up. When we came to the top of the hill, we unexpectedly found an abandoned village. The colonel seemed a bit disoriented. He sent a group of men to scout the area. When they returned with their report, we were told, "Today, we cannot continue. The next camp is too far away, and we would not be able to arrive by nightfall."

After assigning us huts, they fed us. While we were eating, I noticed two large fruits that looked like watermelons. They even seemed to smell the same. We would have eaten them immediately, but we hesitated to ask. When it came to food, Conchita was no longer timid. She went and asked, "Can we eat these watermelons?"

"They are not watermelons, and you must be careful because they will give you diarrhea," one of them answered.

Nevertheless, they handed her a knife with which we cut open the fruit and ate it. On the inside, it looked like green watermelon, but it was flavorless. We didn't care. At least we had something different to eat. As it turned out, we didn't get diarrhea, either.

The next day we walked through a field of sweet potatoes. We were surprised that no one made any attempt to gather any. As I considered all we had been through because of our lack of good food, I shouted, "Everyone should stop and get a sweet potato." The colonel turned and answered, "Don't worry; today, you will have plenty of sweet potatoes."

"OK," I said. "But, if not, I will dig one up myself and cook it."

When we arrived at the camp, the colonel asked the base commander, "Do you have any sweet potatoes?"

"Yes, plenty."

"Oh good, because if not, the menina is going to go back and dig up some for herself!"

As we continued the rhythm of our daily march, we felt more fatigued each day. We felt as though our muscles would no longer stretch, even at night. To my grave concern, I noticed that Conchita no longer produced as much milk for her baby as she did at the beginning. She was feeling more and more exhausted. After only two or three hours of walking, we could see the exhaustion reflected on her face. Sometimes she dropped down by the side of the trail, unable to take another step, with dry lips and sunken eyes, her hunched-over back bent under the weight of her fatigue. The rest of us watched her with concern, thinking, *Conchita, you mustn't give up. You may lose your milk, and your baby needs it.* The greatest hindrance was those broken shoes that were much too large for her feet. When we crossed a stream of water, we would often sink up to our ankles in the mud. For Conchita, it meant that she had to continue walking with dirty, wet shoes.

The lack of water was again becoming critical. In that region, the little water that was available had every color and odor imaginable, and it was nearly impossible to drink. Silently, we all prayed that we would soon come to the place where the trucks were waiting because we felt we could not hold up much longer.

We were surprised at how the guerrillas carried the children, in spite of their weight. They walked with assurance and never stumbled, no matter how difficult the terrain or the circumstances. Not once did they drop one of the children on their backs or fall with them. That gave us much peace of mind because we frequently stumbled and fell. But we could see that the children were safe and sound.

On July 10 we came to another village. Long before we arrived, we heard the now familiar welcome song. Either by radio or from the advance guard, the villagers had been told our arrival, and all the people had come to the edge of the woods to dance and sing. After the ceremonies, we were once again assigned to our huts. They all were old and falling apart. As usual, we received cooked sorghum with honey. I was unable to eat even a little bit this time. The poorly processed sorghum gave me stomach cramps. That afternoon the cramps had been so severe that I thought something must have perforated my intestines. I went to bed but slept very little. I writhed in pain. Finding no relief, I got up and walked back and forth while massaging my abdomen. I was miserable, and even more so when I thought about the next day. I would have to continue walking without enough rest.

The day we were captured, one of the many things that the guerrillas took from my house was a bottle of Kamillosan—an extract of chamomile, which is a good anti-inflammatory medication. Since they didn't know what to do with it, they later returned it to me. We used it to massage our sore, aching feet. Not knowing what else I could do to ease my present suffering, I drank some of the extract, a little sip at a time. I felt little improvement, but I got enough relief that I was able to lie down. That same night, André was sick with a temperature of 103 degrees because of tonsillitis. It was no wonder that the child was sick. The previous night, it had been very cold. We had to sleep outdoors, and by morning there was a layer of frost on our covers.

His parents were extremely worried and did not know what to do. In Ferrán's medical bag, I found a small bottle of antibiotics and a syringe and needle in a stainless-steel box that we had used before. I stoked the fire and boiled the syringe in the little metal box to sterilize it, and then I injected the poor baby. Thankfully, the next day, he was feeling better and recovered quickly. Nevertheless, we were still concerned because having a sick child under those conditions could be a serious problem.

The next morning Conchita was missing a blouse, a diaper, and a towel that she had left by the fire to dry. Neither the Oliveiras nor I knew anything about the missing items. We assumed that they had been stolen. She couldn't hide her frustration because she had very little clothing to start with, and now her only blouse was gone. The colonel attempted to pacify her, telling her that the thief was surely not someone from the group. He assured her that the missing items would soon be discovered, but they never did, and we had to go on without them.

Now we had been walking for a month. With each passing day, our courage sank a little lower. We had no reserve to struggle against discouragement. We were constantly counting the days. Today is day number thirty-two, day number thirty-three, and so on. The counting only served to increase our despair. With our heads down, we plodded along in silence, thirsty and exhausted. Even the burden of our plastic jar of water seemed overwhelming. When we asked a soldier to carry it for us, we were ignored. Ronaldo and Ferrán could barely put one foot ahead of another. Nevertheless, the soldiers constantly attempted to hurry us. "Faster, faster!" they would say. "We have to go faster, or we will never get there."

We were walking through sand again. It got looser as we went along. At every step, our feet sank in the grainy mixture, and when we went uphill, we slipped back, at times seeming to go back more than forward. Sometimes it was so difficult that we wanted to cry in frustration.

Attempting to get our minds off our troubles and gain some courage, we tried to sing the well-known hymn that described our situation, "O the way is long and weary, and our bleeding feet are sore. Is it far to Canaan's land?"

One day, I was walking at the head of the line, wrapped in thought, when I heard some footsteps coming up rapidly behind me. I turned and saw our guard trying to catch up with me. "It's very boring for me to walk so slowly," he said. He could not let us out of his sight, so he had to walk at our pace, which, according to him, was slow and boring.

I had gone on ahead simply to avoid the temptation of talking to my companions about the terrible thirst I was feeling. I knew it was no use because there was no indication that we would have water anytime soon.

The guard and I began to talk, and the conversation soon turned to the political situation in Angola and in the world. I remembered the Red Cross nurse whom they had captured. I tried to find out why. He attempted to give me all kinds of explanations, but of course, none of them were satisfactory to me. "What you have done to us is unacceptable," I said. "Dragging women and little children through these conditions is intolerable."

"When you have the opportunity to talk with our president, you will understand many things," he told me.

"Oh yes, I am sure," I replied sarcastically. "You can be certain I will have an interesting conversation with your president when I meet him."

While we talked, we came to a swampy area, but unhappily we found no drinkable water. We found a little puddle in what had evidently been a streambed. It held a little reddish-colored dirty water. When we tried to gather a few drops, it stirred up the mud and became even thicker. There was barely a mouthful which I drank eagerly, trying not to think about it too much.

When the Sabatés and Oliveiras caught up with us, I could see that they, too, were desperately thirsty. The soldiers, realizing the situation, finally offered us a little of their own resources. They assured us it was clean, but we could see little creatures and all sorts of dirt at the bottom of the container. We closed our eyes and drank. After all, whether we died of gastroenteritis or thirst wouldn't make much difference.

One of the soldiers, trying to show some empathy, asked us, "What's the matter? Why are you so depressed?"

"What else could we be? We have been walking for a month in these conditions," Ferrán responded.

As we continued on our way, we had to cross a swamp so soft and deep that we sank in up to our waists. We could only see the upper half of the soldiers ahead of us, and they struggled to move forward using their arms and legs. The colonel assigned each of us a strong soldier to pull us out of the mud quickly if we were in danger. We moved too slowly in our guards' opinion, so they decided to carry us on their backs. Although Ronaldo preferred to go it alone, the soldier picked him up without asking and began to walk through the swamp. He hadn't gone far when he took a step and sank in so deeply that Ronaldo's legs sunk into the mud. "Why do you have to carry me, if I'm getting into the mud anyway?" Ronaldo protested as he jumped down and continued forward, struggling on his own through the mud.

To make things easier, Ronaldo took off his pants and continued in his shorts. "Check out my husband!" Rosmarie exclaimed.

When, at last, we arrived on solid ground, we found ourselves in a large desert. We briefly stopped so that Conchita could nurse her baby. The colonel warned us, "Be careful to walk exactly behind me because there may be land mines here."

On one side, I noticed two lines of wheel marks in the area. "It looks like some large truck has gone by here recently," I said. "Couldn't they come and pick us up today?"

"No," the colonel curtly responded. "Those are tank tracks left behind by our enemies. Two months ago, they tried to attack us, thinking that we had our camp here, but we had already moved to another place. From our new location, on the other side of the valley, we set up a grenade launcher and began firing at them. Wow! The scare we gave them they still carry in their bones! I think they are still running!"

Later we learned that the government troops had been pursuing them for four months and thought they had them trapped, but somehow, they had managed to escape. When I heard the soldiers talk, I began to get a clearer picture of the colonel's character: He had a strong personality and inspired both great respect and fear. He could be cold and calculating, allowing him to skillfully handle any situation. He was an intelligent man but short-tempered and unpredictable. He believed the end justified the means.

The colonel continued walking at my side. Abruptly, he turned to me and said, "Menina, from here on, you have to be carried."

The soil was becoming soft and swampy. "I prefer to walk on my own, but if you would be so kind as to carry my camera, that would be great," I told the colonel, handing him the device.

I continued on my way, carefully watching where to place my feet in the sticky muck. *Just one false step, and I'll sink up to my neck*, I thought. The colonel must have been thinking the same thing because he ordered a strong man to accompany me and carry me if needed. The other women were all seated on the shoulders of strong soldiers. Since none of us weighed very much, it wasn't a problem. Ronaldo wouldn't allow anyone to carry him after his carrier fell twice in the water and muck.

Before long, we came to a deep, fast-flowing stream. Although it wasn't very wide, it was more than we could jump. Just below the water's surface was a narrow and slippery tree trunk that stretched from side to side. "Let me pass over on my own, please," I begged. But the men insisted.

I saw that the carriers who went ahead of us had a difficult time keeping their balance. They walked close together, holding tightly to one another, forming a chain. They carefully measured each step. As the man who carried me placed his feet carefully, one ahead of the other, I could feel his body tremble. "Not so fast!" he complained to his colleague, who was going ahead. "I can't keep up!"

I imagined myself falling and disappearing into the turbulent water. I was sure I could have crossed by myself with less difficulty. At last, we arrived on the opposite side.

The ground here was generally swampy with spots of grass and dry ground here and there. Instead of setting me down, my carrier began leaping from spot to spot with no thought of the fragile person on his shoulders. "Let me down! Let me down!" I shouted while I struggled to free myself. "If you don't, I'll jump!"

The man decided it would be best to put me back on the ground.

"But why don't you let him carry you to the other side of the swamp?" the colonel wanted to know.

"Because I can't take the jostling anymore, and besides, I want to take some pictures." I found he had given my camera to someone else who was quite a distance away. I missed some good shots.

It took several hours for the whole column to get through the swampy area. At midday, we thought we would stop for lunch, but the colonel ordered us to continue. Next, we came to a sandy area. The midday sun was scorching, so we followed the edge of the woods under the overhanging branches.

As our long column went on rhythmically, stretching toward the horizon, we suddenly heard the sound of a low-flying airplane. We looked up and saw the plane pass directly over our heads. It frightened us, and we looked at the guerrillas, trying to find out what we should do. They stopped walking, but they didn't seem worried, so that calmed us. We watched the aircraft continue on toward the south. Then, just as we started marching again, it turned around and flew directly toward us, even lower this time. The guerrillas ducked into the brush, making themselves invisible. There we stood, alone and out in the open, not knowing what to do. Conchita took off running after the carrier who had her baby. The rest of us froze, too frightened to do anything. Totally exposed, we watched the sky to see what the plane would do next. It circled, flying slowly over us for a brief time and then went on its way southward again, disappearing over the horizon.

The colonel, who had remained at our side, acted as if nothing had happened, and within a few minutes, the soldiers began to reappear. The column took shape again, and we continued on our way. We were afraid that the plane might notify others of our presence and that they might come looking for us, but nothing happened.

As we distanced ourselves from the swampy area, the ground grew sandier and was full of thorn bushes, which we had to march through for hours. Walking was slow and difficult, not only for us but also for the poor carriers who could hardly move forward in the loose sand. The colonel was exasperated and constantly urged them to walk faster. We were obliged to constantly breathe the dust kicked up by those who were ahead of us. Eating their dust didn't lessen our hunger pangs—or our thirst.

Evening came, and they finally fed us. It was so little that when we had finished eating, our stomachs felt as empty as before. As soon as we finished, we had to jump up and continue walking, walking, walking on through the night.

CHAPTER 10

The Jungle Is on Fire!

The surrounding countryside was becoming dryer as we moved along. Soon we found ourselves walking through an area where nearly all the vegetation had been burned off. We saw how quickly wildfires could spring up when the soldiers lit a fire to keep warm or to cook something. A puff of wind and a spark would quickly cause the flames to rage out of control.

At the end of the dry season, it was also common for the cattle farmers to set fire to the grass so that, as soon as the rains came, tender, fresh grass would spring up. Fortunately, since the trees are tall and not very resinous, fires pass through quickly without affecting them much. However, the fires do great damage to the wildlife, especially the smaller creatures that are unable to escape.

One day, we were seated comfortably under a tree where we had stopped to eat. A few yards away, a woman was attempting to start a fire. Suddenly a puff of wind made the flames leap up and sent sparks flying. Before anyone realized what was happening, the tinder-dry grass caught fire all around us. "Put out that fire!" a soldier shouted. Quickly, everyone jumped up and began beating the flames with green branches.

For a few seconds, we sat there, terror-stricken, as we saw the flames racing toward us. Then we jumped up, grabbed our things, and ran. We had barely escaped when the fire reached the tree where, just moments before, we were peacefully eating.

Within a few minutes, the whole terrifying experience was over, and we continued on our way. We walked through great expanses of burned fields. The soot made us cough, and soon our faces and clothes were covered with dark grime.

That night we again slept out in the open. On the horizon, we could see fires burning in several places. The smoke and flames made strange images off in the distance. *I hope the fire doesn't reach us here*, I thought as I drifted off to sleep. We awoke safe and sound the next morning.

According to the commander, by July 15, we would come to a place where we would be met by trucks. We counted the days, eagerly looking forward to the end of our long ordeal.

At the first light of dawn on July 12, we began to get ready for another walk. Ronaldo was in a vile mood that morning. As he slowly moved around, his face reflected his discouragement and accumulated frustration. He took forever to get his things ready. The rest of us were worried as we watched him because we knew the soldiers were in a hurry to leave.

"Well, I'm in a bad mood, and what are you going to do about it?" he growled.

"But it doesn't help! We have to keep up our courage. Just three more days, and we will be there," we said, trying to encourage him.

"I don't want to hear about it. Today, if they start shouting 'twendy twendy,' they will hear from me," he said.

We gave up. It wasn't hard to relate to how Ronaldo felt. It was tough for him and Rosmarie to keep up the pace demanded by the guerrillas. Bombasa constantly pushed the girl who was carrying André to walk faster. His parents had no choice but to keep up for fear they would lose sight of their child. At times, we took turns watching the girl and her passenger so that his mother could worry less about him.

At nine o'clock in the morning, we were finally ready to leave. The late start meant that we would have to walk under the hot sun later in the day. The trail was sandy and difficult. As we plodded painfully along, we couldn't help being impressed by the children who were walking with us. Unlike us, they seemed to have no difficulty walking. We especially noticed the cook's children. They appeared to be no more than five or six years old, yet they walked along effortlessly, singing the revolution song for hours on end. We couldn't imagine how they did it. Nevertheless, their sweet, childish voices lifted our spirits.

The region was extremely dry, and we could smell the odor of gas in the air. Later we learned that there were valuable oil wells and other mineral deposits in the area. We would have preferred water, for that precious liquid was scarce, indeed. I was concerned about the Oliveiras, who were lagging behind. We had not seen them for some time. The girl carrying André was marching at my side. The burden was easier for her if she marched along quickly. But, I knew how much Rosmarie worried when her child was not nearby. Finding her meant leaving the boy, so I remained with him.

After a few more hours of walking, we came to a beautiful river with crystal-clear water where we could drink as much as we wanted. One of the soldiers scooped some with a black pan and offered it to me. I saw that the inside of the pan was covered with the accumulated food deposits of several days. But I told myself, "The important thing is to drink. Dying from dirt or thirst is all the same." I closed my eyes and drank, and immediately, I felt better.

We continued steadily uphill until we came to a wooded area, where that day's walk ended. André's carrier girl sat down beside me. André was quiet and listless. A few minutes later, the Sabatés caught up with us, and about half an hour later, so did the Oliveiras. They were terribly upset because they hadn't seen their child for hours. Rosmarie, especially, was nearly beside herself. She was almost shouting as she rebuked the commander, "This can *not* happen again. You promised me that my boy would always be at my side. I'm a mother, and I get distressed when I can't see him. André is sick, and now it is cold. He has been without a jacket for hours. This is serious!"

The officer exploded like a bomb. "You are not allowed to speak to me like that, *Senhora*! We are not playing games here; we know what needs to be done. Your boy was resting peacefully. If you don't want to lose sight of him, walk faster. Be careful about how you talk to me!"

His tone of voice was so harsh that we were quite frightened. His eyes blazed, and it seemed he could hardly control himself. The rest of us remained totally silent. No one said a word. Again, we were reminded of how careful we must be. After all, we were nothing but hostages at the mercy of UNITA—no freedom, no choice, and no rights. They had the weapons and the power, and we had nothing. At any moment, our story could come to a bloody end. Being suddenly confronted with that fact made us fearful.

That night we slept in the open air, and again, before dawn, our covers were rigid with ice. The next morning, Ronaldo and Rosmarie said little, but they made every effort to keep up and restore the commander's trust. As we moved along the sandy trail, I found it easier to run than to walk at times because my feet didn't sink into the sand when I ran. But on that day, Ronaldo and Rosmarie actually walked faster than I did.

After another incredibly difficult march through the desert, there appeared before us a lush green area with good, black soil. Large, exceptionally well cultivated gardens grew on terraces that extended up the mountainside. Everywhere we looked, we saw people working. Irrigation canals carried water to the gardens. The water was the most delicious and refreshing we had ever tasted. We drank until we could hold no more.

In the gardens were cabbages, carrots, and other vegetables. We were told that the workers were digging more canals to expand the area under cultivation.

After refreshing ourselves for a little while, we continued our walk. Before long, we were once again crossing the desert where there was nothing but dry shrubs and sand, sand, sand. The sand was white, and it seemed even hotter than the yellowish sand that we had crossed before. Little by little, I was running out of strength and getting behind. The Sabatés and their little boy were behind me. The carriers were also exhausted. This group had been with us for three weeks, almost continually walking through sand. Making matters worse, most of the carriers were barefoot, and their feet burned on the hot sand. The deeper we went into the desert, the more difficult it was for them.

One soldier who walked beside me never stopped talking. After a while, it became almost unbearable to hear any more of his chatter. I felt a strong urge to take off running, but where could I go? Furthermore, the boy was not intentionally bad, and I didn't want to hurt his feelings.

Around four o'clock in the afternoon, we came to a real camp. A little girl brought us glasses of cool water on a beautiful porcelain tray. The exquisite glassware was from the Portuguese colonial era.

We realized we must be nearing the place where the UNITA trucks delivered supplies. For the first time, we found a large container with water for bathing in each of our huts. It had been three days since we had been able even to wash even our faces. We were walking through heavy sand, so we had thick layers of dust on our bodies. The mixture of dirt, sweat, and sand made something like caps on our heads. My clothes were incredibly filthy, so I was eager for this opportunity to wash everything.

About twelve days earlier, I had used my last scrap of soap. Since conditions seemed favorable at this camp, I gathered the courage to ask for a little more. We were each given a small bar of blue soap with a nice scent. It was like a miracle to wash again with soap! Without delay, I washed my hair and scrubbed my entire body. Then I attempted to wash my clothing. Naturally, the water was soon very dirty, and by the time I finished, it was useless for cleaning anything else.

To conserve my precious soap, I first scrubbed my jeans and shoes with sand. Next, I wanted to rinse them in the river, but we were not allowed to go to the river without a guard. Our captors promised that someone would soon come and accompany me, but I already knew that "soon" might mean "never"—and so it was in this case. Night fell, and my clothing was still not rinsed. The following day, this would have serious consequences.

We were told that we would get a good supper that evening. The cooks were given canned meat similar to corned beef. For once, we would have meat with our pirão. It seemed like an eternity since we had meals prepared with salt or oil. We had become accustomed to the taste of the bland food, but because we were sweating so much, the salt deficiency caused frequent leg cramps.

We were thrilled at the wonderful news, but we were surprised when, instead of pirão, they brought us noodles with the meat. I never would have eaten such greasy food under normal conditions, but that night it seemed like a grand feast. I didn't hesitate. As usual, I finished before the others, and I was able to get a small second helping.

To our surprise, we weren't finished. To our great delight, the girl brought each of us a gourd with what I first thought was water. But when we tasted it, we discovered it was passion fruit juice.

"An angel has come down from heaven and brought us these things!" I exclaimed enthusiastically. I slowly sipped the juice, enjoying it to the last drop.

Later, we received a pitcher of cacao (unrefined chocolate) diluted with water. It was delicious. We had almost forgotten how good these foods tasted. It was incredible!

We knew that God had answered our prayers. During the preceding days, we had eaten very little. Our evening meals often came when our stomachs were very empty, many hours after lunch. Our legs could almost no longer carry us. The previous day, I had suddenly become so weak that I had to lie down to avoid fainting. It was probably a result of hypoglycemia. Fortunately, Ferrán still had the can with the last of the honey. He placed it in my mouth, and my strength slowly returned. I was able to stand and continue walking. That experience illustrated our poor physical condition.

We learned that when the commander realized our food supply had run out and something must be done, he changed course to bring us quickly to where we could get more food. Otherwise, we would have suffered severe malnutrition as had happened with other prisoners.

After our wonderful supper, the people of the village joined with the soldiers for a celebration. We could hear the songs and the drumming, but we were so exhausted from the previous days of travel that we collapsed in our beds. Around midnight, I woke up with intense abdominal pain. I bent over in agony. I thought I would die as the cramps wrenched my intestines. After so many days of near starvation, I had overeaten and now suffered the consequences. Then, when the cramps had passed, I suffered the worst diarrhea of my life.

The same thing happened to little André the following morning, except that the poor boy was too small to understand what was happening. We had finished our morning devotions and were preparing to leave when a soldier appeared with some chocolate bars and peanut butter. They were military rations furnished by the South African government whenever the trucks came. The chocolate bars were a high-calorie food that allowed the soldiers to walk many hours without getting hungry.

We all ate the chocolate bars enthusiastically. But for André, there were severe consequences. He had an attack of diarrhea so serious that for a while, we feared for his life.

When we left the camp that morning, I had to wear a skirt because the jeans that I had washed the previous day were still wet and coated with sand. We were soon soaked with sweat, as usual, but now, the sand kicked up by our walking got in between my legs and thighs. As I walked, it began to chafe my skin. Before long, it felt as if my skin was on fire. I had no option but to keep going. By the end of the day, the pain was so intense at every step that it was almost impossible to keep on walking. Bombasa noticed something was wrong and asked me, "What's the matter?"

I wasn't comfortable explaining the problem to him in detail, so I simply said, "This is happening because I wasn't allowed to rinse my clothes. If I were wearing my jeans. I wouldn't have this problem."

"When we arrive tonight, we'll take care of it for you," he promised.

"I'm taking you at your word, and I will remind you of it," I replied bitterly.

After some six hours of walking, we stopped at the top of a hill in a wooded area. It was evident that we were going to sleep out in the open again. The carrier girls looked exhausted, but Bombasa insisted that they go rinse my clothes.

I was in agony. The skin between my legs was completely gone—just open sores covered with sand and dirt. Even the slightest touch was painful. I asked our kind cook for some water. She brought very little, but it was enough to wash away the sand and clean my wounds.

The girls soon brought back my clothes that they had rinsed, but they hadn't been wrung out. They were dripping with water. At that moment, we had an idea. Ronaldo and I wrung out my clothes while the Sabatés and Rosmarie caught the water. They had enough to wash themselves and their children and even rinse some clothes. We used the precious liquid, literally, to the last drop.

The night was very cold, so we built a large bonfire and placed our beds around it. The soldiers slept all around us, forming a large circle with us at the center. Whoever happened to wake up in the night would throw more wood on the fire. I made myself a nice bed with a large pile of straw for a mattress, as close to the fire as possible.

I woke up before dawn, and, seeing that the fire was nearly out, I added more wood. I wasn't worried about it because there was only a light cool breeze. Some of my clothes were already dry. To keep them from getting damp from the morning dew, I wrapped them in my red camping jacket that had served so well. I put the whole bundle under my head and went back to sleep.

Suddenly, a loud shout woke me up. "Victoria!" It was Conchita. I jumped to my feet, realizing that my bed was on fire! Right where my head had been resting a few seconds before, flames leaped out of the darkness. Instinctively, I grabbed my bedsheet and threw it over the flames to smother them. I stood back, staring at the surreal scene. I was so startled that I just stood there shaking.

"Watch out! The fire is starting up again!" Ferrán shouted, pointing to more flames racing toward me. I jumped back as I snatched the sheet that covered the straw. My "mattress" went up in the blaze. The flames began licking at the cord from which some of little Ferrán's clothes were hanging. It was a nightmare.

Once the fire had been put out and I had calmed a little, I checked my clothing. One of the sleeves of my jacket was burned completely off. One of my blouses was no longer usable. One of little Ferrán's shirts was charred but intact, and the sheet that had covered the straw had a hole in the corner where my head had been. It was a miracle that my hair hadn't caught fire. In spite of the awful circumstances, we saw that God was keeping his promise to be with us even in the valley of the shadow of death.

"What a miracle that it wasn't worse!" I said.

Conchita thought so too. Her baby usually woke up around four o'clock in the morning to nurse. Because it was cold, she usually did not put her head out of the covers but just tried to make herself as comfortable as possible while she nursed. Then the two of them continued sleeping together until dawn. That morning, however, she uncovered her head and saw another fire in addition to the original bonfire. Startled, she sat up and grabbed Ferrán at the same time she shouted my name.

When daylight came, the commander found me. "Last night, I heard you scream."

"Yes, thank you so much for helping me escape the fire," I said sarcastically.

"Oh, I knew you had a doctor with you, so I didn't need to worry."

"Hundreds of soldiers are walking at our side, but when we need them, not even one is there to help," I grumbled.

On the previous day, one hundred soldiers had joined us. We had to walk three abreast, and that night more than two hundred soldiers were sleeping around us. But when I screamed, nobody moved. That's how well they were taking care of us.

In our devotions that evening, I thanked God for His special care and for the miraculous way he had protected me. When we had finished, the others jokingly teased me. Dr. Sabaté and I had worked very well together, and professionally, we understood each other perfectly. However, outside of that environment, our opinions did not always coincide, and we often had sharp discussions.

Turning to me, Dr. Sabaté said, "You are so mean that fire can't even burn you."

"And you are so unbearable that fire will not even get close to you," I replied. He got up and pretended he was going to throw me into the fire, but I said, "You don't have enough strength left for that." And it was true; the poor man was so thin he seemed like a walking skeleton. We had all lost weight, but Ferrán and I, who were thin by nature, were the most affected.

We were all in good spirits that day because we felt that our long ordeal was nearly over. We still had to cross some difficult terrain, but after another seven hours of intense walking, we finally arrived at the camp where the trucks were to pick us up. Fortunately, we knew nothing of the difficulties that were still ahead.

CHAPTER 11

Seventy People on a Truck

On July 16, I wrote, "We are at a camp where we have been waiting since yesterday for the trucks. Our long march is over!"

Here again, we were housed in dugout huts. They told us it was a protection against bombs.

After putting away our things, we went out and talked with the soldiers who had just come back from headquarters. They told us that we were not far from the border. With this news, our hopes of soon being free rose still higher. However, upon overhearing some things they said, it seemed they might be planning to hold us at headquarters for a while until we could recuperate from the rigors of the journey. Also, they spoke of certain papers that must be prepared first.

While we waited for the trucks, a young soldier in a splendid new uniform came up and greeted us respectfully. He told us he was a junior-grade officer.

To have that rank at such a young age, he must have been an outstanding soldier. He told us about the victories of UNITA in different parts of the country. In his opinion, it would be an easy matter for UNITA to defeat the communist government and throw out the Cuban soldiers.

"No problem," he said. That was an expression we often heard from the guerrillas. They never seemed to have a problem with anything. But to us, it was clear that reality did not always agree with their wishful thinking.

The next morning, we had to wait a long time for breakfast. Ten o'clock came, and we still hadn't eaten. I saw Conchita Sabaté coming toward me with a young man at her side. I walked toward them, and she exclaimed: "Vicky, can you believe who this is? He is Francisco's brother!"

The previous year, Francisco had completed his theological studies at Bongo. He was the right-hand helper of the Sabbath School leader in our church. Francisco was always neat and well dressed. He had gotten married while I was on furlough in Europe, and I brought him a small present.

About two weeks before our capture, Francisco had come to visit me, accompanied by his young bride. At that time, he was working in Malanje, a city in northern Angola. About two weeks before UNITA snatched us from our beds, I heard that UNITA had attacked Malanje, and we wondered whether Francisco had been affected by the attack.

Now, unexpectedly, we met his brother. This young man had finished high school studies at Bongo, and shortly afterward, he joined UNITA.

We told him his sister had been in our hospital as a patient and what had happened to us since our capture. The government troops closely watched the homes of those with relatives in UNITA, so guerrillas cannot contact their families. Francisco's brother was very happy to have news.

After exchanging news, the conversation turned to matters of faith, and Ferrán asked the young officer how he could reconcile his participation in the war with his beliefs. He, of course, defended his point of view. He closed the discussion by telling us that after the war, he would make peace with God. For now, the important thing was to win. When that was accomplished, there would be time for other things.

By this time, it was eleven o'clock, and at last, we were given breakfast. Two hours later, they brought us lunch. It must have been about three-thirty in the afternoon when we first heard the rumble of trucks moving slowly over the sandy roads in the distance. We embraced each other and jumped for joy. At last, the suffering of our long march was over! Little André, though, did not share our joy. He was terrified and ran to the arms of his mother. He had forgotten the sound of a vehicle.

The commander came and told us to quickly gather our things. I took some photos of the underground huts, and we went down the hill to where a truck was pulling up. We were surprised to find only one vehicle. And it was already filled with a large number of soldiers.

We could not imagine how we would find a place on the crowded truck bed. We hostages had quite a few accompanying personnel. A number of native prisoners were also to be taken on the same truck.

But we were not too worried. The relief of knowing we wouldn't have to walk any more offset our concerns.

The soldiers got out of the truck and began to load luggage. For the next two hours, they tried every way they could think of, loading and unloading, to carry as many things as possible. We sat on a log and watched, laughing and talking about what was happening, as cheerful as if we were going on vacation.

For weeks we had been dreaming about that truck. Now, at last, there it was before our eyes, ready for us to get into and continue our journey to freedom. Nothing else was important.

At last, it was time for us to get on. The soldiers pointed to a bench just behind the cab. Conchita and Rosmarie would ride inside the cab with their little ones, along with the commander and the driver. They were crowded, but at least they were protected from the wind. More and more kept getting on until about seventy people were seated or standing in the back of the truck. We were so crowded that no one could even move. It was more like a cattle truck than a vehicle for human transport. The floor was covered with luggage, and there was hardly a place for our feet. Along the sides, there were cans for oil, gasoline, and water. Nothing seemed more unlikely than this truck being able move with such a heavy burden, but at last, it slowly began to roll.

There was no real road, only tire tracks in the sand. Whenever the driver suspected some danger, he simply left the tracks and made his way through the trees, rolling over rocks and through holes, knocking over bushes as he went. At every bump, we were tossed into the air and then would crash back down on our hard seats. Pretty soon, my stomach was upset, and I felt terribly ill. We had not been underway long before we wished we were back on our feet, walking freely through nature.

At around eight o'clock that evening, we came to a village where they told us we would stop for a dish of pirão. The last thing I wanted was food. I quickly ran behind a tree and vomited until there was nothing left in my stomach. I had never felt so sick.

It was very cold, and although each of us was wrapped in a blanket, we shivered miserably. The soldiers lit bonfires, and we sat around them, trying to get warm. Shivering miserably, I tried to get as close to the fire as I could. My head was still spinning. It wasn't long before we had to get back on the truck and continue on our way. My stomach was still upset, I was trembling from dehydration and cold, and I felt faint. I would have preferred a thousand times to be walking and hungry rather than make the journey under such horrible conditions. But I could only obey and climb aboard.

We came to a creek, and the commander told the women in the cab to lift their legs because we were going to drive through the water. They tried their best to protect the children, but the icy water splashed up and soaked them. They rode on, shivering in their wet clothes.

Those of us in the back of the truck had to be constantly on alert to avoid low-hanging tree branches that could whack us on the face or head.

One of the soldiers who was sitting on the sideboard of the truck was looking the other way and took a tremendous blow. At the last minute, he saw the branch and turned just in time to avoid being stuck in the face. It caught him on the back of the head and nearly knocked him unconscious.

We couldn't move. If we tried, we would be crushed, unable to move. The mass of bodies was thrown from side to side while everyone clung to one another to avoid being thrown from the vehicle.

Some of the women had to vomit. They were quickly pushed to the outside so they could heave over the side of the truck. Then came the groans and expressions of disgust.

Around midnight, we stopped. The motor had overheated. After that, we had to stop every half hour or so to refill the radiator with water. Little by little, both soldiers and civilians began to fall asleep. Pretty soon, they were all sprawled on top of one another, forming one massive pile of humanity. I wondered whether we would survive the night. Real sleep was impossible. Yet Ronaldo, in spite of the difficult situation, somehow went to sleep. His head bobbed from side to side. I was afraid he would hit his head against the tanks just in front of us, so I reached out my arm as far as possible and attempted to steady his head a little, wondering how anyone could sleep under such circumstances.

After midnight, a few silver beams of moonlight began to filter through the trees, eventually illuminating the landscape surrounding us. I looked on in silence, wondering how this was all going to end.

At the other end of the truck bed, I saw a soldier who was holding a white bucket in which were two small black pans that he probably used to cook his food. In the beginning, no one had paid any attention to it. But now that everyone wanted to sleep, the bucket was taking up precious floor space. There was no place to set it down because wherever he placed it, it pressed against someone's arm or leg. So, he held it on his lap with both hands until his fingers were nearly frozen. Then, with a single quick move, he pushed it off to one side. The person who received it pushed it onto someone else's lap. The bucket went from lap to lap, from person to person between the soldiers. Under the bright moonlight, I watched the bucket being pushed around the whole truck. Suddenly, it came to a large soldier in the middle of the truck who raised the bucket in the air and asked who the owner was. "This bucket is in the way," he roared. "I'm going to throw it out right now."

"No, no, please," pleaded the owner. "I need my bucket; it is very useful."

"All right then, take care of it yourself." And he threw it over the heads of his neighbors. The owner caught the bucket and again held it on his knees with both hands as we continued on our way. After a while, I saw him quietly put the bucket on the lap of the man next to him, who was sleeping, leaning forward. The bucket was soon making the rounds again. When it came to the big soldier, he was exasperated and shouted. "I don't want to see this bucket again."

At that very instant, the truck stopped to fill the radiator. The man took advantage of the stop, raised the bucket in the air, and threw it out on the road. We had barely begun to move when the owner realized its absence and started shouting and pounding on the cab, "My bucket! My bucket! Stop! Stop! I've got to get my bucket." He jumped off and grabbed his bucket just as the truck began to move again. Then he checked inside the bucket and realized one of his pans was missing. "Stop! Stop! I'm missing a pan," he yelled. The truck stopped, the man found his pan, and we continued on our way.

Almost everyone went to sleep. Except for the noise of the truck, all was silence. Suddenly, my eyes caught a subtle movement, and again, the bucket was on its way. I watched it until it reached the lap of the same large soldier. Cursing, he stood up, ready to throw the bucket as far as possible. Since I couldn't sleep anyway, I quickly intervened. "Give me the bucket. I'll carry it on my lap." He handed it to me, and peace was restored.

In spite of the discomfort, my fatigue won out, and I finally drifted off to sleep. A few minutes later, I awoke suddenly. I began to laugh so loudly that I awakened some of the people nearby. A soldier was sleeping peacefully on my lap with his head inside the bucket up to his neck. All you could see was his bowed back in the moonlight.

"It looks like a calf drinking milk out of the bucket." Ferrán laughed.

In amazement, one of the officers asked how we could find anything to laugh about in such a miserable situation. It seemed like some kind of tragicomic movie in which we were both the actors and spectators.

Suddenly, we heard a shout. A woman had fainted! She was limp and being shaken in all directions, held up by several men. The truck stopped, and several men, one of whom was a nurse, lifted her off the truck and laid her on the grass, hoping she would revive. When the woman did not come around, they asked us to help. In the darkness, I felt around for Ferrán's doctor bag. I searched for the small container of adrenalin that I remembered seeing there. I finally found it in the darkness. Without any sanitary preparation, I quickly gave her an injection, and she revived. They helped her back on the truck, and we started on our way.

While we were helping the woman, the male nurse had gone behind a tree to relieve himself. He came running after the moving truck and attempted to jump back on, but someone had taken his spot, and there was no room for him. Clinging to the sideboards, he tried desperately to find a foothold. He hung in the air, bouncing like a ball from side to side.

Just then, we heard another shout—the woman had passed out again. Somehow, they hauled in the nurse and made a path for him to get to where she was. They banged on the cab, trying to get the driver to stop. But he shouted, "We can't stop anymore. We cannot drive this road during the day because of the heat. If she doesn't recover, throw her out on the side of the highway. I am not stopping again." All that the nurse could do was support the woman and try to hold her head upright so she could breathe.

That poor woman was the widow of a soldier who had fallen in the war. They were taking her to UNITA headquarters where she could earn a living and get some help.

Around four o'clock in the morning, we stopped in a wooded area. With stiff and aching muscles, we got off the truck and tried to stretch. The soldiers lit a fire, and we all squatted around it to warm ourselves. At dawn, we hostages had a brief worship and read our devotional for the day. The Bible text was about Sabbath rest, which reminded us that it was Sabbath. I had saved my only white blouse to wear that day, thinking that we would soon be free, but I now realized it made no sense to change clothes. We were covered from head to toe with black oil from the truck combined with dust and sand.

Exhausted from the miserable night, we wrapped ourselves in our blankets and tried to get a little sleep on the sand. It was to no avail. I envied Rosmarie and Ronaldo. Despite the conditions, they had slept a good part of the night. Now they were bundled together and quickly fell asleep again while the rest of us remained wide awake.

Around eleven o'clock, they brought us a little chocolate diluted with water and a military-ration biscuit. It hardly made a dent in our appetites. It seemed strange to us because we were told that the trucks were bringing a large amount of food.

Just a short time later, they brought us lunch—clean, white rice. No rocks or sand! This was covered with a sauce made from dried vegetables. It tasted fresh and had a very good flavor. It had even been prepared with oil and salt!

Late that afternoon, we got back on the overloaded truck and continued on our way. Around eight o'clock, we came to an abandoned camp. They showed us two beautiful huts where we could sleep for a few hours.

The previous day, while the truck was bouncing over logs and through potholes, we were constantly being thrown in the air and then crashing down on the hard benches. On one of those hard landings, I slammed my back against the cab of the truck. I felt a blinding pain like an electric shock in my spine that brought tears to my eyes. From then on, I couldn't find a comfortable position. We had no painkillers, so I had to grit my teeth and bear it.

Even now that we were lying down, my back pain continued, and I couldn't sit or lie on the hard bunk of sticks and straw. While everyone else slept, I quietly went outside and paced back and forth around the huts. The pain was more tolerable when I was standing up.

At about one o'clock in the morning, they called us to board the truck and continue our journey. It was very cold, so we wrapped ourselves as best we could in our blankets. Seven hours later, we stopped at a river. We were told that we would wait there until a truck on the other side came for us. They would let us know by radio when to cross. It was July 18. We waited all day. I still felt carsick, and my churning stomach showed no sign of getting better. I wasn't able to eat all day. There wasn't much to eat anyway. There was no breakfast. For lunch, they offered us some corn cakes and a little chocolate water.

We were filthy, so we asked some of the carrier girls to bring us a little water to wash. We weren't allowed to go to the river. Hours later, we finally got the water and were able to rinse our hands and faces.

Meanwhile, we looked through the cargo that had been taken off the truck to see if we could find our things. I immediately noticed that one of my bags was missing. It had contained some clothes and a pair of comfortable shoes I had rescued the first day. I resigned myself to the fact that I would have to get by without those things.

André was restless and didn't give his parents a peaceful moment. My nerves were on edge because of the lack of sleep, and I couldn't stand his whining. I took him by the hand, and we went out to take a walk.

While we were walking, we came upon a scene that left me speechless. There, sitting in the shade under a tree, was the commander. He was washing his feet in the same stainless-steel pan that they used to knead the corn cakes and to serve our food.

"What the eye doesn't see, the heart doesn't feel," I told myself and decided not to tell the others.

Because of my back pain, I moved awkwardly. The commander asked me what was wrong. "If we continue traveling this way, by the time we come to the base, you can put us in an envelope and mail us to our families," I told him. He didn't respond. I don't think he was amused, but I didn't really care. Our bodies had been terribly battered.

The heat of the desert that night was intense. We were very tired, but we could not sleep. We waited all the next day for the truck to arrive on the other side of the river. That extra day allowed us to recover a little. On Tuesday afternoon, July 20, we received orders to proceed.

We walked over a mile along the river's edge. Then we cut through a swamp where it was difficult to walk. The Quito River is beautiful, wide, and deep. Small groups were taken across in rubber rafts. While we waited our turn, we washed our clothes and spread them out on the grass to dry. The little clothing we still had, we wanted clean. I decided to walk down closer to the riverside to take some pictures.

The commander ordered me to turn back immediately. "Crocodiles and hippos are waiting for their next meal in that water," he said.

I could tell he was worried by the way he closely watched the boats move back and forth, ferrying his soldiers across the river. Apparently, more than one person had been eaten by crocs there. If one of them were to get hold of a person's leg, it could quickly pull them into the depths with no possibility of rescue.

At last, we were all on the other side, and we climbed the steep embankment into the woods. The beauty of the sunset stood in stark contrast with all the suffering we had been through. What wonderful order and harmony are created by God in nature!

We were nearing the end of our involuntary journey, filled with the hope of soon being free. We were grateful to God because none of us had suffered any serious illness. All things considered, things had gone pretty well.

The truck that was supposed to come to get us still had not arrived, so the soldiers started gathering dry straw for our beds. They gave us an ax to chop tree roots sticking out of the ground. Ronaldo set to work with enthusiasm and had soon leveled a large area to spend the night. Everyone prepared his or her own bed for another night out in the open. We were cheerful, joking, and laughing at anything or at nothing.

Everyone had already finished making a bed, and I still hadn't received my share of straw, so I went to the commander who always slept close by and asked when I would get my straw. I noticed a hole behind him that was about six feet by six feet and a foot and a half deep. There was a fire in it as if they were preparing the fire to roast a pig. Right on the edge of the pit was the commander's bed. "The heat of the fire is better conserved this way," he explained.

"But, commander," I reasoned, "during the night, you might fall into it."

"I don't think so, but if it happens, you will come and pull me out," he answered.

"Yes, if I hear that you are roasting on the coals, I will come and see how you're cooking."

As soon as we had everything ready, we lay down to rest. We had just closed our eyes when we heard the truck in the distance. We couldn't believe it! For two days, we had been impatiently waiting, and now that we had just gotten comfortable for a good night's rest, the truck arrived.

We had to get dressed, gather our things, and prepare to go. As usual, it was another two hours before everything was loaded. While the soldiers were busy loading and arranging our baggage, I talked with Bombasa, who sat beside me. Our conversation soon turned to our capture and the reasons behind it.

"You are very bold," I told him, "to drag women and little children on such a journey."

"Yes, that's right, we are," he replied crossly.

"What if something happened to one of the children? Your reputation in other countries might suffer."

"Yes, of course," he admitted, "but our children also die in war, and no one says anything. If one of your children were to die, it would just be one more child that died in the war," he concluded, matter-of-factly.

"Is it that simple?" I exclaimed, feeling my anger rise. "We have nothing to do with this war. This is *your* war! If you want to fight among yourselves, you have to accept that you will have some innocent victims."

"Anyway, it is the fault of you foreigners that we are fighting," he interrupted.

"No, it isn't! It's true that some countries are getting involved for personal gain, but *we* have nothing to do with that."

"You, white people, are the ones to blame."

"There is a saying in Portuguese: each tries to make the fire reach his own sardine. Each person defends his own interests with no regard for the needs of others. You have reasons to defend your political views, and the others have theirs. But no political cause brought *us* here. Yes, some people are attempting to take advantage of this situation with no concern for your troubles. But we came, at the risk of our own lives, to help in the midst of the chaos," I argued.

We continued our discussion for about half an hour. I felt angry inside. "So if something had happened to one of us, you would simply say that we died in the war, and that's that. After all, no one could prove the contrary."

As I think back on that conversation, I'm reminded to thank God, who cared for us and protected us each day, that most of the soldiers were kind and respectful to us. We later learned that not all their prisoners had been as well treated.

At last, they finished loading the truck, and once again, we squeezed back on. Since the cab of this one was smaller, Rosmarie and André had to sit in back with us. We felt bad that we could do nothing to protect them from the icy wind mercilessly blowing on us.

Directly in front of our knees were two large tanks for water and gasoline. Diagonally, under my feet, was a spare tire. I tried to find a place for my feet on the wheel, but the constant jostling of the truck kept making my feet slip into the hole of the wheel, twisting my leg to one side. It was an extremely uncomfortable position. There was also no place for little Ferrán's basket in the cab, so we had to take turns holding it in our laps.

We had just started moving again when the basket began going from lap to lap just as the bucket had done two days earlier. Dr. Sabaté placed it on my lap, but I already had my nose almost stuck against the tank in front of me on which some soldiers were seated with their legs swinging in my face.

The truck was extremely overloaded. There was no room to move. In the midst of the hullabaloo, I heard the cook fighting for a place for her five children. She was shouting so loud it made us laugh. It went on all night—people insulting one another and fighting for every inch of space. I saw that Ferrán had a little more space than I did, so I put the baby's basket on his lap. But since space was so tight, he kept turning it one way and then another. Finally, he hooked it over his head, covering his face with it. He breathed a loud sigh and started laughing. "What a person will do for his child," he muttered from beneath the basket.

In the cab, Conchita and the baby were also very uncomfortable. The radio was directly in front of her feet, and she had to hold her knees up to keep from breaking it. This kept Conchita from being able to steady herself, and she bounced from side to side like a soccer ball with the baby in her arms. The windshield was broken, so Conchita got a full blast of the cold wind, and sometimes, sprinkles of water or mud depending on what the truck was traveling through. At her side, sitting directly on the floor of the cab, was the commander. He was curled up like a cat, trying to get comfortable in the cramped space.

André got motion sickness and began to vomit. I handed the towel I had wrapped around my neck to his mother so she could wipe off the child and catch his vomit. Poor little boy! He couldn't stop vomiting! I could sympathize—my stomach was churning too. Meanwhile, my legs, crammed into that awful position, began tingling from lack of circulation.

The soldier next to us kept falling asleep and lying across our laps and legs, squeezing us still more. The feeling in my legs was an indescribable mix of pain and numbness. I didn't know how to free them and wondered if, when we arrived, they would need to be amputated. Exhausted, in pain, and feeling helpless, the tears began to run down my cheeks.

I never ceased to be amazed at Ronaldo's incredible ability to sleep. His head bounced from side to side, and he still couldn't stay awake. Poor Rosmarie struggled to hold her baby with one hand and support her husband's head with the other.

Occasionally, the moonbeams filtered through the trees, revealing an almost macabre scene: people bent in every position, rolling onto one another, vomiting, and being tossed around at the mercy of the seemingly demon-possessed truck driver!

It was like something was wrong with either the truck or the driver. He drove like a maniac! He raced along as fast as he could, which intensified the violent jerking and bouncing. He abruptly braked whenever he came to a curve or obstacle. The soldiers who couldn't find a place to sit were tossed around wildly. A couple of times, he very nearly threw some of the soldiers off the truck. The driver refused to stop even when, at times, it was truly necessary.

Around four o'clock in the morning, we came to a military base in the jungle. Long before arriving, we could see the fire. People from the base came through the darkness to meet us, and our soldiers jumped off the truck and greeted their colleagues cheerfully in their native language.

Whenever we came to these bases hidden in the trees, we had a strange, insecure feeling. It wasn't exactly fear, but a feeling of uneasiness when dark, silent figures appeared and disappeared in the shadows, watching us and whispering among themselves in a language we couldn't understand.

When I attempted to stand up, I had no feeling left in my legs, but the circulation began to come back little by little. At the same time, my stomach started to churn. With some difficulty, I made my way off the truck, ran behind a tree, and began retching violently. I felt as if something toxic had come up from my legs to my stomach and was now throughout my entire body. I silently prayed to God.

At last, I began to recover a little. Still trembling from head to toe, I sat down with the others around the fire. The locals looked at us silently and suspiciously. After a few minutes, the carriers brought us more chocolate water from the military rations. I took one swallow and immediately had to run and vomit. It continued until there was nothing left in my stomach. Then I felt my intestines start churning, and I had to find the latrine. The only one available had just one wall toward the camp and was open on the forest side. I felt I was being watched, but there was no other option. Intense nausea and diarrhea forced me to use it without much caring. My bowels convulsed and cramped. My teeth chattered in the cold. Finally, when it all passed, I staggered out and leaned against the wall of a cabin, totally discouraged. I longed for it all to be over.

As I stood there, a wave of seething anger started to wash over me. It was like a balloon that grew larger and larger until I was about to explode. Of one thing I became very sure: I was *not* going to get back on that truck. I would rather die in the jungle!

Daylight was approaching, and they called us to continue the journey. That's when I erupted. "I am not getting back on that truck under these conditions!" I shouted furiously. "Do what you want to me, but I will *not* travel under such inhumane conditions. It is madness! Either get some people off, or I'll stay here!"

The soldiers nearby looked at me, astonished, and hurried to call the commander and told him, "The menina is crying and says she will not get on the truck under these conditions."

In the meantime, Ferrán had also had complained. Collectively, it must have affected the officer. He ordered half the group to get off and wait for the next truck. Under his orders, the driver of the truck was also replaced. They told us later that the first driver was just learning to drive, and it was his first time driving a truck. More than once, we thought our last hour had come. It was a miracle that there was no accident.

Now, with more space, we could at least stretch out our legs and were a little more comfortable. The journey continued through the woods and across the desert, going up and down mountains, passing over roots and tree trunks. We attempted to overcome our fatigue by singing folk songs from our homeland. Rosmarie had a beautiful voice and led us as we sang together with all our might.

Ronaldo, of course, was not in the least uncomfortable. He slept peacefully while his wife attempted to hold him upright. He evidently had a special gift for sleeping under any circumstances. How we envied him! With all that happened, he was aware of almost none of it. Within five minutes of our departure, he sank into the world of slumbers. It wasn't the same for the rest of us, so we entertained ourselves singing, chatting, and reminiscing about home.

The road was so sandy that the truck could not go more than about twenty miles an hour. Nevertheless, we still had to be alert because of the overhanging tree branches.

The soldier in charge of the radio was seated just ahead of me. One time, he wasn't paying attention, and a branch knocked his cap off. "No problem!" he said, smiling, and pulled another one from his pocket. He had barely placed it on his head when another branch snatched that one off too. Just then, we turned and saw our guard lose the cap off his head! It was helpful to have something to laugh about in the midst of so many troubles.

Around twelve o'clock, we stopped in a clearing full of bright green grass. The soldiers attempted to start a fire using a long string with one end lit as they had always done before. It was usually a quick process, but this time they were not able to start the fire. Conchita had a few matches and was able to help them.

While we waited for lunch, I walked around to check out the area. At the edge of the woods, I saw three spindly trees with tropical fruit on them. I had seen the fruit in Bongo. They were green and as round as a ping-pong ball. Inside the hard, thick shell, they had a seedy pulp. The flavor was sour-sweet like wild oranges. I decided to climb one of the trees and pick some.

Ferrán and I ate all we could hold, but the others thought they were too sour. The soldiers warned us that they might cause diarrhea, but we took our chances.

They served us rice for lunch and immediately made us get back on the truck to continue the journey. We were so dirty we were nearly unrecognizable, and we laughed when we looked at one another. A grimy mixture of sweat, oil, and sand covered our clothes and our skin. You could hardly tell what color they had been.

We traveled all afternoon, and it was so hot they had to stop every half hour to cool the engine and fill the radiator with water. About sundown, the engine stopped abruptly. The commander and another man got out to see what had happened.

Just then, the driver from the previous day, who was angry about having been replaced, got up into the driver's seat and pressed the accelerator to the floor, making the engine race.

"Get down from there," shouted the commander. "What are you doing in the truck? Who told you, you could drive?"

The man sat there, glowering.

"Get down immediately! You don't know a thing about driving a truck. I never saw anyone as dumb as you who wanted to drive a truck. You told me you were a driver, but you're only a driver in your dreams. If something happens to these people, it will cost me my head! Get down immediately. You are risking these people's lives."

Angrily, the man got down, and the other driver took his place.

At last, we could go on, but we had gone only a little more than a mile when the truck stopped again. The wheels had dug deeply into the sand, and the radiator was boiling. The driver and several others attempted to cool the motor and get us out of the sand. Eventually, the truck engine started, and we were back underway.

We had gone only another couple of hours when the truck stopped yet again. The men went to work, trying to bring it back to life. They all had their heads under the hood when a huge truck came roaring toward us in the darkness, blinding us in its bright headlights.

We were terrified. What if it was a truckload of government soldiers? If there was a shootout, we would all die.

The commander reassured us, "Take a good look," he said. "That truck has only one headlight. That's a sign. It is an absolute order that every UNITA truck has to travel with only one light. That way, we know it is our people in the truck."

The truck did, in fact, have only one headlight. A few seconds later, it went roaring past us without slowing down. The commander's explanation did not reassure us for very long. We began to think, *What if the government soldiers discovered the sign and decided to use it to deceive the enemy?*

We didn't have long to ponder those thoughts. Soon another truck came out of the darkness. This one had two bright headlights!

The commander stared as if paralyzed as the truck came rushing toward us. Then he jumped out in the middle of the road, waving both arms and shouting, "Stop! Stop!" The driver didn't see him until he was very close. Then he hit the brakes hard, skidding to a stop as the commander leaped off to one side. To our great relief, the driver got out, and the two greeted each other in a friendly manner. It was a transport truck carrying arms and food for "our" side. They explained that they weren't required to travel with only one headlight because it wasn't a military truck.

Before too long, our truck was once again ready to roll. Now, heavily loaded with the recently arrived materials, we journeyed on. Around midnight, the truck stopped again. "The truck has completely broken down, and we have to call for help," they told us. It was very cold. The soldiers built a huge fire, and we all gathered around it. We waited several hours for another truck to come help us. It was our second sleepless night. We tried to lie down beside the fire, but we couldn't find a comfortable position. We got up and sat next to the fire. We paced back and forth. Mostly, we dreamed of warm beds in a safe place.

The cooks made some coffee, but we didn't want any, so they dissolved a few bars of military chocolate in hot water and gave that to us.

While all of this was going on, the Oliveiras slept peacefully in the truck.

The driver came and announced, "The truck is ready to go. Everyone get on. We are going." We started out again, but an hour later, the poor vehicle definitely breathed its last. We got off and were getting ready to spend the rest of the night in the cold when the rescue truck arrived.

The broken-down truck was loaded with all kinds of equipment and supplies. So, although we could hardly believe it, they made us get back on it. The other truck started to tow it with all the freight and baggage, on top of the weight of the truck itself! We had gone only a few yards when we came to a slight rise, and we heard a loud *bang*. Now we had exactly what you would expect: two broken trucks!

Trembling with cold and fatigue, we got off the truck once more, went back, and sat around the fire. The Sabatés and the Oliveiras wrapped themselves in their blankets and were able to sleep a little more.

Dawn found me sitting with my back against a tree in a sandy wooded area. I felt a terrible need to wash, even if just my face, with a little cold water. We were on top of a hill from which we could see the shiny clear water of a stream.

How wonderful it would feel to take a cool bath. Maybe then I would be able to shake off the tired, sick feeling. One by one, all the others fell asleep. Only I remained, sitting with my raw nerves, unable to relax. *A bath would do me so much good!* I thought. I got up and quietly went to the cook, Senhora Isabel, and asked her to go with me to the river. She agreed because she needed water for cooking. If our guard or the commander had seen me, they would have stopped us, but they were asleep.

I quickly found the tiny bit of soap that I still had, and we went down the hill toward the river. When the ground leveled out, we were confronted with a marshy wetland, and we sunk in up to our knees. For a moment, we hesitated, wondering if it might be wiser to go back. But we told ourselves we couldn't be very far from the water and we continued. About a half-hour later, we got through the marshy ground and onto a dry area surrounded by large trees. Then we saw it. There was an obvious path made by animals that led to the river. We followed it, and soon there appeared before us a stream of clean, cool water. Without hesitating, we got in, clothes and all, and began to wash from head to toe. The water was cold, but it felt so good!

I asked Senhora Isabel what kind of animals made the footprints. She told me they were from elephants, lions, rhinoceroses, hippos, and other smaller animals. I had read that elephants could be irritable when they encountered human beings unexpectedly. And what if we crossed paths with a lion?

A chill ran down my spine! After my questions, Senhora Isabel wasn't so comfortable either. We finished bathing as quickly as possible, looking around constantly to see if some large animal was coming in our direction. On top of the hill, I could see the truck and the soldiers quite some distance from us. "Do you suppose they could hear us if we shouted for help?"

"Even if they did, they could never get here in time if we were really in danger. That much is certain."

"Here come the elephants!" I said, half-joking, but I really was afraid. The animals could come at any moment to drink because it was early in the morning. When we finished washing, Senhora Isabel filled a large pan with water and put it on her head. We started back. In our haste, we decided to take a shortcut, but we got into a swampy area where we sunk in at every step. Senhora Isabel, with the extra weight on her head, was sinking deeper than I was. I found a place along the edge of the water where the ground was firmer and we could walk faster, but we noticed that other creatures had utilized the same trail. We could clearly identify the footprints of large cats, evidently lions. Now, thoroughly frightened, I prayed without ceasing, asking God to help us get out of there. I regretted having been so foolish as to leave without military protection and get so far away from the group. We had no weapons and no soldiers to defend us if an animal attacked us.

I began to tremble with fear. My heart was pounding so loudly it seemed as if I could hear it. When Senhora Isabel discovered fresh footprints of rhinoceroses and hippopotamuses in the soil, she, too, was terrified. In the swampy areas, it is not unusual to see a hippo suddenly come out of the water and mud. They do not usually attack, but they are unpredictable when startled. I had started toward the grassy area when I saw a small animal hiding among the reeds. It looked to me like a baby lion, watching us fearfully. I had the impression that its mother must not be very far away. Cautiously we turned and hurried back along the edge of the river. Isabel knew she shouldn't have agreed to bring me. It would cost her head if something happened to me.

Now more frightened than ever, I continued praying: "Dear heavenly Father, I was very foolish. Please forgive me and help us to get back to the camp safe and sound."

At last, we could see the truck, and we began to call for help.

Two soldiers came running. "Yes?" they said. "What do you need?"

"Ah, well, . . . that is . . . I, ah, . . . I was wondering if maybe you could help Senhora Isabel carry this water." We were more than happy to be back in camp, and we didn't tell anyone about our adventure.

CHAPTER 12

Another Camp and Another Friend

For breakfast, we had potatoes and fish. The natives are never in a hurry; it was ten o'clock, and we were hungry, so I decided to help by peeling potatoes.

The UNITA people often asked if I would stay with them. They made me all kinds of offers because they were interested in my services as a nurse.

During the long march, I overheard the soldiers say, "Menina is one of ours. She is a true UNITA. Look at how strong her legs are!" They spoke with admiration of how well I endured the rhythm of the march and my ability to adapt to any situation. More than a few times, I was invited to stay with them. I always thanked them but courteously refused the invitation.

This morning, it was Senhora Isabel, the cook, who spoke, "You would be very useful in the ranks of UNITA," she said. Their insistence worried me because I knew they could force me to stay. If they refused to let me go, I would have no choice.

At last, the food was ready. We each received a large serving of potatoes, which we began eating eagerly. It had been more than twenty-four hours since we had eaten anything.

We had barely finished when a truck pulled up, and we heard the order, "Hurry! Hurry! We have to go! All aboard!" I had my hands full of wild fruit that I had gathered in the jungle with the cook's son. I stashed the fruit, planning to eat it on the journey. It would be a healthy dessert, rich in the vitamins we needed so much.

Supposedly, we were to be given our freedom at UNITA's general headquarters, which was about a day's journey away. The prospect of soon being free made us happy, and our spirits were high. We traveled about an hour before arriving at a base in pleasant green terrain.

The truck stopped, and Senhora Isabel was ordered to get off with her children and the girls who worked with her. Isabel looked at us with a surprised look. All of a sudden, we had to wonder where they were taking us. *Who is going to cook for us now?* we wondered. Our concern deepened when we saw them unload the food and other supplies. Something was wrong. Things were not going as we expected. Why didn't they tell us what was going on?

We were sad as we said goodbye to Senhora Isabel. She had been very kind to us and had always tried to help us as much as possible. Her departure made us feel uneasy about our future.

We continued a while longer and came to another camp. All the soldiers who had been with us for three weeks were now ordered off the truck. Bombasa and the lieutenant colonel also left. We looked at one another with apprehension. Hadn't they told us that this group would accompany us to headquarters?

They introduced us to Major Melgasso, a tall, strong man with a large scar on his right cheek. He and another man got on the truck, and now they were the only ones on board with us five missionaries. The major told us that we would soon be at the end of our journey. Again, we were surprised and wondered what was going to happen to us. We continued on our way, alongside a small stream of water, through beautiful fields of vegetables.

Suddenly, we left the road and headed over some rough terrain into the woods. The wooded area was thick with thorn bushes growing so closely together they looked as if they were woven. When the truck stopped, we could see some old, run-down huts in the brush.

"We have arrived!" they announced. "Get off, please!" Alarmed, we looked at one another fearfully. What are they going to do with us? Weren't they taking us to headquarters to set us free? They showed us three huts and told us that we would be staying in this place for the next two or three weeks. I broke out in a cold sweat. It was as if we had been kidnapped all over again.

As we looked carefully, we could see more huts, well-hidden in the thick vegetation. We saw soldiers walking everywhere.

Our huts had cots made of sticks and straw as we had often used on our journey. One side of the cot was tied to the hut's corner posts, and the other side had legs stuck into the ground. A second layer of branches had been added over the first to make it firmer. A mattress of dry straw lay over the branches. On the other side of the hut was a little table constructed the same as the bed, but without the straw mattress.

The hut didn't have a door, so I hung a sheet in the opening. That sheet was invaluable. I had found it on the first day after we were kidnapped and had been using it to tie my things in a bundle. It was too short to cover the door opening, leaving a gap above and below it. Anyone who wanted could look in. At first, I felt like I was constantly being watched, but I got used to it. At least the cloth gave me a little privacy.

In my journal, I wrote that night, "Major Melgasso introduced us to Father Fernández, a Spanish priest who had been kidnapped eight months earlier. I struggled with a hopeless feeling."

When Major Melgasso brought Father Fernández, I immediately recognized his voice. As I listened to him speaking, I remembered back to April 5 of that year. Early one morning, before going to work, I turned on my radio, and by chance, tuned in to the Black Rooster, the underground station that belonged to UNITA. On the broadcast that day, they interviewed sixteen Portuguese men and a priest, Fernández the Spaniard, whom they had kidnapped. They announced that all of them would be immediately given their freedom.

I was shocked to find myself face-to-face with a man who supposedly had been freed. "How is it that you are still here?" I asked. "Weren't you freed along with the sixteen Portuguese men as they said on the radio broadcast?"

"On the fifth of April," he told me, "they took me along with the sixteen Portuguese men to a rendezvous in the jungle where thirty reporters were waiting. After the interview that you heard, the other hostages were set free. But they brought me back here to the camp. They still haven't told me why. Now four more months have passed, and I still have no idea what they plan to do with me."

When I heard those words, my spirits fell to the lowest they had ever been. All of us felt like crying. We asked one another what we thought might happen to us and how much longer we could be held here. Every day during our long, tedious journey, we had been cheered by the idea that trucks were waiting to take us to freedom and that soon, we would once again be with our loved ones. Now, here we were in the jungle for no apparent reason and without any real prospect of freedom. A dark cloud of confusion tormented us.

Major Melgasso came with a long questionnaire in his hand and assembled us for a lengthy interrogation. He wanted to know where we came from, how long we had been in Angola. He asked where we had worked and wanted to know the details of how we had been kidnapped. He also wanted to know how the soldiers had treated us on the journey and if, during our time in Bongo, we had seen any Cubans. Fortunately, no Cubans had ever come to the mission. In fact, we didn't really know what exactly they were doing in Angola. The major warned us that we had better tell the exact truth and the whole truth about everything we knew. Lying would be punished, he told us. For Christians, telling the truth is a principle of life, so in that regard, our consciences were at ease.

My hut was just at the edge of the woods. That first night alone, surrounded by soldiers and hearing the strange sounds of wild animals, sleeping was very difficult. Fears, uncertainty, and sorrow filled my thoughts. It was the first of many long, sleepless nights.

The next day, I went out to gather some firewood, and in the bushes, I saw a white man accompanied by two soldiers. He came toward me, and I introduced myself. "I am Victoria Duarte from Argentina. I'm a nurse. Who are you?"

Silence.

"Do you speak Portuguese?"

"Yes," he said after a long moment.

"How long have you been here? We just arrived yesterday. We were kidnapped five weeks ago."

"That's not so long," he replied. "I've been here for almost two years."

From his accent, I concluded he must be one of the two Russian prisoners we had heard were being held at this camp. One of the soldiers who were with him turned and went into a hut and called him. The man had to go.

I picked up my firewood, and after I had gone a few steps, I turned to look at the man. At that moment, he was squatting inside his hut. When our eyes met, he placed his finger on his lips to warn me that it was forbidden to speak with him.

About midday, they brought us breakfast: white rice with fried eggs. It was so delicious; we almost felt like we were back in civilization.

The soldiers asked whether in the future we would prefer to prepare our own food. It seemed like a good idea to us because that way, we would at least have something to occupy our minds. We could also schedule our own mealtimes. However, we soon realized we had a problem. They gave us only one tiny pan, a little rice, and a small can of chopped meat.

I had trouble explaining to the girls what we needed, but at last, they seemed to understand and brought us a larger pan. The smaller pan ended up being my plate. The girls also brought us each a fork and a water container.

Every day they distributed the food, which consisted of a half-cup of rice, a tablespoon of oil, and about half of a small can of cornflour for each person. For breakfast, they gave us a small amount of military chocolate because we didn't want coffee. Sometimes they gave us dried fish or canned meat that I had trouble digesting. Twice, I had attacks of dysentery that caused me to lose even more of the little weight I had left.

Worst of all was the idea that we would have to stay in this camp, condemned to inactivity and uncertainty. I often sat in my hut and read my Bible through tears. I determined to study a new Psalm every day, and seek the promises of God for strength to bear the trials.

On the second day after we arrived, the major returned with another form for us to fill out. He was annoyed because Dr. Sabaté had complained at length about the difficulties of the march. I tried to defend him, and as soon as the major left, I ran to the Oliveiras and warned them to be very careful about what they said. We were always careful to avoid saying something that might put our freedom at risk.

The next day, when I met the major again, I asked him if it would be possible for him to give me something to do. I told him it was almost unbearable to sit alone in the hut all day with nothing to do.

In fact, I thought, *Marie, the Red Cross nurse, should be here by now. She was kidnapped fifteen days before we were.* During our long march, I had often asked if she had passed that way, and they told me that she had. Supposedly, in her group, there were some Portuguese, one of whom was so sick he had to be carried.

"Where is the Swiss nurse?" I now asked the major.

"She hasn't arrived yet; she must be on her way," he answered.

His answer seemed strange. *Something is not right here*, I thought, but I said nothing.

I soon learned that there were also two Cubans living in our camp. Supposedly, they had deserted the Cuban army and surrendered to UNITA. At Jamba, UNITA's main base, a Party Congress was underway. All the foreign prisoners who were normally held there had been brought here. However, except for the Russian and the Spanish priest, we hadn't seen any of the others.

On Sunday, July 25, the major came to my hut and told me to come with him. Some foreign journalists had arrived who wanted to interview us. Along the way, he signaled for me to wait while he went to get the Oliveiras and Sabatés. He went off with them and later came back for me. He took me in a different direction. We went way back into the woods until we came to a hut where he stopped and called out. A white woman appeared in the doorway. I instantly knew who she was. She perfectly fit the description given me a few days before our capture by the grandmother who brought her wounded grandchild to Bongo. This could be none other than the Swiss nurse, Marie!

Without asking permission from the major, I asked her, "How long have you been here?"

"I have been here fifteen days," she answered.

I looked at the major, who uncomfortably admitted, "Yes, I lied."

"I can tell," I answered sarcastically.

The major turned and motioned for us to follow him through the woods. We soon came to a clearing where they had set up a flimsy table and two benches. We sat down on a log to wait for the reporters. The major watched nervously, worried that the reporters had gotten lost. Finally, he went off to look for them, and we took advantage of his absence to talk quickly. We whispered quietly in French.

Marie was very worried about the upcoming interview. In the morning of that same day, UNITA officers had interrogated her at length. For more than two hours, they had pressured her about what she would say to the reporters. They admonished her to think carefully before answering their questions. And they reminded her that her freedom depended on what she said.

UNITA was in a sharp conflict with the Red Cross. They complained that the organization worked only on the government's behalf. They contended that if the Red Cross were neutral, it would help both sides equally. Marie's kidnapping was a protest. They pressured her to say things that would defend their point of view regarding the Red Cross.

The poor woman was very nervous. She knew she had to be careful, but now, after so much pressure, Marie was really afraid that she might say the wrong thing. I attempted to encourage her as best I could, but just then, the major arrived with the journalists, and we had to stop talking.

A reporter first greeted Marie and then me, and then asked us both, "What can we do for you? How are they treating you here?"

"Thank you! We are treated well. They're not bad to us."

"Can we do anything for you? Should we inform your families?"

"Oh, yes, please, that would be wonderful."

We gave them our families' telephone numbers, and they promised to let them know about the interview. What a relief! It had now been forty-five days since we were kidnapped—a long time for our families not to receive any news about us.

After the interview, the journalists gave us toilet paper, paper towels, and other useful items. One of the reporters was from a Swiss newspaper. He took photos of the two of us seated on the log. Following them, reporters from an American television program interviewed us. Finally, they said goodbye, and we were taken back to our huts.

In our short conversation, Marie told me she lived with two UNITA girls who were not kind to her. She wanted to ask the major for permission for the two of us to live together, but she didn't have the courage.

When we arrived back at my house, I asked the major for permission to spend some time visiting with Marie. "I'll think about it," he answered.

The next day I waited in vain all day for his answer. In the evening, I went looking for him. He told me, "You can go see her, but she cannot come to visit you."

I ran to see Marie. We were both overjoyed because doing nothing all day was difficult.

Conchita and Rosmarie kept busy caring for their children. They had to cook and clean their huts, bathe their babies, wash their clothing, and so forth. None of it was easy under the circumstances. Every drop of water was carefully conserved. Each hut had a container, which was actually a metal ammunition bucket, that held about three gallons of water. Every morning a truck picked up the containers, filled them from the stream, and brought them back. The precious liquid had to last all day. The desert heat forced us to drink at least two or three quarts of water per day. We had to get by with the rest for all of our other needs. During the long journey here, we had learned to economize, and now we needed to be just as careful. "When we leave here and can have a whole bathtub full of water, we're going to be in danger of drowning!" we said, laughing.

To avoid feeling so lonely, I sang throughout the day—every hymn I could remember. I sang while I was cooking, sweeping, or gathering firewood. One day while I was singing, I turned toward the hut of the Russian and saw that he was staring at me. He gave me signals explaining that I had better be quiet, and if I didn't, I risked being locked up!

Every time I saw him, I felt sorry for him. We, too, were held captive, but at least we were allowed to talk. He couldn't talk with anyone but his guards. He passed the whole day pacing back and forth in front of his hut like a caged lion. His situation made me very sad because I couldn't think of a way to help.

Early the next day, I went to visit Marie at her hut. The base captain's hut was right next to hers, so he could hear everything we said. We spent the morning together, and after lunch, we got together again. We talked until very late, seated around the fire, sharing our adventures.

That night I slept soundly for the first time in a long time.

The next day, I felt very sick after I ate some of the canned meat. It gave me stomach cramps and diarrhea and made me feel very weak. In my diary, I wrote, "All day, I have been very sick. The strange ways of our Lord, who can know them?"

I found a dirty, old piece of paper in the trash, and I used it to write a long letter to Monica Braun, the secretary of the Euro-Africa Division. Of course, I was never able to send the letter, but I kept it as a memento. Among other things, I wrote, "I dream that other people will find out about us. I write and reflect in silence and solitude. I ask myself: why, why?"

I also wrote to my sister with the hope of being able to hand the letter to a journalist who might pass through.

It has now been fifty-five days since we were captured, and we are still living in total uncertainty. There are about twenty of us prisoners, all foreigners, and all of us are in the same situation. We're losing courage. We live in little huts in the middle of a forest. At night, I'm afraid. I hear hyenas, lions, elephants, and wild dogs around the camp. Sometimes large groups of them come through. The captain insists that none of them would ever come into our camp, but I keep the fire in my hut lit all night, just in case.

I asked my sister to get in touch with a UNITA representative in Geneva, but the letter I finally gave to the captain never left the base.

Around the end of July, we received the good news that we would go to the river to bathe and wash our clothes. It was way overdue! Our things were still black with the filth of our long journey in the trucks. When we first arrived, we were given some articles of clothing, among which was a bathing suit. I looked at it and asked, laughing, "What good will this do?" Now, I was happy I had it because it would allow me to bathe and enjoy being in the water.

From then on, they took us once a week to a stream-fed lake about a forty-five-minute walk from camp. The water was clean and clear, and even though we didn't have any soap, we bathed the best we could. We also took advantage of the opportunity to wash our clothes, rubbing them with ashes and sand. The most important thing was the *sensation* of being clean.

Once, while we were there, standing in water up to our knees, a young hippo suddenly rose up out of the water a short distance away! We screamed, and he went back under. We never saw him again.

Little by little, our camp life became routine. Around nine o'clock every morning, we missionaries met together under a tree for our devotions. After that, I would spend the rest of the day with Marie, and in the evening, I met again with the Oliveiras and Sabatés for our evening devotions.

Often, we would stay and discuss our situation. We still couldn't make sense of our capture. There was probably more than one reason, but we couldn't figure out any. Sorrowfully, we thought about all that we had accomplished in Bongo. But now, all we could do was hope that the hospital was still functioning and would not be permanently closed.

I also enjoyed the time playing with the children. Little Ferrán was still a baby, but I really had fun with André, playing in the sand and imitating the soldiers' military exercises. He would stand up straight, raise his hand in a military salute and say, "Yeh, yeh, yeh!" the way the soldiers shouted in their meetings. I would answer, "Yeh, yeh, yeh." Pretty soon, André began calling me "Yeh yeh." It became his name for me from then on.

Now that we weren't walking all the time, André calmed down and rapidly adapted to the peaceful life in the camp. He played and behaved normally, which was a great relief to everyone.

We all talked about what we would do when we got home. No one knew when it might be possible, but we tried to keep up our courage by making plans for all kinds of projects when we returned home. It was good to be able to have these times together. Alone in my hut, I would have lost my mind.

"If you don't give me something to do, I'm going start climbing up onto the roofs of all the huts," I told the major one day. "Anything would be better than just spending the whole day doing nothing!" He promised to see if I could help in the infirmary, but he never brought it up again.

CHAPTER 13

Love and War

One afternoon, when I arrived to talk with Marie, I saw she had a visitor. There, seated next to her on the log, was a young Portuguese man. She introduced us. "I'd like you to meet José Matos Botelho."

He was tall and very thin. Marie explained that he lived with five other Portuguese men on the other side of the camp. Because these men and Marie had been together on their long march, they were allowed to meet with one another. One of the other Portuguese men was a Catholic priest to whom Marie was giving French classes.

"How long have you been a prisoner?" I asked Botelho.

He looked around and then answered in a barely audible voice, "Three years."

I asked him some other questions that he chose not to answer.

"Be careful what you say when the girls who live with me are here," Marie warned me later. "Botelho has been a prisoner for three years, and they don't want to free him. He knows a lot about UNITA that they don't want anyone to know. So we have to be very careful when we talk to him."

Marie told me Botelho had given her a tiny scrap of paper with his mother's address in Portugal. We all expected that Marie would be released first because she worked for the International Red Cross, but Botelho was not sure that he would ever be free.

Now that I could talk to Marie, I no longer felt so lonely, but I still experienced periods of deep depression. My insomnia worsened and became more frequent. It was as if the whole sleep system inside my head was broken. Sometimes I would sleep soundly for an hour or two, and then I would wake up anxious, tossing and turning on my hard bed. By morning, I was tense, tired, and depressed.

On one especially bad night, I tossed and turned for hours on the straw, but I couldn't relax. Suddenly the night silence was interrupted by the howl of a hyena that I could tell was very close. It sounded like the mocking laugh of a diabolical woman. I jerked instinctively under my sheet. Then I sat up, found the stick of wood I always kept at hand, and put it on my fire to make it flare up. I hoped the flame would frighten the animal away.

Fully awake, I gave up on sleep. I looked up through a hole in the roof of my hut. The brilliant African night sky had always fascinated me. With no artificial light in the area, the stars shone in all their splendor. The Milky Way, with its myriad of lights, arched across the firmament with indescribable beauty. Beyond that, I could see part of the Southern Cross. If we followed it, we would come to Namibia and freedom, I imagined.

The moon crept toward its zenith. Just next to it, a little star was flickering timidly. This star accompanied the moon every night, getting a little farther from it each night. It must be close to midnight, I thought.

I turned and looked through a hole in the wall at the surrounding landscape. The dry desert grass and the stunted bushes were transformed into an enchanted forest as the moon bathed every leaf and blade in a pearly glow. I could hear soft rustling in the grass and crackling branches, telling me that the small forest creatures were going about their nightly activities. As time passed and the moon descended slowly toward the horizon, I thought, *Soon, the morning star will appear*. I sat up on the edge of my bed, took out my Bible, and read from the sixteenth psalm:

> I will bless the LORD who has given me counsel;
> My heart also instructs me in the night seasons.
> I have set the LORD always before me;
> Because He is at my right hand I shall not be moved (verses 7, 8).

That text soothed me. I asked God to help me, even in these circumstances, to recognize His guiding hand and to have a heart filled with gratitude and love. My prayer would soon be answered in an unexpected way.

The next day, some soldiers took us to the river. As we passed the hut of one of the Russians, the hopeless look in his eyes tore at my heart. He and his comrades were held in separate huts under heavy guard. The poor men were not even allowed to converse with one another.

We continued on to the stream. Through the tall grass, I could see a white man fishing nearby and a second man a little farther away. From their appearance, I surmised that they must be the Cuban soldiers we had heard about. While we washed our clothes, Conchita and I chatted in Spanish. The baby was lying on a sheet under a tree.

Ferrán wandered nearby. "Watch out, or the hippos will get you!" I shouted as he disappeared behind some bushes. After a few minutes, the soldiers started to wonder where he had gone and decided to follow him. As soon as they were out of sight, the taller of the two Cubans came quickly over to me and asked where we were from.

"I am from Argentina, and my friends are Spanish," I replied.

"And what are you doing here? How did you happen to be captured?"

I quickly told him how we been kidnapped from the mission where we were working.

"What do you plan to do when you are free? Will you go back to back your country?"

"I would love to, but at this point, I'm not sure we will ever be free. And what about you? How did you end up here?"

He briefly told me he had deserted the Cuban army and surrendered to UNITA.

"We will have to remain here," he said sadly. "We can never return home."

"Your family must be worried about you."

"Yes, I am sure they are."

"In your country, they are very hard on the so-called 'reactionaries.' "

"Oh, yes! In fact, it is likely that my family has already suffered for it."

"I am truly sorry for you," I answered, trying to imagine how the young man felt.

"Thank you, but listen! Don't go back to Argentina. Stay here, and we can grow old together!" he proposed suddenly. "We could get married and spend the rest of our lives together here in Angola."

"You Latino men are all alike," I answered, laughing.

Just then, the soldiers returned, and he quickly left.

Ferrán followed along shortly, and the soldiers ordered us back to camp. On the way, we came across some large wild animal footprints, and I wondered what it would be like to meet up with the owners of those footprints. The Cubans passed in front of us without looking in our direction.

That evening I went to visit Marie and laughingly told her about the sudden marriage proposal. She said seriously, "For the Cuban, it probably wasn't intended to be amusing. He has been here two years in the hands of UNITA with no hope of freedom. He sees a young woman who speaks his language, and he thinks, *It's now or never!* His proposal may have been serious."

I could see her point, but I soon forgot the matter.

The next day was Sabbath. Ronaldo said, "In Bongo, you were the Sabbath School leader. I propose that you lead our Bible study today."

I suggested that we sing a hymn that speaks of Jesus as our refuge. He is a mighty Rock offering us shade when we walk on the burning sands of life. His marvelous love surrounds us, and His hand is over us for our protection. That hymn was a favorite of mine because it reminded me of my childhood in the country. I remembered finding baby chicks that had been abandoned by their mothers and taking them home and caring for them. As I held them securely in my warm hands, they chirped contentedly.

We had literally come through a burning desert. Often, as we plodded along, we could see in the distance a single tree. It offered the hope of some shade where we might be able to stop and forget, if only for a moment, that we were surrounded by dry grass, stunted bushes, thorns, and sand. The hymn reminded me that, even though we were at the mercy of our captors, beyond all of it was a loving heavenly Father who offered us shelter and protection, just as I had done for the abandoned chicks.

We invited Fernández, the Spanish priest, and Tiago, a seminary student who had been captured with him in the same ambush, to join us for our worship time. We lent them a Bible so they could participate in our Bible study. We were pleased that we had the privilege of worshiping in peace on that Sabbath in our circumstances.

Afterward, Marie took my Bible to the Portuguese priest, Father Neto, on the other side of the camp. He had asked for one, and though I hadn't met him, I was happy to share it with him. He said it would help him at mass if he could read the Bible texts directly. After that, every morning following our worship, I took my Bible to Marie, and she lent it to Father Neto.

On August 1, I wrote, "Long conversation today with Botelho and Marie about the justice of God."

Both of them had heard us singing on Sabbath, and they wanted to know more. At first, we talked about faith. During his three years of life as a prisoner, Botelho had seen and lived through terrible experiences. It was not strange that he had lost his childhood faith.

"How can you still believe in God?" he confronted me. "You were working for Him at the mission, but evidently He didn't care and left you to your fate. If that wasn't the case, you wouldn't be here!"

"Yes, I still believe in Him," I answered. "I'm happy to have a God I can trust. If not, things would be a lot worse for me."

He insisted, "Yes? That sounds nice, but where was this God when they came for you? Why didn't He protect you? I cannot believe in a God who doesn't show up when you need Him. I'm sorry."

I was silent for a moment, praying that God would give me the right words. We talked at length, and he always came back to the problem of suffering and why there was so much evil in the world. Why does God allow innocent people to suffer and die?

"I don't have the answers to all your questions," I told him, "but the Bible offers some hints in the story of Job and what happened to him. Job was rich and happy. Suddenly he was overwhelmed by trouble. He lost everything in one day: his children, his cattle, and all his wealth! And, to make matters even worse, he soon became gravely ill. At that point, his wife turned on him and said, 'Curse God, and die!'

"Under the pressure of that terrible pain and suffering, Job battled a terrible crisis of faith, and in the end, he was totally out of answers. Then God revealed Himself. He showed Job that above and beyond the mystery of suffering, the universe is filled with mysteries that speak to us of power and wisdom that leave us breathless with wonder and awe. Job recognized then how little he knew and could understand beyond his own limited sphere. When he understood all of that, he bowed his head and said, 'I have heard of You by the hearing of the ear, but now my eye sees You' [Job 42:5].

"This story helps us understand better the meaning of human suffering, but I still need to think a little about how to answer your questions more clearly. Let's meet again and continue our conversation."

That afternoon I went to see Pastor Oliveira and told him about our conversation. "You can tell him about the origin of evil," he suggested, "about how it came to earth and all that has happened since then. Tell him about the plan of salvation and how God is going to put an end to suffering and pain."

I contemplated Botelho's questions, read my Bible, and prayed a lot during those days. Every day we met and talked while sitting on the log that marked the boundary between the areas each of us was permitted to go.

Botelho was also very interested in what was behind the war in Lebanon. Marie had worked in Lebanon and knew the situation well. In detail, she told us about the war between the Palestinians and Israelis. That conversation opened the door for us to talk about the people of Israel in Bible times. Botelho and Marie asked me to tell them everything I knew on that topic.

For several days I avoided the subject because I wanted to be well prepared. I didn't want to give answers without careful thought. I didn't know much about the intertestamental time before the birth of Jesus.

Botelho kept pressing me. One day he said, "You wanted to tell us about the history of the people of Israel in the time of the Old Testament. Have you changed your mind?"

I began with the story of Creation and the events that led to the call of Abraham. Then we talked about Jacob and how his name was changed to Israel.

Eventually, we got to the subject of the angels. "That's another thing I don't understand," Marie said. "Who can be sure that angels really exist?" Starting with that question, we talked for a long time. Finally, we came back to the central theme of how God can allow so much suffering without doing anything to stop it and why I still believe in Him.

"The evidences for faith are all around us," I told them, "and they are clear; but even if I could explain to you the whole Bible in detail, it wouldn't convince you to believe. If anyone closes their heart to the divine manifestations when there is clear evidence, they will never believe. Personally, in spite of all that has happened to me, I'm convinced that it was the will of God that I should be here now in this camp. God has a reason for all of this, even if I don't know what it is yet."

"How can you know? What proof or evidence do you have for your belief?"

They wanted clear and convincing answers. So I told them a story about a man who was driving along a country road when he saw two shepherds with their flocks moving toward each other on the same road. When they met, the shepherds greeted one other and stopped to visit. While they chatted, the sheep mixed together, and to the onlooker, it seemed like a hopeless mess. No one could tell which sheep belonged to which shepherd. The driver stopped his car on the side of the road to watch, wondering how the two friends would sort out their sheep when they finished talking. When the conversation was over, the two men said goodbye and started on their way. Each one gave a short whistle, and the sheep quickly separated themselves, and each went with its own shepherd.

I concluded the story by explaining my point. "Jesus compared Himself to a good shepherd. He said, 'My sheep hear My voice, and I know them, and they follow Me' [John 10:27].

"I know my Shepherd's voice," I told them, "and I will follow Him trustingly, although I do not always understand why He takes me on a certain path. I cannot always understand His will and why this or that happens, but I know that He is never wrong. This can only be understood by faith, and each of us must experience it for ourselves."

The next day we studied the Old Testament maps in my Bible. I told them about the fall of humankind and the promise of the Messiah. In the apocryphal books, we read about the rebellion of the Maccabees and learned more about the life of the Jewish people during that time.

It seemed to me that Botelho was becoming meeker and more interested in learning as we studied the Bible. He continued to tell me I was wasting my time reading the Bible. And when Marie asked Botelho to take the Bible to Father Neto, he made a sarcastic remark. Nevertheless, it was evident that he could not keep from being influenced by our conversations. I could see that, little by little, a change was taking place in his rough personality. Sometime later, I met Father Neto. He told me that Botelho gave him a detailed report of what we had talked about every day.

"Believe me," he said, "your conversations are having an effect. Botelho has changed a lot. He is a different person." Father Neto knew Botelho better than I did because they had been together on the long walk.

At our evening devotions, I told the Sabatés about my conversations with Botelho, Marie, and Father Neto. Ronaldo said thoughtfully, "If even one person in this camp finds his way to Christ through us, all of the suffering will have been worthwhile." I was grateful for my discussions with Ronaldo because, at times, it was hard for me to find answers to the questions of my new friends. As a pastor, he helped me a lot.

One day, when we came to the log, Liberdade, the boy who brought food to us, was sitting with his head in his hands, and he seemed very sad.

"Are you worried about something?" I asked him.

"No, not really," he replied.

We chatted for a while, and then he asked what we did before we were captured. We started to tell him when he abruptly interrupted, "Do you know what love is?"

"Why do you ask?" Marie wanted to know.

"I am just very interested in what you think."

"People often think of love the way it is portrayed in novels," Marie said, "something romantic and passionate. Some people have even killed themselves or somebody else because of love. That's wrong. Love is sweet and serene. It is able to forgive and forget."

Then I told him what the Bible says about love in 1 Corinthians 13, and that love is willing to sacrifice and give of itself.

Liberdade was surprised by our descriptions of love. It appeared as though he expected something completely different. But we could see that our answers brought him relief and great peace. From then on, we spoke with him often, and he always turned to this favorite subject. He wanted to know what we thought about marriage and if it was dangerous to get married to a very young girl. At times we were amused by the questions he came up with. When I was alone in my hut, I tried to summarize our conversations in my diary.

Often, in the few hours I slept, I dreamed of my apartment in Bongo. The same dream recurred again and again. It was always the same: I was in my house, I was kidnapped, but I managed to escape and return. When I got there, the door was open, and my things were scattered across the floor.

"Every time, it is like I'm watching a movie," I wrote in my journal. "I see the house where I lived. Outside is the garden with its flowers. Inside the house, some of my plants are missing, and I can't find my books. I see other people wearing my clothes. When I awaken, I'm always sad."

In the course of our conversations, Botelho told us about his capture and the long time he had spent at other camps. He was born in Angola, the son of a wealthy landowner. He was surrounded by all kinds of luxury. He had his own car, a personal tailor, and an apartment in Luanda, close to the university. When the hostilities began, his mother and younger sister left for Portugal, but he remained with his father on their large farm, where many natives worked for them. One morning in July 1979, UNITA came and set fire to everything. Botelho's life was spared, mainly because UNITA wanted him as a teacher for their jungle schools.

He recounted living through difficult times. He was often hungry. "When we killed a cow, we ate it all, even the hide," he told us. "We soaked it until it became soft enough to rub off the hair, then we boiled it and ate it. We also ate cassava, peeling and all." Raw cassava contains cyanide, so they soaked it in water for twenty-four hours and then cooked it. They threw nothing away.

Botelho witnessed many terrible things while traveling with the guerrillas. But he had to be careful what he told us. We talked so softly that we could barely hear one another, always watching to see whether anyone was nearby.

When someone approached, Botelho would give a signal, and we would start talking about something trivial. His long experience in the jungle made him wary and very alert. He was always aware of what was going on around us. We learned a lot from him. Soldiers often passed by our meeting spot because we were close to the house of the major. That forced us to keep up our guard. Sometimes, Botelho would write a message in his hand or with his finger in the dust. Then we would erase it with our feet.

One evening, at worship, Ronaldo showed us a typewritten message. "Look at what the major gave me. Here is a record of everything that

UNITA has done in the last fifteen days!" We read the report. It read something like this:

"July 17: Our brave soldiers planted a mine on Route __. It was set off by a truck carrying fifty civilians who were blown into the air, truck and all. On our side, everyone OK.

"July 20: Our troops attacked and freed fifty civilians from the hands of the enemy and recovered ten heavy weapons. Losses by the government: twenty men. On our side, everything in order. Long live UNITA!"

While listening to him read, I got a sick feeling. My mind went back to Bongo. I could see the bodies blown to pieces. I could hear the cries of the wounded and the terrified wailing of the children looking for their parents. I remembered seeing the looks of horror in the eyes of the survivors.

"And it was for this kind of report that they stole the paper from our print shop," Conchita complained.

By the time he finished reading, night had fallen. From where we were, we could hear the radio in the major's house. They were probably listening to UNITA radio, the Black Rooster.

Suddenly, we saw a soldier burst out of the major's house running and shouting something in Umbundu. Another soldier responded and repeated the message until it seemed the whole camp was shouting. The soldiers came running out of their huts, shouting, gesturing, and repeating continuously, "Long live UNITA! Long live UNITA! Long live UNITA!"

"They must be celebrating a victory somewhere," Ronaldo remarked.

"I sure hope we can get out of here before the war gets any more compli-cated," said Conchita, very concerned.

The shouting faded little by little. When everything was quiet again, I went back to my hut. I was shivering, and my stomach ached as the terrible cruelty of this war confronted me in all its harshness.

Earlier that day, I had asked a soldier for a knife to open a can. Instead of a knife, he handed me his bayonet. As soon as the soldier was out of earshot, Botelho said, "Do you realize they use those to kill people?" The bayonet dropped from my hands.

Later, the major came over, and we began to chat. The major told us how much he missed being at the front of the battle. Unfortunately, he was too old for that.

"Do you really like to hurt and kill people?" I asked him indignantly.

"Of course, I do. That's our life! That's why we're here!" he answered, surprised by my apparently naïve question.

Now, lying in my tent, I thought about the people capable of such cruelty, who had us in their power. They were kind to us; they gave us food. They had even carried us on their shoulders when we had to pass through the deep and dangerous rivers. *Could it be that they will soon show their true colors?* I thought. I stayed awake pondering for a long time while I tossed in my bed. Finally, I got up and wrote in my diary, "Why, Lord? How can people be so cruel to one another? What is happening to our world? Please, Lord, help me understand these things."

CHAPTER 14

"The President Wants to See You"

On August 4, I recorded in my diary: "The major came to me and said, 'The war will soon be over. Some of you are going home. Marie and the Brazilians will probably go first. That's why I don't want you to move in with her, because you will be sad when she leaves.' "

Our conversation continued. "And, by the way, we are expecting important visitors who will be coming from headquarters. They want to speak with you," he told me. Then he sternly added that we were not to tell anyone that we were prisoners.

"Is that so?" I answered incredulously. "Will you kindly tell me what is the proper term we should use to describe our situation? You say we are not prisoners, but it sure doesn't seem like we are free, either!" I insisted, emphasizing the irony.

"Ahh, well, just say that you were evacuated."

"Evacuated! What a fine word to describe us! Evacuated!"

Despite my impertinence, the major couldn't help but laugh.

About that time, Marie and I discovered that Botelho would be having a birthday on August 8. We decided to surprise him by making him an especially delicious Portuguese cornbread called *broa*. In view of the fact that we ate cornbread every single day, we decided to ask the captain for some extra ingredients. When his birthday arrived, we had been given three eggs, two chocolate bars from the military rations, a little bit of sugar, and twice the usual amount of corn flour.

We dug a hole in the ground and built a fire. Working with the fire in the hot weather made the sweat run down our faces and backs. When the fire had burned quite a while, we removed the coals, and placed the corn dough, shaped into two cakes, in an old aluminum kettle, with an improvised lid and covered it with part of the hot soil.

Half an hour later, we dug up the kettle and opened it. To our delight, the cakes were brown and crisp. We called Liberdade and asked him to go tell the major we wanted to talk to him. Of course, it was unheard of for an "evacuated" person to summon the major to their house to talk. But at times, we thought it appropriate to break protocol. The major soon arrived with a curious look on his face. We greeted him cordially and asked him how his family was—the polite thing to do, according to African custom. After talking about his family for a while, we made our request. "Our friend, the young Portuguese," we said, "is having a birthday today, and we want to surprise him with a little celebration in his house. Would it be possible for you to allow us to meet there?"

The major seemed amused, and putting on an air of generosity, he responded, "Of course! Yes, that would be fine. For such a special occasion, we can make an exception. You may go, and I will join you later."

Before long, we were there along with the major, the captain, and Liberdade. The camp's male nurse, who lived in the same house with Botelho, had cleaned and swept the place, made the beds, and put everything in order. We placed the special broas on the little table, and the men went to make some cereal coffee. Liberdade and Marie called for Botelho, who was visiting Father Neto. When he arrived, we all shouted, "Happy birthday!"

Botelho took a step backward and exclaimed, "What's going on here? Have you all gone crazy?"

"We just wanted to help you celebrate your birthday!" we answered, laughing.

Botelho was overwhelmed. Our surprise had turned out very well. After hugs and birthday wishes all around, we sat down to eat the scrumptious sweet broas and coffee. We had a great conversation while the major and the captain regaled us with interesting trivia about the different tribes of Angola and some of their adventures with wild animals in the jungle.

At some point, the conversation turned to the topic of our food scarcity. For days, we had received only dried fish, cornmeal, and beans. The spaghetti, rice, and even the little bar of military chocolate had long since disappeared from the menu. Three times a day, it was the same meal—a truly unique diet. Because the soldiers had just been telling us about how they set up ambushes, we told them that if we didn't get more food, we would ambush Liberdade and hold him hostage. "Chocolate or your life!" would be our condition.

We laughed riotously. From then on, whenever Liberdade brought us our ration, which, in fact, was even less than before, we would threaten that he had better watch out.

"I am starting to be afraid for real!" he told us one day. "Don't worry, though, the truck is coming soon with lots of good food." It sounded encouraging, but the days continued to go by, and our reserves continued to shrink at an alarming rate.

On August 11, I recorded, "Our menu consists of corn mush, corn cakes, and corn drinks. We have organized a *Vitaparcours* [a 'fitness trail,' something like an obstacle course] where we can exercise and, at least, move our limbs a little bit every day."

About fifty yards from the camp, there was a huge shade tree, in the trunk of which someone had carved some rustic seats. We asked the captain for permission to walk to it, and he granted it. We were pleased with the change in routine.

Over time, I was able to get acquainted with the other Portuguese prisoners. Marie was allowed to visit them, so I accompanied her. I stayed with her a little farther each day, and since neither the captain nor the major said anything, I was soon going as far as the middle of the campground to meet with them. We discovered that Father Neto was a very cultured and pleasant person who knew how to relate to young people. We grew fond of him, and often, we sat and conversed.

It had been a week since the long-promised visit from headquarters. When we asked soldiers whether President Savimbi was coming, they always answered, "We don't know."

We were all too familiar with that sort of answer, so one day I said to the captain, "So! You keep telling us you don't know anything about whether the president is coming, but surely, he must be. When we were kidnapped, they told us: 'The president wants to talk with you.' And here we are, ready for the interview. We have walked seven hundred and fifty miles to honor his request. We have been here for a month now, and he has not spoken to us yet." The captain didn't respond.

That very night, we heard the rumble of trucks in the distance. The next day, the major came and told us that he had some good food for us and that the visitors had arrived. We cleaned up our huts as much as possible and then waited.

Later, they came for us and took us to a large new yango that we had never seen before. A large number of soldiers stood guard in front of the yango. A tall, strong man with a thick beard and a military beret came over, greeted us, and invited us to come in. The yangos are round like the huts, and, because they are generally used as meeting places, they place log benches along the walls for people to sit. The area in the center of the circle is left open.

We were seated in a specific order: the Portuguese, me, Conchita and Ferrán Sabaté, the Oliveiras, Father Fernández, and then Marie. The man who had greeted us when we arrived stepped up onto a sort of podium they had placed in the center. He sat down on a chair that was built in the same way as other camp furniture—using crossed sticks padded with fresh straw.

Without introduction or instruction, the man began speaking. He seemed to have a strong, stern character, and his intimidating look made the atmosphere tense. We were confused: Who was he? Why were we here?

First, he addressed Father Fernández. "Ah, you have been with us for some time, haven't you? If I could have, I would have sent you home a long time ago, but I have no plane available. I like what you said to the reporters." He went on for a moment, commenting about Father Fernández and his understanding of the struggle and interests of UNITA. The priest answered, but I wasn't listening. I was too busy studying the speaker and considering our strange circumstances. An idea popped into my mind: Could this be none other than President Savimbi himself?

Next, he turned to Marie, "You are a special case," he said, his voice rising as he spoke. "I mean, you really do insist that the attitude of the Red Cross is right, don't you?" Then he launched into a long, angry tirade in which he vehemently attacked the Red Cross and all it represented.

Marie tried to defend herself, but he didn't allow her to get a word in, shouting her down as he continued. He made all kinds of accusations about the Red Cross, condemning Marie's attitude and criticizing her statements to the reporters. "What do you think UNITA is?" he shouted. "The Red Cross talks about neutrality, but they are nothing other than supporters of communism and pawns of the dos Santos government! If they were neutral, they would help both sides. But no, they work with the MPLA while they refuse to even speak to us. What kind of neutrality is that?"

He continued ranting like that for some time, while Marie, trembling and terrified, struggled to keep back her tears.

Then suddenly, without giving her a chance to speak, he stopped and turned to Ferrán Sabaté. "And *you*, you had the nerve to say that UNITA had kidnapped you. You try to create propaganda, don't you? Who do you think you are? What did you come to Angola for—to cooperate with the Cubans? You missionaries are nothing but hypocrites. You pretend you are helping the people, but all you are really doing is cooperating with the communist regime and supporting the government."

Ferrán still hadn't realized who was speaking. Irritated by the speaker's accusations, he raised his own voice and shouted back, "Wait just a minute!

Don't talk to me that way. We did *not* come here to cooperate with any government."

"Who do you think you're talking to?" the other man exploded, shouting even louder and leaning toward Ferrán with his eyes flashing. "Who do you think you are? Nobody dares to talk to me that way!"

A cold sweat started down my back. Pressing against Conchita, I tried to reach Ferrán´s shirttail, hoping to make him be quiet. Indescribable terror came over me. I silently pleaded with God to make Ferrán be quiet. I knew we must remain silent. One wrong word from us could complicate things terribly. *Ferrán, Ferrán, please shut your mouth, please!* I begged silently. *Our freedom is at stake.*

At that point, it all came clear to Ferrán. It dawned on him who he was confronting.

"Excuse me," he mumbled as his face went ashen. "I am so sorry. I didn't know I was addressing President Savimbi."

Savimbi, however, was not appeased. He continued to rage like a flamethrower, hurling accusation after accusation against the missionaries. "Why do you come into my dominion without permission?" He continued spewing hatred at a fevered pitch, accusing us of receiving and treating Cubans, of supporting the MPLA party, of serving the communist president, Eduardo dos Santos, and on and on.

"You call yourselves pacifists," he shouted. "Of course! As long as the Cubans are not in *your* country, it's OK. But if they were invading your country, then you would move heaven and earth to find support. Naturally, since they are coming to Angola and not your country, you don't care what they do here. Here you are pacifists, and you don't want to get involved in our conflicts. Nobody invited you to come and work in my territory. You came to my territory through the door opened by the government, and you think I am going to stand for that?

"You should be very grateful if I decide to release you. Truly, I should have left you to your fate. In the future, I won't waste my time kidnapping people. Whoever comes into my domain and into the war zone, getting involved in matters where they have no business, will have to suffer the consequences whether they are missionaries, Red Cross workers, or whoever it is. If a bullet goes through their head, it's their own fault. I did not invite any of you into my territory!"

We continued listening in silence, frightened and helpless. I was trembling from head to toe. "Oh, dear Lord," I prayed silently, "now what is going to happen to us?"

Suddenly, it was as if he flipped a switch. He began speaking to the

Portuguese. I listened in amazement, as Savimbi, in a quiet, kind voice, spoke to them as if they were old friends. He asked them where they were from, where they had worked before they were kidnapped, and how old each of them was.

"I am sorry that things have come to this point," he told them kindly. "But, well, you will soon be free. You can return to Portugal and start your lives over. All is not lost. One can always start over again."

Then looking to Botelho, he smiled and said, "I heard about the good work you did in the camps where you were before. I'm happy to meet you personally. What do you plan to do when you are free?"

"I plan to go to Portugal, where my mother lives with my little sister. My father has remained in Angola, knowing that I was in the hands of UNITA."

"How old are you?"

"Twenty-six."

"Oh, you are very young! I am thirty-eight, and I still have plenty of life ahead of me. You can never lose hope. I will soon set you free. Then you can go back to your mother, and she can know for sure that she still has a son."

He next addressed the Oliveiras. He greeted them in a friendly fashion and inquired about their welfare. "The best professor I had in my childhood was Brazilian. He was more like a father to me. All that I am, I owe to him." With a reassuring smile, he continued to recall positive things about his relationship with the Brazilians. Ronaldo, who had been dreading this meeting due to the bad relations between his country and Angola, now smiled in relief.

Savimbi turned to Marie, and again, his anger flared. He told her she was foolish and stubborn. He insisted that she had not given the reporters her own opinion but had spoken only as a representative and defender of the Red Cross's evil designs.

Marie was crushed and trembling as he continued shouting at her. He said nothing about her freedom. She stopped trying to hold back the tears and sat there weeping in silence.

Finally, Savimbi leaned toward me. "And you are the young woman from Argentina. Did you hear about the war between your country and Great Britain?"

"Yes, just before our capture," I replied. "I heard about what was happening."

"And are you also aware that the war is over? Argentina surrendered and signed a peace treaty with England."

"Yes, the major we met along the way told me about that."

"And what do you think about it?"

A red flag went up in my mind. I knew I had to be very careful with my words. I didn't know how things were in Argentina. The hated military government that had gotten our country into the war was responsible for the disappearance of thousands of young intellectuals. Many of them were innocent, and some had simply dared to denounce the military and its tyranny. I felt I should somehow avoid answering the question.

"It has been a long time since I lived in Argentina, and I'm not very much up to date on the present political situation."

He nodded. Then we chatted for a moment about the origin of the conflict over the *Malvinas* (the Falkland Islands). "My country has a strong anti-Communist ideology," I assured him. *Thank God for that*, I thought, because if it didn't, that might be the end of me. After a few more comments, he straightened up and said, "All right, I will soon let you go."

"May I ask you something?" I asked.

"Yes, of course. Go ahead."

"How has our freedom come about? Is it because of the intervention of our home countries or the intervention of the Adventist Church?"

"Well, your church has been very worried about you. There is nothing they could have done that they have not done. They even offered to send an airplane directly here to pick you up. I was surprised by their efforts and all they were willing to do to obtain your freedom. They even offered to pay me twelve thousand dollars for you. That irritated me a lot. I didn't kidnap you for money; that is not how UNITA works."

I learned later that things were not as clean as he was pretending, but I was happy to know the church had been doing everything possible to secure our freedom. After losing the war, my country had so many other concerns that the fate of a kidnapped missionary in Angola was a low priority for them.

Often, as I reflected on those events, I realized I could've remained there in the jungle forever if UNITA had insisted on negotiating only with Argentina. The other prisoners sometimes teased me, saying that they would send me some small gifts after they were freed so that I would not feel so sad.

"May I ask you another question?" I requested of Savimbi.

"Yes, please, go ahead."

"How are things in Bongo?"

"Everything is OK at the mission. I heard that government soldiers went there and put some people in jail for cooperating with us. Aside from that, everything is in good order. And what do you plan to do when you leave here?" he asked, smiling. "Do you, by any chance, plan to become a reporter? You seem to ask a lot of questions."

I laughed and returned the favor. "If I do, you are the one who has the answers. Let me ask you something else."

"Just go ahead and ask, menina," he answered.

"What are your intentions for the Bongo Mission? Do you plan to attack it again?"

"At the moment, we are not interested in the mission. I don't think we have anything more to accomplish there. If the people who live there behave themselves and don't get involved in my business, nothing will happen to them," he answered, reassuming his attitude as the absolute master.

"Please take care of the mission," I pleaded.

Then, with a wistful expression, he looked off into the distance and said, "Most of my people grew up at the evangelical mission of Donde."

The Donde Mission was one of the most important in Angola. Thousands of young people had been educated there over the years. They had a school for girls, another for boys, a hospital, and a leprosarium. During the weeks that we lived with the people from UNITA, we learned that many of them had been educated at the Donde Mission. Savimbi's father and brothers had received their formal education there, as had Jonas Savimbi himself.

"We love that mission," he said. "We carry it in our lifeblood. That mission was the heart, the very seed of Angola, right up until the beginning of the war, and then the communist government converted the mission into a military base. It was very painful—intolerable to us. We preferred to destroy the mission rather than see it transformed into a military base for the MPLA. So, one day we placed explosives around it and blew it up.

"It was our intention to establish a great university there, where our sons and daughters would continue to receive an education, but when the enemy set up quarters there, it was more than we could stand." The man slowly spoke as if talking to himself. The pain he felt could be perceived in his voice. We knew that things had really happened just as he said, and we listened, deeply moved by his words.

Finally, the president concluded his political discourse, and we were dismissed. One of the Portuguese asked if it would be possible to have his picture taken with Savimbi. "Yes, of course, not a problem. But is there anyone here who has a camera?" Savimbi asked, looking around.

"Yes! The menina has one."

"Oh yes, the journalist! Here, Miss Journalist, get your camera."

Everyone posed with the president in the center while I took several pictures.

"Now, someone else take the pictures because I want the young journalist to stand by me."

That is how it came about that I still have a memento of that significant day—a photo of me standing beside President Jonas Savimbi.

Finally, the president told us, "I know that there is not much food left in the camp, but I do not want my prisoners to go hungry. My soldiers have agreed to go without their rations so that you will not lack anything. Today I brought you a large supply of food; I hope you will enjoy it." Then, he ordered his men to unload all the food from his truck and put it in Liberdade's cabin.

The following morning the boy came looking like Santa Claus. He brought condensed milk, canned meat, crackers, cornmeal, wheat flour, potatoes, jam, sugar, oil, and dried vegetables. We couldn't believe our eyes! It seemed almost too good to be true. In my diary, I wrote, "What a wonderful Sabbath! God is so good to us."

For a long time afterward, we talked about our meeting with the president. Marie and Ferrán were naturally quite concerned, but the rest of us were hopeful. The Oliveiras were especially happy. In his sermon that Sabbath, Ronaldo told us that he had recently been reading some of the psalms that describe the mercy and love of God for us. "We can now see the light at the end of the tunnel, and for that reason, we are going to praise and bless the Lord," he said.

It was a marvelous worship service that Sabbath. We were especially happy because Savimbi had clearly stated that we would be set free due to the efforts of our own Adventist Church.

CHAPTER 15

We Learn to Make Buns

After our visitor left, we unexpectedly received authorization for Marie to move to my hut. The soldiers set up another cot for her, and although it greatly reduced the available space, we were both pleased with the new arrangement. Marie hadn't felt comfortable living with the UNITA girls because they often treated her rudely. They wouldn't let her prepare her own meals, and her food preferences were very different from theirs.

It was also a blessing for me to have her company. I suffered a lot from insomnia, especially because I could hear the sounds of the wild animals prowling during the night. Lack of sleep and uncertainty about our future were affecting my psyche, and I suffered depression and fatigue more frequently. Once Marie moved to my hut, I immediately felt better.

We had been together for two days when Liberdade showed up in the morning with three fresh buns. We were surprised. We had no idea that bread could be made here in our remote camp. He told us that he made the buns himself. With a little margarine and jam, they were delicious!

Later that day, when the major came to visit, we showed him the buns and told him the story of Hansel and Gretel. We told him about the wicked witch putting them in a cage to fatten them up so she could eat them. "That is what's happening to us. First, UNITA starved us, and now they want to get us fat."

"Not to worry," laughed the major, "we are not going to eat you."

For the rest of the day, we talked about those buns. The next day, Liberdade told us how he made them: he mixed the flour with yeast, water, and salt and kneaded it well. When the dough had risen, he placed it in a can, covered it with another can, and then put it in a sand "oven," similar to the one I had used to make the broas.

We had some flour that they had given us, and we wanted to try it ourselves, so that afternoon, we set to work. We dug a hole in the sand and built a fire, which soon became a thick bed of coals. We made the dough and impatiently waited, but it didn't want to rise. Finally, we decided to bake the bread the way it was. We placed the dough in two cans. Then we buried the cans in the hot sand and covered them with live coals. With eager expectation, we sat down to wait.

After about half an hour, we smelled something burning. *Well, it couldn't really be burnt; we didn't put on that many live coals*, I thought. We waited a little longer and then decided to check to see how it was doing. We lifted out one of the cans with its precious contents. By that time, it was night and completely dark, so we pulled some straw from the roof and lit it from the live coals to make a torch. With the light of the torch, we looked inside the can. We saw nothing that looked like bread! What we saw was a lump hard as a rock and as black as midnight! Marie was bitterly disappointed, almost to tears. I certainly didn't want to make her feel worse, but I couldn't help laughing.

The next morning, we cut off the thick charcoal crust and found a little bread that was still edible, although it tasted burnt.

One of the Portuguese prisoners was a professional baker, and when he heard our story, he asked for permission to visit. He taught us how to make good bread with homemade yeast. To stretch our precious white flour, we mixed it with cornmeal that we had previously cooked to a thick mush. We learned that we needed only a small fire and a few coals to achieve the ideal temperature for baking the bread in the sand.

When we tasted our bread with a little jam, we could almost forget that we were prisoners. The Sabatés and Oliveiras thought we had a great idea, and soon we were all baking bread.

Despite the president's visit and his grand promises, nothing really changed. We were still in the dark regarding our future. As the days went on, we began to wonder whether we would ever actually be released.

Ronaldo was the most optimistic. He constantly projected new dates when he thought we might go home. The Sabatés, Rosmarie, and I were more cautious, and Marie was totally pessimistic. Because of what had happened during our meeting with Savimbi, she had almost no hope of regaining her freedom. The Portuguese were hopeful, except for Father Fernández. Based on his previous experience, he had no expectations of freedom any time soon. On the other hand, Botelho was confident that the president's promise would soon be fulfilled and he would be free. He always tried to put on a tough front, claiming to have no personal feelings and facing life with a hard, realistic attitude.

"How do you feel now, knowing that you probably will soon be free?" we asked him.

"Nothing, I don't feel anything in particular," he claimed, trying to disguise his feelings.

The three of us continued to meet together to discuss all sorts of subjects. Botelho told us about his home and growing up in luxury with servants to meet his every need. We could tell he imagined he would return to the same lifestyle when he got to Portugal. We tried to caution him and warn him that he might be disappointed because things had changed drastically in Europe.

On the Portuguese side of the camp, the men did not cook for themselves. A soldier was assigned to cook for them, and he always used the same method of preparation. In one large kettle, he prepared either spaghetti or rice porridge, and in another, he made a sauce, *conduto*, as it was called. The sauce was simply a mixture of things, with no condiments other than a bit of salt and oil. It might contain meat or vegetables, depending on what was available. The cook stirred everything together with a long stick while it boiled. A stick was used for lack of a spoon. Apparently, no one washed the rice because it always had so much sand in it that it was practically inedible. The spaghetti was usually cooked into a gummy mass. How grateful we were that we could prepare our own food!

After meals, the men had to clean the kettles and common utensils. That week it was Botelho's turn to do kitchen duty. He told us dejectedly that it was the first time in his life that he had actually had to wash a pan.

"That's wonderful that you can learn to wash dishes," we told him. "In Europe now, every man has to do it. Women study and practice their professions. They no longer spend the whole day at home, washing and cleaning. Because of it, the men have to help."

Botelho looked at us, shocked. "No! Never!"

"In Europe," we insisted, "you're not going to find a woman who is willing to be your servant, and servants are extremely expensive. You might as well get those ideas out of your head. In Europe, marriage is a partnership with equal rights and responsibilities. Sometimes the men go to the market to buy groceries, and they take care of the children." We goaded him mercilessly.

"No! The men buy groceries? No way!" he said, almost desperately.

We never missed a chance to tease him about the subject. We kept trying to get any illusions of going back to his spoiled lifestyle out of his head. Poor Botelho! We had fun at his expense because we could see how worried he was about it.

One morning he told us he hadn't slept well the night before.

"Well, that must be because you are afraid you will have to wash dishes!" we told him, joking sarcastically.

One day, when I had nothing else to wear, I put on a blue dress that I had snatched up the day I was kidnapped. I had never worn it because it was too delicate for our rustic environment.

"Victoria, you are as beautiful as a bride!" exclaimed Father Neto when he saw me.

"A bride without a groom," I shot back.

"Well, right here is your groom," said the priest, pointing to Botelho.

"No, she doesn't want to marry me," he said.

"That's for sure," said Marie. "She'll never marry a man who doesn't know how to wash dishes."

Marie and Tiago began to join us in our devotions. Every day at sundown, we gathered to sing and pray. It was the best time of the day. Seated around the fire, we would sing, study our Bibles, and pray for freedom. Every week, Ronaldo taught us a beautiful new hymn in Portuguese.

Tiago read the Bible and joined our singing with enthusiasm. Sometimes, he asked to borrow the devotional book and a Bible so that he could take them home to study. Often, when he went for water or was busy preparing meals, Father Fernández heard him cheerfully singing the hymns he had learned. On those occasions, we missionaries could see that God was using us, even in those strange circumstances, to help people find a closer relationship with Him.

One day, after visiting the Portuguese, Marie came back extremely upset. "Botelho is going to be taken to Jamba," she told me almost in a whisper. "He wrote a message to me on his hand so that we would know what is going on. Botelho is very dejected, almost to tears. He has no idea why they are taking him. But we must be very careful. We can't talk to anyone about this."

We were both extremely upset. We tried to think of a reason why Botelho would suddenly be taken away. Could it be that they had decided to get rid of him because he knew too much about UNITA? What about the president's promise that he would soon be free? No matter how much we tried to think of a reason, nothing made sense.

That afternoon, we went to our usual meeting place. Botelho came like usual, acting as if everything was normal, but when we sat down on the log, he began speaking softly, "I can't understand why they are taking me. I am so afraid." We, too, were filled with fear and sadness. My throat felt dry. It was clear that something like this could happen to us too. At any moment, they could just say, "You are being transferred to another camp," and nothing would be heard of us again.

"It's impossible that they won't release you!" we reassured him. "Imagine if they send us home, and we will tell everyone about you. UNITA can't afford that!"

However, we all knew in our hearts that this hope was as fragile as the tiny flicker of light we could see shining from a hut in the distance. We had already seen that in war, there are neither laws nor morals. We were in their hands, and they could do with us whatever they pleased.

Could it be that they would force Botelho to work for them as a teacher in the Jamba schools? Or, perhaps, they wanted to offer him a place as a representative of UNITA abroad. It could be that they had decided to keep him at their headquarters indefinitely, or perhaps they would just eliminate him.

"This is worse than the day I was kidnapped," Botelho told us. "I could do nothing to defend myself, but everything happened so fast I didn't even have time to think. But today, I am terribly sad, mostly because I will have to leave both of you. During my three years here in the jungle, I never had anyone to talk to. Now I have you, and I've just begun to know you, and then to leave in such a sad way." Tears ran down his face as he spoke.

We listened in silence, trying to hold back our own tears.

Just then, we saw two soldiers running toward us, and one of them yelled, "Nurse Victoria, come, come! The commander wants to talk to you!"

I was nearly paralyzed with fear. *This is it*, I thought. I got up and followed the soldiers. My heart was beating so hard I thought the messengers could probably hear it. When we reached the commander, he very calmly said to me, "We're here to repair your bed."

Oh! So that was all! My bed was broken, but that was hardly out of the ordinary. In the middle of the night before, some of the branches it was made from had broken and dumped me on the floor. My bed had actually been a problem for a long time. But it just now occurred to them to repair it!

There was a long pause before I recovered enough to explain to the men that it was only a matter of lifting off the sheet and the straw and doing the work. As soon as I could, I hurried back to reassure the others because I knew they were very concerned.

Botelho had been ordered to be prepared to leave at any time because the next truck that came by on its way to Jamba would take him. We were still engrossed in conversation when we heard the distant rumble of an approaching truck.

We grew pale, and, without saying much, we got up and quickly went our separate ways. A few minutes later, we heard them call Botelho and saw him walk toward the truck. Sadness came over us, and we felt helpless, once again confronted with the fact that we had no control over our lives.

The next day we didn't even leave our huts. We knew no one was waiting for us on the log. Father Neto was concerned, so he came to check on us and get the Bible that we always lent to him. Almost in passing, he said, "Greetings from Botelho. He said he'd come to see you later."

"What! He didn't go?"

"Go see him later," the Portuguese priest answered simply.

I quickly found my devotional book and opened it to a page where I found the text from Romans 8:28. "We know that all things work together for good to those who love God."

"Give this to Botelho and show him the page," I asked the priest.

Since then, every time I look at that page, I remember those events. Botelho's hands were dirty when he read the text. I can still see his charcoal fingerprint on the page where he held the book open.

That afternoon, we met at our usual spot, and he told us that the truck that we saw was not going to Jamba, so he would have to wait a while longer. It seemed that he was no longer quite as upset and had gotten back some of his courage.

It had been quite a while since our rations had included any military chocolate, but we still had a bar we had been saving. We decided to give it to Botelho along with a little piece of bread that we had prepared the night before.

"No, no!" He objected. "I know how precious these things are to you. Keep them, please." But we insisted, and he finally accepted.

The next few days were spent in constant tension. At night, we would hear a truck and think. *This time they have come for him.* But, when we went to our meeting place, he was there as usual. Then one morning, Liberdade told us, "Your friend is gone."

We were speechless. That afternoon, the commander told us, "You are alone now. The young Portuguese is gone."

Now that it was no longer a secret, we told the others what had happened. Around the fire, with the light of the flames illuminating our faces, we all sat in silence. It felt as if danger was lurking all around us. What would happen now to those of us who remained? What did the future hold?

About that time, we became acquainted with another camp resident, a boy named Elias. He just showed up one morning and asked if he could join in our worship. We discovered that he was an Adventist who had been brought to the camp and forced to work for UNITA. He told us how difficult it was to live his faith. He had no Bible or songbook and no contact with other believers. During his time with UNITA, he encountered frequent conflicts of conscience and was forced to decide whether to obey God or man. As soon as we could, we asked the commander for permission for Elias to attend our regular meetings, and it was granted. However, when the time for worship came, the captain always found something for him to do, and he was never able to attend. One day very early, he came secretly and told us what was happening. We quickly took out our Bibles and read a few verses. Then we sang a few songs and prayed with him.

Unfortunately, the captain somehow discovered what he had done and ordered him not to come again. So, we had to find another way to help him. We found out that Tiago and Elias were friends and saw each other often, so we loaned Tiago our Bible and songbook. The two of them started meeting every day at sundown. That way, they could study the Bible together and sing. Tiago would bring the books back to us early the next morning. (The day we were set free, I gave Elias my songbook.)

The camp hadn't received any food since President Savimbi's visit, and rations were getting scarcer every day. Liberdade told us one morning that we must carefully ration what we ate. We told them it was no problem for us because we had found a solution. Curious, he wanted to know what our solution was. We kept them guessing for several days.

Then, one morning we told him, "It doesn't matter that we don't have enough food. The main thing is that you must stay in good shape."

"Why?" he asked innocently.

"Because, when there is nothing else to eat, you'll be next! We'll ambush you and roast you!" We laughed out loud.

However, we noticed that Liberdade didn't think it was all that funny.

Every morning when he brought us our food, which was less every day, we threatened him. "You know what's going to happen when the food runs out; we are *not* going to go hungry."

One day the captain overheard us and said, "We will have to take good care of Liberdade, so you don't eat him."

"Just make sure we always have enough food," we warned. Our threats, however, didn't do any good. Before long, we were living almost entirely on beans.

The short supply of water was another problem. I described our situation in my diary.

Every one of us can use only two containers of water per day. It is not easy to get along with so little, but we have learned some coping strategies. When we wash our saucepan, we do it carefully with clean water so we can make a soup with the water later. When we have to wash all our dishes, we begin with the cleanest; then, we pour the used water into the dirtier dishes until everything is washed. By the time we're finished, the water is so thick and dirty that it can no longer be used for anything and must be thrown out.

The previous day, after we had washed our feet, we found little bits of carrot between our toes. Then we remembered that the day before, we had used the water to wash the tin box in which we kept dehydrated vegetables. We had to laugh. "We have sunk to making soup with the water that we use for washing dishes and washing our feet in the water we used to clean our vegetable box," I said.

"It will be even worse when we end up making soup with the water we used to wash our feet!" Marie replied.

Summer was approaching, the weather was getting warmer, and we were thirsty. We only got six liters of water per day for both Marie and me, so we had to ration it carefully. We reserved three liters for drinking, and the rest had to get us by for cooking, cleaning, and washing. We perfected the art of saving every drop. In spite of the scarcity, we kept ourselves clean. We cleaned our teeth with ashes and scrubbed the pans and dishes with sand. We also scrubbed our clothes with sand. Once in a while, they gave us a tiny scrap of soap that we saved for personal hygiene.

We managed to acquire two pans. One was totally black, and we cooked in that one. The other one we sometimes used as a bowl. We also had a jam can, six old corned beef cans, two plastic mugs, and a fork and spoon that belonged to Marie.

We constantly reminded each other: "Don't let anything go to waste." We truly learned how to get by with what we had.

CHAPTER 16

"Guantanamera"

The month of August was slowly drawing to a close. For nearly two interminable months, we had been at the UNITA camp. If someone had told
us how long our ordeal would last at the time of our capture, we would
have been overwhelmed with discouragement.

One day they told us we would have a visitor on August 26. We weren't
told who was coming or why. The day came and went. We had no visitor.
Then, on the twenty-ninth, the commander woke us up at six o'clock in
the morning. "Get up quickly and get ready. We have important visitors
from headquarters!"

About an hour later, two men came to our hut. They introduced
themselves as Dr. Valentín and Dr. Jakajamba. They gave us a friendly
greeting and told us that, at the request of the president, they had come
to confirm that we would soon be free and to tell us something important,
individually.

First, they spoke with Marie and told her that the Red Cross was
doing everything possible to secure her freedom. They told her that when
she arrived in Switzerland, the news reporters would no doubt want to
interview her. They said she must patiently answer all their questions and
present the situation as it really was in order to help UNITA liberate
Angola.

Both men had studied political science and administration in Switzerland, and they spoke so highly of the country that Marie almost felt as if
she were a guest of honor rather than a prisoner.

While awaiting my turn, I felt more than a little apprehensive because,
after the president's visit on August 13, I had called the major and told
him I had a message for the president.

As related earlier, in his talk to us, Savimbi attacked the Adventist

Church ferociously, calling it an accomplice of the Russians and Cubans and a pawn of the communists in Angola. "You say you are Christians and apolitical, but you are nothing more than communists and servants of the government," he roared.

Of course, we all remained silent at the time, but I was not happy. I felt that I couldn't allow this man to insult the church that way, no matter how important he was. I kept mulling over his words in my mind. I thought about David and his courage in defending the name and honor of God. Finally, after praying fervently, I decided to send a message to Savimbi with the major who would soon be traveling to Jamba. I didn't tell my colleagues about my plan because I did not want to involve them in the possible consequences of what I had said.

The major came and sat down in front of me with a recorder on his knees and listened attentively. With conviction and without thinking of the consequences, I said that I had to respond to President Savimbi's accusations against the Adventist Church. I expressed my surprise at his words because he told us that he was acquainted with every one of our activities and everything that happened at the mission. "If that is the case," I said, "the president must know that at the mission, there are neither Russians nor Cubans, and we do not participate in any type of political activity. We never ask anyone what party they belong to. We treat all patients equally, regardless of their ideology. As you well know," I continued, "the Adventists are an apolitical organization. Our mission is to help our fellow men and alleviate the suffering, without regard to their religious or political persuasion. Our mission is to save, as Jesus did. We could never be communists as the president has stated because communism denies the existence of God, and we believe He is the Creator and Sustainer of the world."

I touched on each one of his accusations and concluded by asking the president to change his position regarding the Adventist Church.

When I finished, the major assured me that he would transmit every word to the president. I thanked him for his patience, and I saw him leave with a flicker of respect in his eyes.

The major had no more than gone when I started thinking about what I had done. Soon, I felt that my head was not at all secure on my neck. How would Savimbi react, and what would be the consequences? Would my friends have to suffer because of my boldness? For several days, I worried and continued to pray, placing the matter in God's hands, until I had a sense of peace and assurance that I had done the right thing.

Time passed, and I had nearly forgotten about my message to Savimbi. But when these two men arrived, I couldn't help but feel apprehensive.

What did they have to tell me that was so important? Did this have anything to do with my message to the president?

As it turned out, they were surprisingly kind to me. We talked a long time about various subjects, especially about religious freedom. That seemed to be the principal reason for their visit. In Free Angola under UNITA, religious freedom would be guaranteed. Every church would be free to preach and develop in the country. "The missions educated us, and we want them to continue their good work," they emphasized. It seemed clear to me that their objective was to change my image of Savimbi because of his discourse. Nevertheless, I cautiously avoided any reference to the subject.

The men wanted to know what we would do to support their cause once we were free. With enthusiasm, they described their heroic objectives in a very attractive way and almost apologized for having taken us as prisoners. Finally, they warned me, "Of course, many reporters will be interested in you and your story. What will you tell them about us? Keep in mind that it is not normal for guerrillas to deal so kindly with their prisoners, especially with a young woman. That is certainly noteworthy. You have not been subjected to any kind of abuse or mistreatment," they repeated.

"Naturally, I will take these things into account when I speak with the reporters. I do greatly appreciate the things you mention. You may be sure I will say only the truth about all that we have experienced here. I will be careful about what I say to avoid causing any problems for my Adventist brothers and sisters in Angola. After all, there are fifty-six thousand members in this country, and I would not want any of them to suffer because of what I say. That is why I will be very cautious."

Finally, they called the Sabatés, the Oliveiras, and the Spanish priest and once again confirmed that we would all soon be released. "Because the Adventist Church has done all it could to obtain your freedom, in a few days, you will be flying home," they assured us.

After they left, we were in high spirits. A few more days! That could be tomorrow or the day after tomorrow, or, at most, another week!

Two days after their visit, I wrote, "Today, the major brought me a spoon. A spoon! After 2½ months as a prisoner, I have a spoon! Is this a good sign or not? Will I still need this spoon for a long time more? We will wait and trust."

On September 1, I wrote, "Letter from the Cuban." An unexpected event changed the routine of our life at camp, at least for Marie and me. On Wednesday night, I had a strange dream in which I was getting ready to leave the camp. We were leaving for freedom, filled with happy expectations. We picked up our few belongings, and before leaving, I looked toward the camp of the Cubans. I saw them standing in front of their huts, looking at us sadly. *It's good that you can't leave*, I thought. *You deserve it because you have made me really angry.* Immediately, I felt ashamed for my thoughts about those men who were suffering the same sorrow and uncertainty that had tortured us during the past months. I felt very bad: *I must be a heartless person with no feelings*, I thought. Filled with humiliation and remorse, I turned slowly to leave. At that moment, I awoke, happy to know that it was only a dream. I went back to sleep. When I woke up in the morning, I only remembered having dreamed something strange, but I couldn't remember the dream itself.

We had just awakened that morning when Father Neto came to visit us. We talked a little, and then, suddenly, I thought about my dream, "Last night I dreamed something very strange that I do not remember right now, but it seems to me that it had something to do with the Cubans," I said.

"Victoria, could you give me a piece of paper and pencil," he said, suddenly looking disturbed about something. I handed them to him and watched, surprised as he wrote, "The Cuban left a letter for you with Guerrero, the Portuguese baker. Please go ask for it."

"Oh, no! That can't be true!" I exclaimed. "Please tell Guerrero I can't read that letter. He must return it or do whatever he wants to with it. The captain has forbidden us to have any contact with the Cubans."

Two weeks earlier, when we were going to the river, I took a shortcut and found myself unexpectedly, almost directly in front of the Cubans' house. I did not know that they lived only a hundred yards from us on the other side of a little wooded area. The older of them was outside. He greeted me and said something that I didn't understand. So, I barely acknowledged his greeting and continued rapidly on my way. Just then, a soldier came from nowhere to take me back "the right way" without saying anything.

Later, the major was visibly upset. "Did you understand what the soldier said to you?" he asked.

"What soldier?"

"I sent a soldier to tell you something very important," he answered impatiently.

"No one said anything to me," I assured him.

"Well, the thing is this: there are a couple of people here in this camp with whom you are not to have any contact!"

"Are you referring to the Cuban that I greeted today? He did say something, but I did not understand, so I went on my way and paid no attention."

"The Cubans are not prisoners, but I advise you definitely not to make any attempt to contact them," he ordered emphatically.

"Very well, I will keep that in mind," I answered, although I was surprised.

"But what if the Cuban comes to visit us at night?" Marie asked after the major had gone.

"Well, we will have to scream. The Cubans need to understand that we do not want to have any contact with them."

Now, on that September morning, here was Father Neto telling me that the Cuban had sent me a letter!

Marie and I were very upset and tried to decide how we should respond. We really didn't know what to do. In the afternoon, we went to visit Father Neto and talked the matter over with him. "Guerrero still has the letter. Don't you want to read it?" he asked.

For a moment, I wavered between fear and curiosity, and finally, I said, "All right. Get it for me." A moment later, I had the letter in my hands and was attempting to read it while Marie stood guard. It was difficult to do anything secret in Father Neto's place because his little hut was made of vertical sticks with no straw in the cracks so that from the outside, anyone could see what was going on inside, and vice versa.

The message from the Cuban was a love letter. He wanted to tell me that because of me, he had experienced much turmoil lately.

"Dear Miss Victoria," he wrote,

Ever since I saw you at the edge of the river, I cannot get you out of my mind. My heart is filled with love for you. I want to ask if you would be willing to marry me. For a long time, I have wanted to send you a message, but that is not allowed. Finally, it occurred to me to send a letter with the boy who brings your food. I waited anxiously for a reply. The boy came back with the message that you did not have paper or pencil. I wrote another letter and attached some paper and a pencil. This time a little note came back saying: "I have to think about your proposal. Give me time." Filled with hope, a couple of days later, I sent you another message. This time the soldier brought me the answer saying, "Within two days, you will receive my reply." Those two days seemed like centuries to me, and when they had passed, my letter carrier, the boy who brought the food, was not there; he had been transferred to another camp. I continued waiting and expecting to resolve the matter. Finally, I realized that the captain was mocking me and that, in reality, my letters never reached you, the boy had given them to the captain, and he was the one who wrote back. I became very upset and angry and went to see the captain because he had scorned me in this way, and I asked him to allow me to speak with you because, after all, I am not a prisoner. The captain answered that he had strict orders not to allow us to speak with the prisoners, but he was going to ask for orders from headquarters, and he would let me know, but that in the meantime, I must wait and be patient.

The man had agreed to wait, but in the meantime, he was in a constant state of anguish, thinking that at any time, I might be given my freedom without his having an opportunity to speak with me. He was also worried because Marie and I no longer went over to our exercise area close to the large tree where, without our realizing it, he was observing us every day.

In fact, for no apparent reason, the captain had suddenly forbidden us to go to our favorite spot under the tree. At the time, we didn't understand the reason for the prohibition. Now, with this letter in my hand, it became clear.

Miguel—that was the Cuban's name—asked me to write a reply and bury it in the sand under the tree, to cover it with my feet, and mark the spot with a cross so that he could find it easily.

This man must really be out of his mind, I thought. I didn't know whether to cry or laugh at the crazy idea. We could not move a single inch without being closely watched. If I were to bury anything at all under a tree, I would hardly leave the place before someone would be there to dig it up.

After I read the letter, I returned it to Guerrero and asked him to return it at once and tell Miguel that we were strictly forbidden to have any contact with them. As a missionary, I could not possibly get involved in such things. I would agree to converse with him only with the captain's definite consent and in a place where everyone could see us.

To tell him directly that I couldn't respond to his feelings of love didn't seem like the right thing to do. I thought that, in his emotional state, he wouldn't be able to handle it and might do something foolish.

I did feel sorry for the poor man because he was on a dead-end street.

Judging from the way he expressed his ideas in the letter, he seemed to be intelligent. He knew he could never return to his country and would probably never see his parents again. It wasn't right that the soldiers had mocked his feelings expressed in the letters. That only made things more complicated and reinforced his delusions.

I really hoped that Guerrero would find the right words to say to him. The two of them could only meet at night, secretly, because the Cuban was forbidden to speak with any of the prisoners.

Our expectation of freedom soon made everything else secondary in importance.

On Friday, September 3, the major came early in the morning and said to us, "Go to the river immediately, bathe, and prepare to leave. You will be taken to another camp."

We hurried to the river and got ready. On our way back to the camp, I pretended I was about to take the path that passed directly in front of the Cubans' houses, which was much shorter. Immediately, our guard called me and ordered, "Not that way, no!"

We took the path indicated by the guard, and just a few steps farther, we came around the corner of the hut and nearly collided with the Cubans, who were sitting in the shade playing cards with the soldiers. I nearly laughed at our comic encounter, but the guard quickly pushed us back in the opposite direction. "This way, no. By the other path." Then he took us by the path he had first forbidden us to take.

This sort of thing angered me. For the last few days, we had been closely watched. They followed us everywhere. The situation made me feel uncomfortable and annoyed, but there was nothing we could do about it.

So, that morning, with our things gathered together, we sat down to wait, imagining that they would take us someplace near the border with Namibia where they could send us on quickly as soon as our freedom was approved.

We waited all day. When it was dark, we unpacked our bedsheets and lay down to sleep. Around midnight, we were awakened suddenly by the sound of truck motors. But nobody called us. At dawn, some men came to get our things and put them on the trucks.

Since it was Sabbath, we decided to go ahead with our worship service while we waited for further instructions. We were just finishing when the same men came back with our things, accompanied by the major. "Today, we will not travel. But don't give up hope. You will be freed for sure, but headquarters just told me that it is not good to move you right now."

Very disappointed, we sat and wondered whether we could believe anything they told us. With every setback, keeping up our hopes became more difficult. At times, we had the impression that we would never leave.

That night, Marie and I were so worried about our situation that we couldn't sleep. We went outside and sat on the log that served as a bench beside the fire. We began to sing. Marie knew some Spanish folksongs, so together, we broke the silence of the night with our voices. It was very late when, suddenly, we heard someone from the other side of the woods also singing in Spanish.

It was a romantic love song. It seemed comical to us, and we made the foolish mistake of responding with the same melody. We sang other songs, including "Guantanamera," a Cuban song that Marie knew very well. While we were singing, a group of passing soldiers stopped to chat with us. They stayed and entertained us with stories of their adventures in the jungle and their encounters with serpents, lions, and other wild animals.

Impressed by what we had heard, we lay down to sleep that night. A few days earlier, the soldiers had killed a huge snake close to the hut where Marie had lived. The horrible reptile was about six and a half feet long. Several mornings, we had seen tracks that the snake made in the sand when it went down the path during the night. The soldiers found it and killed it. Thinking about such a reptile coming into our house made us feel uneasy.

Tense from the emotions of the day, we lay on our beds, listening to the strange night sounds, talking softly. At some point, however, I must have fallen sound asleep because I suddenly awakened, startled by loud noises that sounded like falling trees. Marie was sitting up, trembling on her bed.

"Victoria, I called you several times, but you were sleeping so soundly you didn't wake up. Something is moving out there. And here in the hut, I heard some steps and something moving in the wall and coming toward my bed. I was so afraid. I thought it might be a snake. I couldn't sleep," she explained, almost crying.

I thought for a moment. "But if it sounded like steps, it couldn't be a snake; snakes don't have feet," I said.

"I know, but there is something there."

I, too, heard the steps, but then everything was silent. We almost stopped breathing as we listened intently, but we could hear nothing. As we peered through the cracks, we couldn't see anything moving either, even though the bright moonlight was brightly shining all around.

The wind made an eerie sound in the branches and rustled the leaves as it blew, but there was no movement outside our hut.

Just then, we looked toward the Sabatés' hut and saw that the wind had revived the campfire. With every gust, the flames grew higher and higher until they were flaming dangerously toward the straw house. We didn't even want to think about what would happen if the forest with its carpet of dry leaves and dead branches were to catch on fire. Someone had to put out the fire! We hesitated because we would have to cross the open space on the narrow path that ran through the thorny bushes. If we met up with some night predator, there would be no escape. Finally, we gathered our courage and ran to the Sabatés' hut, where we put out the fire with sand. Then we quickly ran back to our own hut. We went back to bed, and

Marie fell asleep at once, but I didn't close my eyes for the rest of the night.

After breakfast and morning worship, Marie and I headed for the Portuguese camp to take a Bible to Father Neto, just as we did every day. As we reached his little hut, we saw two prisoners standing by a nearby hut. They were being guarded by two UNITA soldiers who were playing cards with the Cubans. Startled, I said to Marie, "Let's get out of here. We don't want the major to think that we came to meet the Cubans."

We ran to Father Neto's place, gave him the Bible, and whispered, "The Cubans are there in the village playing cards; we have to go quickly."

When we passed by the same spot, my suitor again looked at me. For an instant, our eyes met, but he was not smiling. He had a stern look, and his jaw was clenched with fierce determination. It seemed that he might take any risk to meet with me, even if it caused a problem for the whole camp. A cold sweat ran down my back, and I was terrified. The rest of the day, I could think of nothing else. The premonition that something bad was about to happen hung over me like a dark shadow. I spoke to Marie and the others about it, and we were all very worried. When evening came, I said to Marie, "We better not sing tonight. The Cuban might think we are dedicating our songs to him, and one of these nights, we will have him here in the hut!"

So, we went to bed early. Marie was soon fast asleep, but I was still worried and couldn't relax. The rats had dug a tunnel through the straw at the edge of the hut looking for crumbs from our scarce rations, and they were making a tremendous fuss. We figured out that these rats were what had frightened us so much the night before. Sometimes it actually sounded like someone was walking. You could hear leaves crackling and branches falling as the rats dug their holes. I shivered with disgust.

My thoughts constantly returned to the Cuban and the expression on his face. It revealed that he had made up his mind to do something. There was no doubt about it, even if it put us all in danger. UNITA had very strict rules and did not hesitate to hand out harsh punishments to anyone who broke them.

I lit the kerosene lamp and tried to read my Bible but couldn't concentrate. The thought of what the man might do made my hair stand on end. Soldiers guarded these men at night, but the guards always fell sleep in the open doorway of the hut. If the Cuban could so easily step over the sleeping guards to go to Guerrero's house at midnight without being seen, it wouldn't be hard for him to pick up a rifle and come after us. He could force me to go with him someplace where he could do whatever he wanted. Fear made it hard to breathe, and my head was spinning. "Please, Lord, help me!" I prayed. "Don't let this man do something evil. Help us find a solution to this problem without someone getting in trouble."

I sat up and again tried to read my Bible and to pray. It must have been around midnight. The moon illuminated the landscape, and I could see everything through the thin walls of the hut. Nothing was moving outside, and, except for the rustling of the rats, there was absolute silence. Nevertheless, the premonition of imminent danger—fear that something was about to happen, had me on edge. I turned my back to the door and pulled up my sheets. I knelt there on my bed and prayed, asking God for protection and wisdom.

Suddenly, instinctively, I whirled around and looked at the doorway, and my heart nearly stopped! There, between the doorpost and the sheet that covered the door, was the Cuban! I stifled a scream and sat upright. I exclaimed in a whisper, "No, no! Go away! Please! You can't come in here!"

He came in a step, and, pointing toward Marie, he asked, "Who is sleeping there? Is it an African?"

"No, no, that is my friend Marie."

He came into the hut and sat down on my bed. "No, get out of here!" I insisted. "Why did you come, especially at this time of night? It is extremely dangerous. Go away. If the soldiers see you, it will be the end of you."

"Did you get my letter?" he asked.

"Yes, about a week ago."

"No, the one I wrote today. I gave the Portuguese a letter to give to you."

That morning we had gone to visit Father Neto, and when we passed by Guerrero's hut, he was lying on his bed. The other Portuguese were talking with him. He must not have dared to give me the letter when they were there. Now, I recalled that he had moved his feet in a strange manner as if he wanted me to notice something.

"I did not receive anything today," I replied.

He cursed and said in a low voice, "In that letter, I let you know I was coming tonight."

"You are completely out of your mind. You can't come here. The major lives right beside us; every time he talks to someone, I can hear. If he can hear us, he will know that you're here, and it will be the end for all of us. You are putting your life in jeopardy and ours too."

"Don't worry, no one saw me. Just keep calm." He took the kerosene lamp off the table and set it on the floor. When he did that, Marie woke up. She sat up with a start and threw her arms into the air. She looked at us with wide eyes and then lay down again.

"No! This can't really be happening!" she exclaimed.

"Did I scare you?" Miguel asked with an air of innocence. "That's why I wrote the letter; to let you know that I was coming tonight so you wouldn't be afraid. Look, I love you, and I want to marry you. What do you say?" he asked hopefully.

"I say that you are crazy."

"But why?" He laughed. "Tomorrow, some people from UNITA are going to come here, because I asked them to come. They already know that I want to marry you and so they are going to talk to us. When they come, they will call us both, and I want you to commit to me."

"How could you even think that? It's impossible for me to marry you. I am a missionary. You simply show up here and risk getting us all in trouble. If you are discovered, not only will you have trouble, but we will too. You have to leave."

"I know. But tell me, will you marry me or not?"

"Listen, we are missionaries, and furthermore, we are prisoners. It is impossible for me to marry you here and under these circumstances."

"But why not?"

"You know that we are in a completely different set of circumstances than you. Please leave now and be certain that I cannot marry you."

"But why not? Tomorrow, the people from headquarters are coming. You must be at my side."

I felt I had to placate him so that he would leave. "That depends . . ."

"Depends on what? On you or on UNITA?"

"The decision is mine!"

"I can't lose you," he said.

Just then, we heard footsteps outside. In a soft whisper, I said, "If someone discovers you right now, I will definitely tell them that I did not call you and that I have asked you to leave."

He took the kerosene lamp and hid it under the bed. We sat in absolute silence. The footsteps came nearer until they were almost directly in front of the hut, and then they slowly went away. Soon, we heard the major's voice. Apparently, he was speaking with two people in front of his house.

"You have to go *now*! Immediately. You cannot stay here another second," I insisted in a quiet whisper.

"Will you go tomorrow if they call you?" he asked again.

"Of course, I will go, but we can't continue talking here in the dark. We are forbidden from talking to you, and here you are intruding in my hut. Leave *now*!"

"All right, I'll go, but tomorrow when they call you, you have to be by my side," he insisted.

"OK, I will go, and we will see how things go."

"So, we are going to get married?"

"We'll see about that tomorrow. Please go!"

My nerves were about to explode. At any instant, some soldier could stick his head in the hut, or even the major himself might come and ask why we were still awake.

"Give me a photo of you," he said.

"I don't have any," I told him, although it was untrue.

"All right," he said, standing up. "Give me a kiss."

"No!"

Turning, he extended his hand to Marie and told her goodnight. He started to leave and then turned around again and said, "I can't lose you! Do you understand that?"

At last, he left, and Marie and I both heaved a sigh of relief. The nervous tension electrified our bodies.

"Let's turn off the light and go outside as if we need to go to the bathroom," suggested Marie. "That way, if someone sees us, they won't ask why we are still awake."

We scurried outside in the darkness. My whole body was trembling in a state of shock. Since the time of our capture, I had not trembled so much. I shook uncontrollably.

Finally, we returned to our beds and talked about what we should do the next day. We felt sure that no one would come from headquarters to consider Miguel's marriage request. We thought we should do something to ensure that he didn't come back the following night. It seemed clear that talking to the major would be risky. The only thing he would do is punish Miguel severely, and, after all, he hadn't mistreated us. We decided to see what happened the next day. If nobody said anything to us, we would know that nobody was aware of Miguel's visit, and we would let sleeping dogs lie.

Long after Marie was asleep, I was still awake and trembling. Every time I heard the slightest sound, it gave me a start. A couple of times, I got up and anxiously looked outside. I prayed the whole time that God would help me be calm and do the right thing.

I was terribly worried, thinking about the next day. In Angola, it is customary whenever you meet someone to engage in a lengthy exchange of greetings. In Bongo, the custom had, at times, gotten on my nerves. It went more or less like this, "Good morning! Did you pass the night well?"

"Well, yes, and you? Did you pass it well?"

"Yes. And the day, is it going well for you?"

"Yes, thank you."

"And the family? How is the family?"

"They're doing well, thank you, and how is your family?"

And so it would continue. It's possible to spend quite a bit of time, which seems strange to our pragmatic Western mentality.

Each morning, every person who passed by our hut greeted us in this manner. No one wanted to be impolite, so they stuck their heads in our door, greeted us, and questioned us about our well-being. There was one particularly friendly soldier who always carried on this way. He spent about ten minutes every time he came by.

I had just had a horrible night. I hadn't slept a wink. I was barely out of bed when the first soldier appeared and began his routine of friendly greetings. With my nerves jangling, I could hardly respond.

Then around nine o'clock, the major stopped by, and he, too, wanted to know how we had passed the night. We couldn't tell if he knew about our night visitor. We watched his expressions, trying to guess what he was going to say and expecting the worst.

"Last night," he began, while my stomach twisted in a knot, "I could not sleep well. In the middle of the night, a soldier came to see me."

When he said that, I nearly stopped breathing. Then he went on, "And the soldier said, 'The girls are crying.' He also told me that he has been observing you lately, and he said, 'The girls seem very sad, and last night they didn't even eat their supper.'

"I wondered what could be the problem," the major said, "so I sent a soldier to check on you and see whether there was a problem."

My head was spinning. That must have been the soldier who had come up to our hut and stood there listening.

The major continued, "The soldier came back and said 'No, they are not crying; they are only conversing.'"

There could be no way that this wasn't a miracle! Normally, whenever someone wanted to ask us a question or tell us something, they just said a quick, "Excuse me," and then stuck their head in the door or came right on in. But when the Cuban was with us, the soldier just stayed outside and listened instead of coming in.

As the major related what had happened, we realized that he knew nothing about our night visitor. A heavy load lifted from our hearts, and I praised God for saving us from a catastrophe.

That afternoon, we went to visit Father Neto. We had decided not to tell him about what had happened. However, when he greeted us with his usual friendly smile and asked us about our welfare, all my stress returned and closed my throat like a vise. I was unable to speak and began trembling again. I felt compelled to tell him. I found a scrap of paper and quickly wrote, "The Cuban visited us last night."

"No! That can't be!" he exclaimed. "That is extremely dangerous."

"Come later to our hut; we need to talk to you," I wrote again. Soldiers were always milling around his open hut, and it was nearly impossible to talk without being overheard.

Later, back at our hut, I quietly told Father Neto the details of what had happened. When I finished, he said to me, "Whatever you do, don't tell the major. If he finds out, Miguel's punishment will be terrible. At the minimum, they will lock him up, but that wouldn't be the end of it. The bigger problem was caused by the captain—the one who filled Miguel's head with delusions by writing those stupid letters. Now the poor fellow is in such a state that he might do something crazy."

I fully agreed and wished I could tell the captain to his face, but of course, I knew that wasn't a good idea.

We couldn't ignore the possibility that Miguel might try something else, and the next time it might not turn out so well. Then it would be my fault for not having said anything. I felt I wasn't safe anywhere.

The three of us considered numerous options. Finally, Father Neto suggested, "Why don't you ask the major for an interview?"

"But how can I do that? He will undoubtedly suspect that someone brought me the letters. And if he does, even you might be in trouble."

Finally, we decided, and that afternoon, I spoke with the major. "Lately, we have felt very restricted in our freedom of movement," I began. "Marie and I have the impression that everyone thinks it is their mission to watch us all the time. We can't go outside the camp in any direction. The path behind our house is blocked by a pile of thorny branches, so we can't even get firewood for ourselves without going a long way around. If we go to the river, we have to go the long way to get there too. It's all very hard on us, and we want to know why we are under such heavy surveillance. It has occurred to me that maybe it's because of the young Cuban that we met at the edge of the river who asked me to marry him. Maybe you're afraid that he will try to get in touch with me in some way. If that's the case, wouldn't it be better if I could talk directly with him and get all those delusions out of his head so he can be at peace? That way, the entire camp would not need to be in a panic every time I got twenty yards from my hut. In your presence, I could tell him that I have no intention of marrying him, and that would put an end to it."

The major was clearly uncomfortable that I had directly addressed the subject. He hesitated a moment before answering. "I can't allow you to speak with him. I have strict orders not to allow any contact between you and the Cubans. But I do understand. We are soldiers, but we also have hearts. I am going to ask if there is anything I can do, and I'll let you know," he promised.

I expected a reply like that. At any rate, now the major knew my position, and if something happened again, he wouldn't suspect that I had instigated it.

Up to this time, I had been having a problem with insomnia, but after Miguel's night visit and my talk with the major, it was even worse. Every noise near our hut made me jump. Even Marie, who usually slept well, couldn't relax and get to sleep that night. We imagined all kinds of different scenarios.

Then, we had an idea. In our doorway, a cloth hung above the threshold to give us a little privacy. It occurred to us to set up a warning system. We stacked our water bucket, our kettle, and pans on top of each other just inside the curtain. Anyone who tried to come in would inevitably stumble over them, which would make a loud clatter that we hoped would scare the intruder away.

We were quite pleased with our invention. After setting it up, we continued to talk about the events of the previous night. Suddenly, we heard loud footsteps coming our way, and a voice said, "May we come in?"

Startled, we looked toward the door. Two soldiers looked in at us. "Get up and come with us," they said. "A photographer is passing through, and he has to leave right away, but he wants to take some pictures of you."

Relieved, we began to laugh. "A midnight photo! Only UNITA! At midnight they kidnap you, and at midnight they come to take your picture."

We dressed quickly and followed the men to the edge of the camp where they had built a huge fire. The other missionaries were already there, awaiting their turn in front of the camera. Finally, the photographer finished, and we all returned to our huts to sleep for the rest of the night.

The next day, the major brought us some bad news. "I have to tell you that you are no longer allowed to go over to the Portuguese camp. I received an order that all contact with them is strictly forbidden."

"But why? What happened?" we asked. "Are you afraid that maybe the priest will fall in love with one of us?"

"No, no! It's nothing like that. But we can't continue allowing the visits."

It was like a dark cloud came over us. It had now been ten days since the men who promised we would soon be free had been there. Since that time, we had heard nothing more about it. Discouragement came over us. Father Neto was our friend, and we enjoyed visiting him. He was courteous, well-educated, very spiritual, and had a gift for relating to us.

"You don't allow us to go into the front part of the camp, and now we can't go visit the Portuguese. What are we going to do with our time? We can't spend the entire day doing nothing. It would be unbearable."

The major tried to give us some consolation. "I know that the Portuguese priest always borrows your Bible. If you want, I can take it to him every morning and bring it back in the afternoon."

His offer didn't make us any happier, and we told him so. After he had gone, Marie said, "We have to figure out a way to get the Bible to Father Neto. The major wasn't really going to take it to him anyway. Father Neto will miss it, especially now that he'll be alone."

We considered our options. The only solution we could think of was to give it to Tiago, who often went to visit him. But we abandoned that idea because someone would eventually find out. Then they would probably forbid Tiago to visit the priest.

The next day we went to ask the major if we could at least have an area to run and do exercises. He said, "Yes," and pointed to an area we could use. Strangely, it was a path that went right past the Portuguese area over by our large tree. That was our opportunity! I took my Bible, wrote a short note to the priest, placed it in the Bible, and tucked it in my blouse.

We told our guard we were going out for a little exercise. We quietly passed the captain's house and then began running until we reached the Portuguese camp. Without saying a word, I ran right inside Guerrero's hut, left the Bible on the table, and kept on running. Guerrero immediately understood and took it to the priest. That evening, Father Neto sent it back with Tiago. We continued doing the same thing for several days, leaving early each morning before the captain was awake. One of the Portuguese would be waiting by the side of the road, and, without slowing down, we handed off the Bible and continued running. Every day we wrote a little note—a Bible text or some news about our situation and what the captain was doing. We knew that the priest received the Bible, but he never replied. So, one day Marie wrote asking how he was. That evening his brief reply came. "I apologize for not answering. I know that silence is a bitter reply, but what can we do? I am well, although I am disheartened. God will soon set us free."

By "return mail," I wrote "Psalm 68:6, 'God sets the solitary in families; He brings out those who are bound into prosperity.' He will surely not fail to answer our prayers."

The next day, we had nothing to write about, and since we were a little late, I took the Bible, placed it under my arm, and went running as we usually did. The major was standing outside, near our hut, and he greeted us. We replied and quickly resumed our pace. Without slowing down, we delivered the Bible and continued on our way, but we knew the major was watching. It was good that we hadn't put anything in the Bible that day!

"We really do have a guardian angel," we agreed. The one day that we didn't put a note in the Bible was the day the major saw us.

The next day, Guerrero met us on our daily run. "Don't put notes in the Bible anymore," he whispered. "They are checking it."

"There's nothing in it," I replied, without slowing down.

On Sabbath, we went out simply for a walk along the same path. In the distance, we saw Guerrero coming toward us. We decided not to stop to talk, fearing we would get in trouble.

But it was too late. Guerrero came up to me and said, "Here is a letter. It's a little old." He extended his hand as if to shake hands and pressed a tightly folded paper into my hand. I closed my hand around it, worried that some soldier might have noticed. When we returned to our hut, I discovered that it was the letter that Miguel had written before his night visit. I had previously sent a message to give the letter to the priest, suggesting that he burn it, but evidently, he hadn't done it.

"My love!" I read. "All that I am going through is for your sake. Tonight, I will come to visit you. If that's OK, sing 'Guantanamera' twice after the baby cries." He was referring to the Sabatés' baby, who usually woke up crying around ten o'clock to nurse.

That night I hadn't sung. I hadn't even heard the baby cry, but he came anyway. He wanted to see me, his letter said, so that we could talk and make plans for our life together.

He seemed to take it for granted that I would marry him. But now, he knew my position, and since a full week had gone by, I felt safer. I assumed he had finally accepted my no and wouldn't show up again.

I wondered how the Cuban was able to get his letters to Guerrero. I found out his method was very risky. In the middle of the night, he quietly stepped over the guards while they slept and went to Guerrero's house. He split the end of a long stick, stuck the letter in the split, and then pushed the stick through the straw walls of Guerrero's hut.

CHAPTER 17

"We Were Like Those Who Dream"

The night is dark, and the moon has not come up over the horizon. The dry branches make the flames of the campfire flare up. The usual night sounds: the crackling of dry branches, the swishing of the leaves, the call of the tom-tom, the melancholy voices of the soldiers, and the far-off cry of the hyena. Counting: 188, 189, 190 steps to the big tree by the crossroads close to the house of Adelino, the cook. Beyond that is where the Russians live: forbidden territory for us. Now, back again: 188, 189, 190—like some kind of zoo creatures, pacing restlessly back and forth, back and forth, in our cages.

For six weeks, we have had nothing to eat but cornmeal, a little rice, dried fish, and canned meat. We haven't seen soap for two weeks. How many days, how many weeks has it been since we were promised our freedom? Every passing day is a new disappointment.

Will we be home for Christmas? Or maybe for New Year's? For some time, we have felt a growing sense of resignation; there is nothing more than an exhausting sense of hopelessness.

We feel totally cut off from the world, forgotten in the depths of the jungle, where time seems to stand still, an eternity between the lines of thought.

Each is imprisoned in his or her own thoughts; insignificant things transform into gigantic problems. The camp rules become tyrannical to us. I look at the night sky. The Southern Cross seems to mock us, pointing us always to the south, the pathway of freedom. September 13, 1982. Marie Brunier.

When Marie wrote those words, our courage had reached its lowest ebb. When we were together, we no longer had anything to talk about, and we would stare at each other in silence. Sometimes Marie did not want to go with me on the walks even when we had once again been allowed to walk along the path that went to the front of the camp.

One Sunday morning, I was jogging along the pathway when I heard someone singing. The music came from one side of the house where the Cubans lived. It was Miguel, singing in a sad voice, "To the devil with loneliness! I met her by the river, and she had the same pain in her heart as I did, but she did not want to risk a relationship with me. Leave everything and fly away with me! Together we will forget the misery of this solitary life."

It seemed that the Portuguese were also becoming more and more dejected. Father Neto asked us constantly if we had any news about our liberation. Every time we met the captain, we asked him the same question. He always answered, "No, nothing new," and then he would leave quickly.

In my diary, I wrote, "We were told that we would soon receive visitors. Again, they have forbidden us to go to the front part of the camp. I feel like a monkey in a cage. We walk around and around the hut. And we sing to keep from crying."

To Marie and me, it seemed that the others were even more down than we were. So, we tried to think of something we could do to cheer them up. Thinking our situation might drag on for months, and we could end up getting sick, we decided to organize an evening of activities to add some spark to our lives. We decided to build a huge bonfire to gather around, where we could sit and tell stories, act out skits, and do other entertaining things to cheer each other up and break up the dull routine.

However, before we could execute our plan, some new developments turned our lives in an entirely different direction. Early on the morning of September 14, we were still in our hut trying to wash up and thinking of ideas for the social activity when Marie noticed the major in the distance. Several days before, he had left for Jamba. Before leaving, he told us that when he got back, we would be freed. And now, here he was. We almost stopped breathing. We dressed quickly and ran outside, "Do you have any news for us?" we wanted to know.

"Well, I found out that in a few days, Miss Brunier will fly home. You missionaries will have to wait a while longer. Your home countries have not yet met our conditions."

"No! I can't believe it; that is impossible! If your president does this to us, I'll go on foot to his headquarters and tell him personally what I think of it. He promised us before witnesses that, because of the Adventist Church's efforts, we would be given our freedom. He said nothing at all about our home countries."

"Hmmm, we'll see about that," the major said, and he quickly departed, giving us a mischievous look.

That afternoon he called all of us to the yango. Dr. Valentín and Dr. Jakajamba were there. They told us that due to the Adventist Church's admirable effort and commitment, they had decided to free us.

"And to assure you that it is sincere this time, we will remain here with you until you leave. Arrangements have been made for you to travel via South Africa. Zambia refused to take you, and if we were to go through Zaire, you would have had to walk another three months," they told us.

Dr. Jakajamba looked at me with a mischievous twinkle in his eye, "However, I understand that the menina actually wants to stay here, isn't that right?" He was referring to Miguel, but I pretended not to understand. He didn't mention it again.

The visitors told us that several journalists who wanted to interview us had come with them. They invited us to a cultural program in the evening. The rest of the day was filled with emotion as we prepared for our departure. It had all happened so unexpectedly, just at the point where we had almost lost all hope.

Suddenly I thought of Botelho! I ran to the house of the major and asked, "Major, what happened to the young Portuguese man, Botelho?"

"Oh, Botelho! He came along with us, and he will be freed together with you."

That was wonderful news, indeed. We could hardly wait to see Botelho again and share news of what had happened while we were separated.

That evening, we all gathered around a large campfire in the spot where almost two months earlier, shortly before the interview with the journalists, I had met Marie. Now we were taking part in a great fiesta. To celebrate in style, they even offered us milk. The guerrillas sang their revolutionary songs. Afterward, they asked each of us to do something that represented our own country: sing a song, recite a poem, or something else. The priest, Fernández, shared some challenging riddles. Botelho told a story.

Guerrero, our old Portuguese friend, was seated next to me. He leaned over and asked in a whisper, "A while back, you asked me to burn the letter I was holding for you. How did you know I had it?"

"I'll tell you that when we're free," I whispered back. There were too many soldiers nearby, and I wasn't sure I could speak softly enough to make sure they didn't hear.

Marie told us that August 1 is a holiday in Switzerland when the whole country lights bonfires similar to the one we had that night. Finally, it was my turn. I sang a traditional song from Argentina. When I finished, everyone applauded enthusiastically. It really was a beautiful evening; above all, we were happy that we would soon be free.

The next day I wrote, "It is incredible; I feel reborn! Today, we will be interviewed by journalists."

Many journalists had come. They were especially interested in interviewing and filming Marie and me because they wanted to show how the guerrillas had treated the two female prisoners. They filmed us inside and outside of our hut. Afterward, they had us sit by the fire where a kettle of beans was cooking. With the cameras rolling, the kettle, as if on cue, fell over, and some of the beans spilled out on the sand. Some might have thought it was especially dramatized for the cameras. I got up quickly and grabbed a cloth to pick up the hot kettle and put it back on the fire. The whole scene was recorded.

Then, turning their cameras to Marie, they started to question her. More people from UNITA surrounded our location and listened carefully to make sure we didn't say anything inappropriate. The interviews went on. Anyone with common sense knew that the beans would soon begin to burn, but no one took the kettle off the fire because of the cameras. Finally, Dr. Valentín couldn't stand it any longer. He got up and quickly took the kettle out of camera range.

They continued asking questions for a long time. Finally, they were satisfied. After they left, we invited Dr. Valentín and Dr. Jakajamba to eat with us. We wanted to visit with them because we knew they had ties to Switzerland, where we had both lived.

We had only burned beans to offer, but they appreciated our invitation and brought two cans of fruit that we enjoyed for dessert.

That evening the major asked me jokingly if I really didn't want to stay and marry the Cuban.

"Tell me what you know about him," I asked.

"It's like this," he explained. "The young fellow saw you at the river and fell in love with you. He is determined at all costs to marry you. It was just that fast."

"We have to understand where he's coming from," I said. "He doesn't have any possibility of meeting a girl. Furthermore, he knows that at any time, I might be freed, and that only makes him more desperate."

"We will have to kidnap some Cuban girls; then those boys will have someone to marry," the major teased.

"Yes," I said. "They aren't prisoners, yet they can't leave, and they are very lonely. That's how they get such crazy ideas in their heads. But they never threatened me in any way." Of course, I never told the major about the night visit and the letters.

"Very well," said the major. "Tomorrow, I'll pay him a visit and explain your position."

The next day, we were keyed up with travel fever. We had to put up with a few more interviews and political lectures. But, finally, they brought each of us a form to sign, promising that we would not return to Angola as long as the war continued. We signed it with sadness in our hearts. We all felt that the experiences we had gone through were insignificant if we couldn't return to the mission soon.

They told us we needed to be packed and ready to go by midday. Unexpectedly, we heard the sound of singing. It was a chorus of young women who had come from Jamba to accompany us to the border of Namibia and sing at the liberation ceremony.

We sat on our baggage and waited. The afternoon went by, but nothing happened. We didn't know what to think. We started feeling upset and discouraged. Was this going to be yet another disappointment?

I saw the major coming from the side of the camp where Cubans lived, so I ran to ask him about his conversation with Miguel.

"Yes, I spoke with him," he told me. "The poor guy was very sad. For some reason, he seemed very afraid, but I tried to reassure him and let him know that I understand how he feels. I reminded him that you are a prisoner who will soon be free, and we couldn't allow things to happen here that would damage our image. I think he was relieved, and he seemed less worried after our conversation. I don't think you need to worry about him anymore."

Of course, the major didn't know why Miguel was so afraid. If I had told him about the night visit and letters, the situation might have been very different for Miguel. I was also more at peace.

Since it was now evening, Marie and I wrapped ourselves in our blankets and went to sleep. Unlike what usually happened, we fell asleep at once. We were sleeping soundly when we heard a loud voice that awakened us with a start. It was the major outside our door.

"Get up! Get up! It's eight o'clock. This is the third time I've called you. Are you deaf?"

"That can't be right. It's not possible!" I said in a daze, trying to ascertain what was happening.

"All right, hurry now! Get up! We have to leave right away!" he insisted.

When he had gone, I said to Marie, "Wait! We have to pray first."

We knelt together, and I fervently asked for God's guidance and protection for whatever lay ahead. Then we quickly got ready and went to the edge of the woods, where three trucks were waiting. A huge number of people would travel with us. The Sabatés got on the first truck, which was already completely filled with the soldiers and journalists, so that Conchita could sit in the cab with her baby. The rest of us, including the major and a group of soldiers, got on the second truck. UNITA took advantage of the way opened by the Adventist Church to free the Portuguese men and the priest, Fernández. The UNITA women's chorus climbed aboard the last truck. It was about ten o'clock when we finally started rolling.

Our truck looked so odd that we couldn't help but laugh. It had no cab, so it looked like a big old box. The driver sat up front with the major while the rest of us stood in the back.

The three trucks traveled slowly and laboriously in single file over the sand. When we had been underway for about two hours, we had to stop because the truck that was following us broke down. Our driver helped the other driver make the repairs, and we continued on. But before long, we stopped again. We continued to stop for repairs every few miles.

The constant jolting, speeding up, and slowing down soon had its effect on our stomachs. Before long, both Ronaldo and I were leaning over the edge, vomiting.

At some point, we realized we had turned around and were heading back the way we had come. We were shocked. "What's happening? Where are we going now?" we asked.

"We have to find a mechanic. The truck that was following us broke down completely," came the reply.

We protested as forcefully as we could. It would have been so much more comfortable for us to remain with the broken truck rather than to go jostling all the way to a mechanic and back. But, of course, no one asked us for our opinion.

They found a mechanic at a camp that was about a half-hour closer than the one we had left. By the time we finally got back to the broken-down truck, it was four o'clock in the morning, and we were only two hours away from our original camp. We were very cold and tired. While the truck was being repaired, we tried to warm up around a fire. We were already covered with oil and sand, so we didn't hesitate to lie down directly on the sandy desert floor. It seemed impossible to get any dirtier than we already were. We couldn't even think about sleep with the cold wind blowing through our clothes, so we focused on staying close to the fire.

Someone brought coffee in an aluminum pot and passed it around. We all took a big drink of the hot, comforting fluid.

At sunrise, we got back on the truck and continued on our way. The soldiers warned us that this part of the journey was dangerous because now we had to travel by day, and it was an area often patrolled by enemy aircraft. If we were spotted, we would probably become targets. All morning, we watched the skies fearfully. Marie, Botelho, and I pressed into one corner and sat on the floor. We attempted to make the time pass more quickly by sharing what had happened to each of us over the last few weeks. It was still hard to talk because there were soldiers everywhere. But we revived our old methods, and despite the bumps and jarring, we were able to share. As the day wore on, the heat of the desert sun beat down on us mercilessly. There was no escape from the burning rays. Botelho, at least, had brought a large turban that he wrapped around his head. It made him look like an Arab, but the rest of us had nothing to cover our heads, and we were miserable.

At about nine o'clock in the morning, we stopped for a few minutes. Everyone was given a chocolate bar and some dry cookies, and then we continued on our journey. Thinking that we would arrive at our destination early in the day, the soldiers hadn't brought any drinking water. We got very thirsty. The burning sun made it difficult even to think, and we lost track of time.

The heat must have damaged the motor because it started spewing a fine spray of jet-black oil that rained down on us. We closed our eyes and kept our heads down. With no defense against the shower, we rode along in silence.

André started crying miserably. I took a blouse from my bag and gave it to Rosmarie so that she could cover his head. I still had a little water that I gave to him. He drank it eagerly, but he was so thirsty that he continued to cry at the top of his lungs for more water.

The landscape got drier as we went along; the sparse grass was brown and, in some places, black, looking as if it had been burned. It was especially horrible when we went through areas of white sand that reflected the bright sun into our eyes, forcing us to keep them closed. It felt like our heads would explode at any moment. We knew that there was water in one of the tanks we had on board. But that precious liquid was reserved for the truck's motor, in case it was needed, and it was contaminated with oil, gasoline, and rust. At first, it seemed undrinkable, but by midday, we imagined we would be happy to have at least a drop of any kind of water! When someone offered me a jug of the questionable fluid, I drank some, and so did Marie. The Oliveiras rejected it at first, but after a while, they, too, overcame their aversion and drank deeply.

"If we have survived this far, nothing can kill us," someone said. But we still didn't dare to let André drink the solution, even though it was painful to watch him suffer from thirst.

His mother started to cry along with her child, and her nose began to bleed. With a small damp towel, we made a cool compress and pressed it on her forehead to protect her from heatstroke. A little while later, we saw a big tree that the truck would pass directly under. We were able to snatch some branches from it and make our own little bit of shade.

It was nearly sundown when the miserable journey finally ended. We had arrived at a camp on the border of Namibia. The people there were concerned about our late arrival, knowing that we had no reserve water.

Our clothes and faces were black with the oil and sand that had sprayed on us. Reporters and photographers recorded our arrival in detail. We had to provide them with some graphic, memorable images.

The only things on our minds were water and sleep. We saw some barracks that had recently been built with fresh straw. Our eyes quickly fell on a container filled with clean, fresh water. Marie went off to look for a glass. I couldn't wait. Kneeling down, I desperately drank like a thirsty dog.

They brought each of us a basin of water to clean up as best we could. Later, when we were somewhat refreshed and wearing cleaner clothes, the journalists came for more interviews. We were extremely tired and went to bed immediately afterward.

Even though we hadn't closed our eyes all night the previous night, I woke up at midnight and couldn't go back to sleep. The anticipation of freedom was simply too much for me. I could hardly believe that we would very soon be free.

My mind went back over all the experiences we had lived through in the past three months and how God, in His mercy, had protected us. So many of our experiences could have been much worse. There had been moments of danger and sorrow, but the Lord had seen us through every one of them. The first month in camp, before Marie came, was very difficult for me. During that time, the sixteenth psalm had been a great comfort. I identified with the psalmist in many ways. Despite the harrowing experiences we had lived through, the Lord had never forsaken me, and furthermore, He had allowed me some deeply enriching experiences.

Especially meaningful were the conversations with Botelho and Marie. In the final days of our captivity, Marie often read my Bible, and she confessed that it was the first time in her life. I saw that our conversations about faith had not been without effect. We even had favorite texts that we repeated when we felt discouraged or afraid. For instance, when jungle animals prowled around our camp and we heard their roars, divine promises were our safeguard and hope. The most important thing that I realized was how, during those months, my relationship with God had grown closer than I had ever experienced before. I knew that our God is a personal and present Friend and Comforter, a present Help in time of trouble. My trust in Him had grown and strengthened greatly.

I thought about all of that as I turned restlessly in my bed, waiting for dawn. Around six o'clock, I heard the sound of a helicopter approaching from the direction of the river.

Although we had constantly asked the major, he never told us how we would get to Namibia. All kinds of possibilities had gone through my mind. We were all afraid we might have to face another long journey on foot. But when I heard the sound of the helicopter, I knew our walking was over. "Marie! Marie! Listen!" I shouted, beside myself with joy. She sat up in bed, listened for an instant, and then we embraced as tears ran down our cheeks.

Then she said something that made me very happy, "Vicky, wouldn't you like to say a prayer and ask God to accompany us to the very end and that everything will turn out all right?"

Right there on our beds of straw, we knelt and prayed, thanking God for His protection, for all that He had done for us during the long journey, and for having brought us safe thus far. We trusted Him with our future and all that was yet to happen, certain of His protection and care.

Together, we read our precious book of devotions. Then we quickly got ready for the journey. I decided to give Tiago my blanket and the old jeans that had been so useful during the long march. We had barely gathered our things when the major appeared. We had breakfast, and then the truck carried us to the rendezvous point in the clearing.

Every resident of the camp was there, the women's chorus sang, and we were taken under the shade of a tent and given a seat. Numerous reporters were also there. They took pictures of us from every angle. The natives danced and sang their revolutionary songs. The improvised podium for the authorities was colorfully decorated with the UNITA flag, paintings of guerrillas in their battles, and the image of UNITA's president, Jonas Savimbi.

Dr. Valentín stood up and called us to follow him to a pasture where there was a large herd of cows. Apparently, he wanted us to know that UNITA had cattle as well as enemies. After we had sufficiently admired the healthy animals, we went back to our places and eagerly awaited what would happen next.

While we waited, we saw half of the young women from the choral group board a truck that headed off toward the river. They returned half an hour later with the truck full of journalists. Among them, we saw two men who stood out. They appeared to have different roles. They greeted General Bocca, who had been introduced to us the night before. Someone introduced one of the visitors to us. "This is the head of the South African Red Cross. He has come to receive the prisoners."

Then General Bocca launched into a long political harangue. He spoke passionately about the cause of UNITA. He recounted how they struggled for freedom and justice and how it was being demonstrated by the release of the prisoners that day. After him, the head of the Red Cross spoke. Finally, they read the names of all the prisoners and ceremonially handed him the paper with our names on it, thus formalizing the act of our liberation.

The head of the Red Cross thanked the general and handed him a letter for President Savimbi, to whom he sent his respectful greetings. The choir sang enthusiastically, "Thank you very much! Thank you very much!" Everyone applauded and shouted, "Long live President Savimbi! Long live President Savimbi!"

Then I saw the other man who was with the head of the Red Cross. He had not been introduced. He came around behind the group, approached us, and held out his hand to me first because I was closest, and said in English, "I am a Seventh-day Adventist minister."

I couldn't believe my ears! I must have looked totally confused because he leaned in closer and repeated, "Adventist minister."

I jumped to my feet and hugged him with all my strength. Immediately, the others came and did the same, with great joy. It was as if an angel had come down from heaven to carry us off with him. From that moment on, we were unaware of anything else that was happening. We were so thrilled! The pastor started speaking to us while Marie translated, "Now it's confirmed. You are, indeed, free. Our members all over South Africa have been praying for you from the day we first heard of your capture."

When I heard those words, I couldn't hold back the tears. It was wonderful to know that our brethren in the faith had been praying for us, not only in South Africa but also around the world, as the pastor assured us.

"You are going to fly to South Africa, where you will be our guests. My wife is preparing our home to receive you."

Once again, I was overwhelmed with emotion. *Preparing a home!* Those words were the sweetest I had ever heard! To be in a real house! A home! To once again be in a home, to belong to someone!

The pastor opened his briefcase and took out two beautiful red apples, the first we had ever seen in Angola, and he gave one to each of the children. André took his and began to eat it at once. Surprised, his mother exclaimed, "Look how he is enjoying the apple!"

The pastor told us that in South Africa, ambassadors from each country were waiting to receive their citizens. As for us missionaries, the Adventist Church was taking the responsibility of receiving us and caring for us while we were there.

Apparently, we still looked very dirty because the pastor reached into his briefcase again and offered each of us a scented cleaning wipe to refresh ourselves. Then he opened a bag of trail mix and passed it around so we could each take some. My emotions had so tightened my throat that I couldn't even swallow the wonderful food.

Later we were interviewed for the UNITA broadcast on the Black Rooster. Marie had already been given a note from the Red Cross of Geneva warning her to be very careful about what she said. It caused her some concern over her interview. The rest of us reassured her, and everything came off well. The native women danced with their children in their arms.

Conchita was so taken up with the scene that she picked up one of the children and began dancing with them, to their great delight. Finally, we boarded the truck and were taken to the Okavango River, which marks the border between Angola and Namibia. The UNITA women's chorus was waiting for us there. They sang again with renewed enthusiasm. The group from UNITA embraced us and wished us good luck. A South African Army boat took us across the river in small groups. Marie and I were last. As we stepped onto the boat, one of the guerrillas placed his cap on my head.

As soon as we had set foot on the other shore, it suddenly seemed more real. "We're free! We're free!" our voices echoed across the desert.

Marie pointed out a large tent pitched at the top of a hill. "Let's go see if there is something for us there." To our surprise, we found an enormous table covered with all kinds of food and drinks, a true cold buffet, out there in the desert. I ran back to the others and shouted, "Come! See how many good things there are to eat!" Overwhelmed by such abundance and all the beautiful colors, we went around the table again and again, not even knowing where to start. One of the journalists who was in charge of making sure that we were in Pretoria by five o'clock was getting worried. "Hurry quickly!" he urged us. "If not, we'll be late." We needed no more urging.

As we ate together, we realized that we would soon be in South Africa and that we would have to say goodbye to one another, maybe forever. We quickly told one another, somewhat awkwardly, many things we had not been able to say before, and we exchanged addresses. Botelho told us that when they took him to UNITA headquarters in Jamba, they showed him all the wonderful things available to him there. They tried in every conceivable way to convince him to stay voluntarily and work for them. When he told them that he would not be able to accept their proposal because of his poor health, they asked him to serve as a representative of UNITA in Portugal. Botelho felt that if he wanted to get back his freedom after so many years of captivity, he must accept the proposal. Immediately, to his surprise, everything changed. They began to treat him very well and make all kinds of concessions. He was supposed to forget all the suffering he had endured during his years in the jungle and defend UNITA's interests with total conviction.

When we had finished eating, they took us to a tent where a young physician gave us a medical checkup. Then they put us in a huge helicopter that took us to a small town in Namibia. We were surprised by the cleanliness of the place. While we were waiting, I looked for a restroom. The Adventist pastor, Eric Annandale, asked around to help me find one. A soldier signaled for me to go with him and directed me to a Jeep. As we pulled away, Botelho, very perplexed to see me leaving, shouted, "Where are you going?"

I turned and shouted back, "To the bathroom!" His astonished look made me laugh.

The soldier took me to a small house nearby. The bathrooms were brand new and spotlessly clean. Everything was finished in good taste. The facilities were so clean that I was almost afraid to use them. Only one detail was lacking: there was no water! When I mentioned it to the soldier, he laughed and said, "That's so you don't forget that you are still in Africa."

A little later, they took us to board a military plane for our flight to Pretoria. They seated all of us on the floor and strapped us in tightly with our backs against the side of the aircraft. When we landed, a crowd of reporters was waiting. Dr. Sabaté made a short speech thanking the South African Army for bringing us. He thanked the journalists for making the world aware of our plight, and finally, he thanked the South African Red Cross for its help. The president of the Red Cross presented each of us with a small medal as a memento of our liberation.

Except for the Argentinian ambassador, ambassadors from each of the nations of the captives were present. Our plane had landed earlier than expected, and my ambassador was unable to get there in time. We decided not to wait. We said goodbye to the Portuguese men, to Father Fernández, and to Marie. They were taken away by their ambassadors. We climbed into Pastor Annandale's car, dirty as we were, with him and his wife.

When we arrived at their home, the first thing we noticed was a bouquet of roses on a table by the door. We were delighted by the beautiful colors of the flowers after so many days in the arid desert that had almost no color.

When we entered, we eagerly went and sat in the inviting living room chairs. What a sensation of comfort and freedom! Pastor Annandale brought me the bouquet of roses and said, "These are for you, Victoria." I looked at him, astonished. Who would have sent me a bouquet of roses here? A little card with a name I didn't recognize hung from a branch.

The Annandales showed us to our rooms. They had rearranged their home so that there were rooms for all of us. They even managed to have cribs for the babies. On each bed, they had placed bath items we might need—things that we had been missing for so long: soap, shampoo, lotions, and other toiletries. They had even bought underclothes and pajamas for us. I placed the beautiful bouquet of roses on the nightstand beside my bed. Just then, the doorbell rang, and they called me. There was the ambassador from Argentina, Alfredo Oliva Day, and the consul. They introduced themselves, and then I knew who had sent the flowers.

"Victoria, what were you doing in Angola?" the ambassador asked, placing his hands together in a gesture typical of Argentina. "And how did you fall into the hands of the guerrillas?"

I answered his questions, and we talked for a long time. As they were leaving, they invited us all to lunch at their house the following Friday.

In the meantime, Mrs. Annandale had prepared a delightful meal for us. Sitting at a table filled with delicious food, eating from beautiful plates, and using all the proper utensils seemed almost too good to be true. Afterward, we each attempted to contact our family members by phone.

When Ronaldo heard his mother's voice as she answered the phone in Brazil, he only said, "Mother!" and then began to weep uncontrollably. His wife had to take the phone and explain their situation to his family.

I called my sister Mary. She gave a shout of joy when she heard my voice and knew that I was really free. Then she told me something that broke my heart: in July, my four-year-old nephew Christian was playing with a pointed stick and accidentally pierced his cheek, severing his optic nerve and leaving him blind in his left eye. My beloved nephew, with his big black eyes, had always been such a cheerful and loving child! I was overwhelmed with grief and began to sob.

Still saddened by the news, I hung up the phone. The Oliveiras and Sabatés surrounded me and hugged and comforted me. That moment made me aware of how close we had grown during those three months and revealed how strong the bonds of love and empathy had become.

After each of us had called our families, Mrs. Annandale showed us the bathrooms where, after all this time, we would be able to bathe properly. Naturally, we could not avoid giving one another some good-humored advice such as, "Be careful you don't drown." It seemed like a dream to be able to place my whole body in a tub full of clean soapy water. When I was finished and had drained the dirty water, I couldn't help laughing. I called the others to come and see the dirty ring around the top. The thick oil from the truck clung there as a witness to our ordeal in the desert.

What an indescribable feeling it was to lie down in a soft, clean bed! My insomnia disappeared as if by magic, and I had scarcely laid my head on the pillow, when, for the first time in a hundred nights, I slept deeply, without fear.

How grateful we were to the Annandale family for their love and care for us! They cared even to the point of getting us new clothes, and they made sure we lacked nothing during our stay.

On the evening of our arrival in the Annandales' home, after our baths, the pastor called us for family worship. When we were all seated in the large, pleasant living room, we sang some hymns. Afterward, the pastor asked, "Would any of you like to request a special text?"

"Yes, I would like you to read Psalm one hundred twenty-six," I said.

While the pastor looked for the text and began reading it, I thought back on how much strength and assurance I'd found in the Psalms during our captivity. At times, it seemed that they were addressed directly to us. Every day, I read a psalm and meditated on its words, underlining the promises and begging God to free us as He had His people Israel. On September 16, our last day in the camp, while we were sitting on our luggage waiting to leave, I opened my Bible once more and read Psalm 126. When I finished reading, I ran to where Ronaldo and Rosmarie were sitting on their luggage, singing a hymn. With deep conviction, I exclaimed, "That is our psalm!"

Now here, seated comfortably in the Annandales' living room, we listened once again to the words. Free at last! Every word that the pastor read touched our hearts. We were deeply moved because we, too, were like those who dream:

When the LORD brought back the captivity of Zion,
We were like those who dream.
Then our mouth was filled with laughter,
And our tongue with singing.
Then they said among the nations,
"The LORD has done great things for them."
The LORD has done great things for us,
And we are glad.

Bring back our captivity, O LORD,
As the streams in the South.

Those who sow in tears
Shall reap in joy.
He who continually goes forth weeping,
Bearing seed for sowing,
Shall doubtless come again with rejoicing,
Bringing his sheaves with him.

CHAPTER 18

Life Goes On

In Pretoria, we said goodbye to the Portuguese men who, two days later, returned to their own country.

After a busy and intensely emotional week, we came to the Sabbath, September 25. The Adventists in Pretoria had given money for us to get new clothes. During the Sabbath worship service, Pastor Annandale introduced us to the church, and Ferrán expressed the gratitude that all of us felt. The love and heartfelt care of our brothers and sisters once again proved how deep are the ties that bind our hearts together in Jesus.

After the service, we were invited to the home of a widowed father and his three young sons who lived together in a large, beautiful older home. The father spoke French, so it was easy for us to communicate. We invited Marie, and she came to spend the afternoon with us. We all laughed a lot as we shared some of our adventures in the UNITA camps.

After sundown, we went to the Johannesburg airport, where we would go our separate ways. For the last time, we joined in a circle to pray. Ferrán thanked God for His protection during our tremendous odyssey and placed our future in His hands. I was the first to leave. Ferrán and Conchita's flight was to leave two hours later, as was the Oliveiras'. As I was going through customs, I heard Ferrán shout, "Victoria, we love you very much!"

Those words were still echoing in my heart as the plane took off. During the sixteen months we worked together in Bongo, we had become an extraordinary team. Ferrán had a special gift for organization and administration. Conchita represented, to my mind, the perfect teammate: beautiful, well-balanced, cheerful, and always willing to help. I admired her skill as a midwife and loved working with her. Finally, there was me, energetic and possessing a strong will that, more than once, had upset

206 | KIDNAPPED IN ANGOLA

Ferrán. At times, we had argued intensely over the details of how we should care for our patients, but we quickly forgave each other and continued working unitedly in our efforts to save lives in the midst of the chaos that surrounded us. We had lived through so many difficulties and fears together! What joy when things turned out right!

During one of our last conversations, Conchita said, "When I think about how everything happened, I can't believe it. Why did something like this have to happen? Did we do something wrong?" Her face reflected her perplexity. The same unanswered question echoed in the minds of all of us. Now our team had been broken up, perhaps forever. Only God knew what would happen afterward.

Seated next to me on the flight was a young couple conversing in German. It reminded me that I was flying toward Switzerland and would soon be truly free.

Freedom! I took my old, soiled, and oft-read book of devotions and wrote on the last page:

Freedom, I love you so much! Before, I never stopped to think about you. I just enjoyed you. I had you and used you as I pleased, but I never stopped to think about who you really were and how much you meant to me. I finally understood how precious you were one night when you were suddenly torn from my arms. Then, at last, I realized how much you meant to me. I cried out, calling you desperately, but you were gone and could no longer hear me. I missed you terribly, I longed to have you back, but it was impossible. I had lost you, and I didn't know where to find you.

But Today! Oh yes, Today, I have found you! I have gotten you back, and I never want to lose you again. Freedom, I love you so much!

I closed the book and attempted to sleep. As I did, my thoughts went back to Angola. I was happy for my newly restored freedom, but on the ground far below were people who had lost theirs, perhaps forever.

A vision of the hospital appeared before my eyes, its rooms filled with malnourished children, weeping mothers, war-wounded citizens, and some that we could not save.

I realized more than ever how far I was from being able to answer the question, Why? How much easier it would have been to bear the difficulty we lived through in the preceding months if we had known for sure that we could go back to Bongo!

Now the flight attendants were handing out the evening meal, but I didn't take mine. Far below, people were living amid great suffering. I could see their faces with cheeks sunken from starvation, the faces of children swollen with edema due to the lack of protein, and I lost my appetite.

At six o'clock the next morning, we landed at Zurich airport. Lost in my sad thoughts, I hadn't thought of the reunion awaiting me there. With my tiny suitcase in hand, I went through customs and out into the large waiting area. There, I spotted my sister Mary and my brother-in-law, Walter. They greeted me excitedly, and waiting behind them was a large crowd of my friends and acquaintances. Half of the Schaffhausen church was there! Now they were all hugging me. How often I had thought about each of them, wondering whether I would ever see them again!

As we left the airport, the sun was shining in all its splendor. Seated in my brother-in-law's car, I watched the green countryside pass by. "So green! The fields and the trees are so green!" I exclaimed again and again.

"They always are," answered my sister, somewhat puzzled.

After our long march through the desert in the last part of our journey, the brilliant colors of Switzerland seemed almost too beautiful to be real.

With an incredible outpouring of love, my sister and some friends had prepared a breakfast banquet in the little Waedenswil church. Some members of the church band from Schaffhausen brightened the atmosphere with their music. A profound sense of gratitude flooded my soul, and the words of the twenty-third psalm came to mind:

> You prepare a table before me in the presence of my enemies;
> You anoint my head with oil;
> My cup runs over.
> Surely goodness and mercy shall follow me
> All the days of my life;
> And I will dwell in the house of the LORD
> Forever (verses 5, 6).

A new life was beginning for me, completely different from the one I had imagined when I left for Angola.

In the days that followed, I was incredibly tired. I slept late every morning, and I got up only to lie down again and rest some more. I was thankful I didn't have to go back to Argentina yet. Psychologically, I didn't feel up to answering questions from reporters and incessantly talking about the ordeal. Furthermore, Argentina had just been through a war, and I was afraid that some of my friends had fallen. I wasn't prepared to deal with more grief just yet.

The first time I had to go into the city to buy some things, I felt like an extraterrestrial. The rush and noise of traffic and the smell of exhaust were almost unbearable—the crowds of people hurrying here and there, so unconcerned and selfish, each shut up in his own little world of personal interests. I was irritated to the point of anger when I saw someone throw away some food. I simply felt out of place.

I called Conchita, and she told me that she was having the same problems. "It was difficult there," she said, "but here in the city, I can hardly stand it. There is too much noise! Everything is so different!"

In the following days, many of my friends invited me to their homes, and I visited them. It was always a great joy to get together and be able to talk, yet I had an emptiness inside that they couldn't fill. The enormous question remained unanswered. Depression slowly began to wrap me in its web, and I couldn't break free.

I tried to be strong and ignore what was happening to me. I should have sought help, but I didn't. Gradually, I began to lose all desire to study the Bible, and my prayers became empty words. Whenever I thought about it, I felt guilty, remembering the marvelous way God had cared for me. However, I did not know how to resolve the conflict of my inner feelings.

One day I received a letter from the Euro-Africa Division of our church inviting me to work in La Lignière Clinic in Gland, Switzerland, at the end of my furlough. The invitation only added to my gloom. I just wanted to go back to the mission field, to go to someplace where I could really make a difference and feel useful.

The tension grew within me day by day, and by the end of my first month, I was lost in profound sadness. Insomnia, which had characterized my nights in the UNITA camp, came back, and I simply could not sleep. Hour after hour, I would toss in bed. I looked for medical help, but sleep medications made me feel worse. It was as if the sleep center of my brain had ceased to function.

Finally, I decided that I needed to be alone, and I went to spend some time in a cabin in the Swiss mountains. I attempted in vain to find myself and recover my psychological equilibrium, but my longing for Angola grew stronger every day. I missed the black faces, the friendly, trusting people with their cheerful smiles and uncomplicated lifestyle. Especially, I missed my patients. I had accustomed my life to theirs and was lost without them. I didn't know where to turn.

Doubts and disappointments filled my spirit. I felt a heaviness in my chest and the continual desire to weep. Had I gone to Angola only to become aware of the suffering of its people and then been forced to leave them to their lot? What would happen to them? I did not doubt that God had cared for us during the time we were hostages, but did it have to end like this? Did I have to simply resign myself to work at the clinic in Switzerland and bury all the hopes and ideals I had cherished since childhood?

Only God could answer my questions, and although I had lost the desire to do so, I decided to turn to Him for help. Sometimes my prayers were humble pleas, asking for help and understanding. At other times, I shed tears of grief, begging him to care for the mission and the hundreds of suffering people who were seeking help there. Again and again, I came to the Lord, asking, "Why did you allow all of this to happen?"

Time went on, and although I didn't receive an answer, little by little, my doubts and sadness were replaced by peace and confidence. By the end of my furlough, I felt stronger and comforted. Doubts, questions, and painful memories returned often, but I felt as if a powerful hand was holding me up and freeing me little by little from the gloom and sorrow. Nevertheless, it would be years before I recovered any ability to sleep well. In fact, insomnia would remain as a permanent result of the experiences I lived through.

I had just returned from my time in the mountains when the phone rang. A teacher friend was calling to ask if I would be willing to share my story with his students. And another teacher wanted me to give a talk to her students in a girls' school.

"But my German is not that good," I protested.

"Of course, it is," they assured me. "You speak it very well."

I know enough about German grammar to be aware of my deficiencies in that difficult language. When none of my protests availed, I turned to the Lord. "You know that my German is not good enough to speak in public, but if You really want me to do this, please take charge of all my needs." Sharp pain in my stomach warned of the toll that these talks could take on my already exhausted nervous system.

Before long, a list of invitations crowded my calendar: Biel, Hamburg, Bern, Gland, and other places. Before each talk, I was stressed and nervous. Speaking to a large audience in a foreign tongue was an intimidating undertaking. Additionally, recounting the experiences brought back memories, and it was like living it all over again. At the end of each talk, I wanted to run behind the curtain and weep, but the audience eagerly waited to meet me and ask questions. After sharing at these events, I would go to bed and lie awake for hours. When I finally fell asleep, I was tormented by nightmares.

I began receiving encouraging feedback from some who heard my story. One young man said, "For a long time, I have wanted to be a missionary, but could not fully decide. Now everything is clear: I will be a missionary."

"My daughter is studying nursing," one woman told me. "Ever since she heard your message, she wants to be a missionary."

Those words filled me with joy, and I was comforted. But I still felt anxious and down. Who was I to be influencing these people? When I thought about myself, I could see only a strong-willed person who had many flaws in her own character. I felt so unworthy to witness for God and to influence other people's lives. The responsibility was too much.

I instinctively refused all contact with reporters. When I couldn't avoid them, I found it very difficult to respond kindly to their endless questions.

At the beginning of December, I traveled with my sister and her two children to Argentina. I cannot describe the happiness I felt to be back with my friends, my mother, and my brothers and sisters. We had barely arrived when I was asked to speak at a medical council that was meeting in Buenos Aires. Some dear friends, such as Dr. Wensell and others, had made arrangements for me to share my story there.

Many of my friends had followed the story of my kidnapping with anguish and alarm. I could tell that they had suffered on my behalf. Many of them had known me since infancy. We had grown up together, and suddenly, they lost me in the Angolan jungle. Some of them clung to me and wept when they saw me.

My mother and my brothers and sisters showed their love and joy in a completely different way. They silently listened to my stories, asking no questions. For them, all that mattered was that I was alive and home again. And I was so grateful to have them!

Little by little, the news media learned of my presence in Argentina. Many interviews and speeches followed. I accepted their invitations because I felt it was important for the young people in my country. There was still an atmosphere of fear and unhappiness from having lost the war. I wanted to offer a message of hope and assurance. I wanted to assure the young people that God is a present God, and He watches over those who serve Him.

Nevertheless, I was relieved when I could return to Europe. During the month in Argentina, I gave eight speeches and many reports. I responded to countless questions everywhere I went. By the end of my time there, my voice was hoarse.

When I was back in Europe, the Euro-Africa Division sent me to the Adventist seminary in Collonges, France, to study advanced French. The Spanish-speaking students at the seminary took me into their circle and gave me an enormous amount of help and encouragement. They knew about my struggles, and they prayed for me every time I traveled somewhere to speak. When I returned, they always welcomed me joyfully. When I was with them, I felt like a colleague, just another student. I felt happy and free in their company. I still feel gratitude when I recall their support and encouragement, especially when I received an invitation to go to Washington, DC, and was completely overwhelmed.

I often said, "I feel like a little shepherd girl who was taking care of her sheep in the wilderness when suddenly she was snatched up and placed in front of a large crowd where she now must speak." Only God knows how difficult that period was for me and how many prayers ascended to heaven before and after each meeting.

Slowly, I learned to leave all my worries and concerns in the hands of my loving God. I began to understand that my poor German and my feeble French and the difficulties of my own character were nothing more than—to use the words of Paul—a "thorn in my flesh" so that I would not become proud. I clearly understood that I am only a tool in the hands of God. Any good that comes is His doing and to His glory.

CHAPTER 19

How to Be a Missionary

While I was still at Bongo, someone once asked in a letter, "How can I be a missionary?"

First, we must understand what it means to be a missionary. Of course, all of God's children have a mission to fulfill. They are "a royal priesthood," called to "declare the praises of him who called you out of darkness into his wonderful light" (1 Peter 2:9, NIV). We are charged with making "disciples of all the nations, baptizing them in the name of the Father and of the Son and of the Holy Spirit" (Matthew 28:19). That is the universal call to mission.

But not everyone is called to fulfill the mission in the same way. Each one is to serve "according to his own ability" (Matthew 25:15), "according to the measure of Christ's gift" (Ephesians 4:7). Each individual is assigned a "place in the eternal plan of heaven. . . . Not more surely is the place prepared for us in the heavenly mansions than is the special place designated on earth where we are to work for God."[1] God gave Moses a message for the king of Egypt (Exodus 3:10–14). An angel touched the lips of Isaiah with a live coal from the altar and sent him on a mission to his own people (Isaiah 6:1–8). Saul of Tarsus was a "chosen vessel" to take God's name "before Gentiles, kings, and the children of Israel" (Acts 9:15). Thus he became a model for all who would be called to service outside the boundaries of their own ethnic group. The person who wrote to ask how to be a missionary, of course, had in mind this type of service.

The first thing I wrote in reply was, "Be a missionary only after you have spent time talking to God about it and are sure you cannot do anything else." The one whom God calls to cross-cultural service must have not only the assurance of the call but also a great capacity for adaptation to very diverse circumstances. He or she must show much love and willingness to accept people as they are, to serve them and treat them as equals. The colonial concept of mission never was right, and today it is worse than ever. One who is sent on a mission is not a commander but a servant. And when God is the sender, the commission is to carry a message from God to others, to serve those people according to *their* needs. The mission to be accomplished may be difficult. It may be disagreeable, complicated, and even dangerous, but if it is God who has sent us, He will take care of us, and He is responsible for the results.

In recent decades, most African countries have obtained their independence through violent revolutions, and there have been radical changes in nearly every region. The majority of foreigners caught up in these conflicts were forced to flee for their lives. Mission stations were closed. Schools and hospitals were invaded and turned into military camps.

Due to the lack of basic supplies and qualified personnel or, in some cases, because of the disorder and lack of discipline of those suddenly charged with directing them, factories were closed, great plantations were abandoned and overrun with weeds, and tourism disappeared. Ethnic (tribal) differences, held in check during the centuries of colonial occupation, reawakened, destroying the hopes of national unity that is so essential for consolidating the recently acquired independence. Power struggles, resulting in deadly violence and civil war, destroyed what little remained after the fight for independence. Hunger and fear hovered like an evil shadow over the land.

That was the situation that when we came to Angola. We found a people who were rejoicing in their freedom but were still not sure how to handle it. They were accustomed to obeying orders. They didn't know how to take the initiative or undertake any activity on their own. On the other hand, they were unwilling to submit to any foreign authority. They were an independent nation, struggling to move forward in spite of the difficulty caused by the civil war.

Missionaries who go to Africa today must be aware of these dynamics. They must learn to treat people and authorities with respect, and if they do, they can have a positive influence on those whose lives they will touch.

Whoever wants to be a missionary today must have common sense and much wisdom. They do not need to adopt the local way of thinking and acting, but they must know and understand the traditions and customs so they can offer help in the right direction and in the most useful way. They don't need to transform the people into Europeans or Americans, but they can help them be better citizens of the countries that they are trying to develop.

Some Angolan traditions and customs are beautiful and helpful. Others we found difficult to integrate into the demanding rhythm of work at the hospital. For example, the long absences of our workers, caused by the African funeral and mourning traditions, were a serious problem. Once we understood those traditions, we had conversations with the personnel and came to a consensus as to how many days they could miss and what their attitude should be toward their work. With some flexibility on both sides, we were able to achieve an acceptable work program and care for the patients while still allowing the workers to fulfill their family responsibilities in harmony with their customs.

In Europe and America, it is common to hear people say missionaries are no longer needed in Africa and that what the Africans learned from the whites has only harmed them. This is the view of armchair experts, who hold to Rousseau's vision of the "noble savage." In the first years of independence, some Angolan ethnic groups had a similar idea. They were determined to throw overboard everything they had learned during the colonial period, but they came to realize that this was not really possible. Four hundred years of living with whites had changed their worldview. The education they received, mostly from the missionaries, now formed an integral part of their lives and way of thinking. An ideological syncretism had been developed and transmitted for generations. They needed to first identify the positive elements in their ancient culture and the positive ones they had acquired. Then they could forge an identity satisfactory to themselves and to the international community to which they now belong as a new nation and as independent individuals.

The distrust that had been sown with regard to everything that had to do with whites had its consequences. The shortage of physicians and medicine resulted in a resurgence of witchcraft and traditional treatments that brought great harm to the people, especially to the children.

Often, children were brought to us at the last minute with clear signs of poisoning. We could only imagine what sort of treatment the poor child had received. If the patient did not improve rapidly, it often happened that the family would sneak into the hospital and snatch them away to place them in the hands of some miracle worker, thus signing the death decree for the victims.

The new missionaries have tried to reopen schools and hospitals and create jobs. Everyone was aware of the fragility of the situation in the midst of tribal conflicts and civil wars in the countries where they were working. They made great efforts to educate the local people so that they could assume greater responsibilities to be capable of making wise decisions for their own good and the good of their people.

Sadly, in our case, we were not even able to complete the nurses' training program we had started, a course that would have allowed the young people to take care of the patients more effectively. After we were snatched away, the political instability and the lack of medical professionals resulted in the closing of the Bongo Hospital, to the great loss of all who lived in the area.

It is vital that the native church focuses on the integral formation of its youth so that they can achieve greater effectiveness in their ministry and require less of the costly aid from outside. Training is one area where outside help from new missionaries can be especially useful.

But there must be some important changes in the training of professionals. Their education should be oriented to the reality and needs of the people they are going to serve. In Africa, the pastor has great power over communities and exercises a strong influence. If used well, it can become a powerful agent for change.

In the past, the Bongo mission had a clear vision and commitment. It dedicated great effort to integrate the education of native youth. At the school, they not only taught theoretical knowledge but also gave great importance to technical education, offering instruction in sewing, cooking, carpentry, shoe making, and agriculture, among other things. But today, this emphasis seems to have been forgotten. In an effort to improve the academic level of their pastors, the leaders have made agreements with foreign institutions that allow the African pastors to achieve university-level training while setting aside the preparation so essential to meeting the real needs of their own communities.

It is important for a pastor to know Greek, but it is more important for him to speak the native language correctly. It is good for him to know exegesis, but it is also essential for him to understand the intricacies of the traditional practices and customs of his people so that he can contextualize the message of salvation in a way that they will understand it in all its beauty. The pastor, the teacher, or the professor must know the rudiments of first aid and principles of hygiene and nutrition. Together with a solid theological formation, the pastor must know how to cultivate the soil and know the nutritional values of the different foods grown in the area so that he can teach his people the right way to produce and prepare them. Pastors, teachers, and foreign missionaries need to know how to teach the rural communities they are serving in such a way that their message will catch the interest and promote real change in the lifestyle of their members.

They must know how to create community projects that will really improve the quality of life for the members of the community. Their wives should be promoters of health, hygiene, and child education. The gospel is a comprehensive message that takes in the whole sphere of human existence, and it must bring about significant and positive change in the lifestyle of the new converts. If it does not achieve this objective, something fundamental is lacking in our methods.

Africa is in a state of rapid change, and both foreign and native workers must continually adapt their methods of work to the circumstances in which they live. Projects are needed to increase soil productivity so that the people have food in spite of climate change and the growing water shortage. It is necessary to educate people about the importance of protecting the environment so that communities do not continue to self-destruct.

Instead of promoting large and costly institutions that only an elite few can attend, our efforts should be directed toward education that is available to the majority. The education should contribute to a better life for Adventist families, providing them with tools for work to support themselves. The creation of technical schools where our young people can learn trades, such as construction, ironwork, plumbing, agriculture, sewing, or barbering, is a great need that is being ignored.

These schools should not be concentrated in one location but placed in different provinces of the country like the ancient schools of the prophets, allowing many to benefit, not just the few who have enough money to travel and pay for an expensive education.

It is a grave error to neglect the education of children. The children of our believers there are left in the hands of people who know nothing about the love of God and the lifestyle He wants for His children. Those educators provide the basic formation that will direct the life of a person. The results are plain to see. There is a great need for the creation of primary schools and community centers to strengthen the spiritual education and manual skills of the children. We must remember that if we want to promote real change in a community, we must apply all kinds of strategies to educate the children. They are the best agents for changing the society in which they live.

There is a wonderful motto: "Every church, a school." To achieve this objective, workers need to contextualize the message. They also need commitment, vision, faith, love, and total dependence on God.

Yes, Africa needs missionaries, both native and foreign, with the qualities required to carry out the plan established by God for mission in this world of change and conflict in the end time in which we live.

I am deeply grateful to God for the sixteen months I was able to work in Angola, and I thank Him also for the hundred days during which I was a prisoner because that experience enriched my life and taught me to value what is really important.

Although I never found an answer to the big question, "Why?" I at least know one thing: when I went as a missionary, I went with a desire to do my best for the people. I did the best I could. I worked with love and willingness, but the people who were in bondage for hundreds of years and who now faced a horrible civil war needed more than physical help; they needed understanding and empathy. In Bongo, I lived in a pleasant, clean house. I was well-dressed and lacked nothing. Enclosed in my impenetrable Western mentality, how could I feel for those people and understand their ways?

A week before we were kidnapped, I said to one of the students at the seminary, "I love Angolan people very much, and I'm willing to adapt everything to your way of living. I want to understand why and how you react to each situation. Just one thing: please don't ask me to eat pirão (the gruel made by stirring manioc flour into a fish or meat-based broth) or drink *kissangua* (a drink made from corn flour). That is not for me!"

Just a few days later, I held out my hands, eager and grateful to receive a plate of pirão. And, after being tortured for hours by thirst, I would have given anything for a swallow of *kissangua*. Through my experience, I no longer look at suffering from the outside but as one who suffered with them and like them. Like them, I had to flee for my life. Like them, in a single hour, I lost everything but a few things I could carry in my hands. Suddenly, our roles were reversed. They were the ones who gave orders, and I had to obey. I had to sleep on the ground, dealing with dirt and insects. When I was tossing and turning on my straw mattress, unable to sleep, or when I drank water from a dirty kettle, when I was exceedingly happy for a straw roof over my head at night to avoid sleeping out in the open, I learned to know the people and could understand them in a way I never had before. Now I was one of them, and nothing separated us. That's how I learned to truly appreciate and love the people of Angola.

I thought again of Psalm 126:

> Those who go out weeping,
>   carrying seed to sow,
> will return with songs of joy,
>   carrying sheaves with them (NIV).

Those words are a prophecy that was fulfilled for us in two different ways. We planted in Angola with tears, and through that experience, the Lord planted assurance and greater confidence in our hearts, and He reaped a harvest in us of greater love and a different attitude toward Africans. We expected to harvest the fruit of our labors in the new earth, but the Lord designed that, through this experience, we would be prepared to offer a better service to the humanity that surrounds us here and now.

Now I understand better the meaning of Jesus' sacrifice for me. He voluntarily separated Himself from His Father to come and live on this earth as one of us. He was the greatest example of contextualization that has ever existed. He became a human. He was born the poorest of the poor, and He participated in the joys and sufferings of humanity, thus revealing His understanding of our condition and His sympathy for us in all things. His love for us was so deep that He was willing to sacrifice even His own life, dying on the cross to save us. Today, a risen Savior, He stands before the Father as the perfect Intercessor, One who can sympathize with us because He knows by experience the rocky path that human beings must tread as prisoners in this world of sin. He is a loving God who is there for us, concerned about our needs, and willing to hear our prayers. His greatest desire is to free us and take us home with Him to heaven.

---

1. Ellen G. White, *Christ's Object Lessons* (Battle Creek, MI: Review and Herald®, 1900), 326, 327.

Epilogue

The intense experience I lived through in Angola changed my life forever. It was an ever-present reality in my mind. I often wondered whether I would ever be able to go back to the Bongo Mission.

My home country had just been freed from a harsh military regime that came to an end with the ignominious defeat of Argentina in the Falkland Islands. Unbridled inflation, unemployment, and corruption brought the country to an unprecedented socioeconomic crisis.

In December 1982, I decided it was time to go home to Argentina. Walking down the streets of Buenos Aires, I was troubled by the immense number of street children. It seemed that they were everywhere I looked, wandering aimlessly, begging, or sleeping on cardboard cartons on the street. Nobody seemed to care. I wondered whether I could do anything for them. That was when I began to see the need for a center for at-risk children.

I returned to Europe and went to the Adventist Seminary at Collonges to study French. After that, I worked for a while at La Lignière clinic in Switzerland; but I was not happy. I felt out of place there and with that class of patients. My thoughts constantly turned to the mission field, and I longed to go back. But the news from Angola was discouraging; the armed conflict continued. Many of my friends fell during those terrible years. The possibility of returning to Bongo seemed to be practically nil. Furthermore, we had signed a document promising never to return to Angola as long as the civil war continued, and it seemed like that would be never.

While at Collonges, I met João Augusto dos Santos Neto, the youngest son of a devout Catholic family in Portugal. He had immigrated to Venezuela, and while there, he embraced the gospel of salvation by faith and became a Seventh-day Adventist. This brought a cataclysm of wrath from his outraged family. His father, Adelino dos Santos Neto, felt humiliated by João's decision. Like the youngest son of many a good Portuguese family, the boy was destined to become a priest. Determined to make clear his repudiation of his son's decision, Adelino launched a bitter letter-writing campaign of persecution that lasted for more than twenty years. It was painful for João to read the insults in his father's lengthy letters, but the truth was precious to him, and he was not willing to give it up.

When we met in April 1984, the life experience of João, his faithfulness to the Lord in the face of trials, and his noble character won my heart. On June 9, 1985, three years to the day after my capture in Angola, we were joined in marriage, promising to be faithful to each other and to serve the Lord together as long as we lived.

In October 1988, we, along with Jessica, our two-year-old daughter, went as missionaries to Senegal in the Niaguis Mission and served there for five years. Our sons Gabriel and Joel were born in Senegal.

During those years, we often spoke about Angola and the experiences I had lived through there. As time went on, I began to lose contact with my friends in Angola, but I could never forget them. Sometimes, when we would go to Portugal, we would meet brothers and sisters from Angola, and I would bombard them with questions, eager to hear any news of the people I knew and the mission I loved.

During our five years in Senegal, we came to love the people of that country and to identify fully with them. We dressed like them, and I carried my children on my back, African style. But when school age came for our children, we needed a place for them to receive a formal education.

In 1995, after spending a year in England, we returned to Argentina and, in an act of faith, pioneered a ministry for the street children in the city of San Carlos de Bariloche. God blessed our work, and in August 1995, we opened the Centro Esperanza (Hope Center) on the outskirts of the city. With far more faith than resources and through more than a few trials, we carried on this work for sixteen wonderful years. The Centro Esperanza became a place of refuge and hope for hundreds of children who entered its doors. The gospel of love in Jesus changed their hearts, transforming their lives and their behavior forever. We loved those children with all our hearts.

Despite how rewarding our work on behalf of the children was, I could never forget Africa. I always wondered whether it would ever be possible to go back to the beloved continent. Our children were growing up and leaving home to study in Adventist institutions. Finally, the day came when the nest was empty, and João and I began to think about the possibility of returning to the mission field. The Centro Esperanza was such an integral part of our lives that I couldn't get up the courage to leave. However, the stress of maintaining the institution in difficult times was undermining my health. I needed to replace those activities with something less demanding.

By 2008, I felt physically and psychologically drained. It was evident that I could not go on much longer managing the institution. I had to make a decision. With the help of our donors, we traveled to Europe for a month's vacation, followed by a month spent visiting all our donors, giving them reports of what was happening at the Centro Esperanza. Upon our return, we decided to restructure the institution so that we would be able to leave by the end of 2011. We began praying daily for a person who could assume the responsibility of directing the center.

Sadly, our donors weren't willing to wait for God to bring the right person. They thought they knew better, and made a decision that brought fear to my heart. In December 2010, with deep sorrow, I turned over the leadership to the person they had chosen, knowing it would be the end of the beloved institution. And, in fact, within three years, to the dismay of the community, the Centro Esperanza closed its doors. The property was sold, and nothing remains but a memory of the work that had been done there on behalf of so many children. I wept bitterly, but there was no turning back. God was calling us to use the experience we had gained there for the benefit of His cause in a place far from there.

After we left the Centro Esperanza, we began to receive mail from different places inviting us to join in ministry at other institutions similar to ours, but we wanted to go back to the mission field and, if possible, to Africa. We had a number of options, but João knew where my heart was, and he said to me, "All your life you have wanted to go back to Angola. Now is your chance; why don't we try it?"

Angola! Why not? After so many years, we had lost contact with all the people we knew in that country. We only knew that the war had ended in 2001 with the death of General Savimbi and that the mission was abandoned and in ruins. With a good deal of doubt and hesitation, I began using both phone and computer and spent a week contacting various mission fields: Switzerland, Zimbabwe, South Africa, and others. Finally, I made a most providential call.

My call went through, and a feminine voice answered.

"This is Victoria Duarte," I said. "With whom am I speaking?"

At that, the voice on the other end of the line exclaimed, "Victoria! Just yesterday, we were talking about you!"

"Who is speaking?" I repeated.

"This is Ivonne, the youngest sister of Isaura," she answered. Isaura had been one of my students in the nursing course at Bongo. I was overcome with emotion. At the time of our sudden departure twenty-nine years before, Ivonne was a child of eleven or twelve. We spoke for a few minutes, and to my surprise, she still remembered the Bible text I used on the first Sabbath talk I gave after arriving in Angola.

I briefly explained that we were willing to come back if there was a place for us. Ivonne transferred the call to the Angola Union offices in Huambo, about forty-five miles from the Bongo site. The president of the Angola Union was pastor Teodoro Elías, a friend from our time at Collonges.

"Yes, we want to rebuild Bongo!" he exclaimed.

"And we want to be there!" I responded.

Things happened quickly after that. Five months later, on June 20, 2011, we arrived in Angola.

Two days later, Pastor Elías took us to Bongo. We got out of his vehicle, and there we stood. There before us were the ruins of what had once been the Bongo Adventist Hospital. Everything was destroyed. Bushes and weeds grew out through the doors and windows. Goats jumped around in what had been the hallways of the hospital. With intense emotion, I stared at the ruined rooms, remembering scenes that we had lived through there. It seemed incredible.

During the first years after our kidnapping, I had a recurring nightmare. In my dream, I would go back to Bongo and look for my house. I would see it with the door ajar. I would push it open and go in, and there I would see the dressers open, the bookshelves falling apart, and my books and papers scattered across the floor.

Now, standing next to Pastor Elías, I looked at the row of small buildings in front of the hospital and asked him, "Which one was my house?"

"That one." He pointed. A wave of emotion swept over me. The door was ajar. I pushed it open and went in, and there was the whole scene before my eyes: the dressers standing open, the ruined bookcases and the old books and papers scattered on the floor, just as I had seen them so many times in my nightmare.

The joys, the emotions of my return, and all that happened afterward would require another book. Suffice it to say that our first Sabbath in the Huambo central church was especially difficult. I hadn't foreseen the flood of emotions that would pour into my heart. The members invited me to go to the front and give a brief testimony. I looked at their faces. Here and there, I recognized friends from my youth. Seeing them unleashed a flood of tears that I had been holding back for all those years. I have no idea how I finished my short speech. I sat down beside my husband, overcome with such strong feelings that my throat was closed. I wept uncontrollably. My chest was aching, and my eyes were burning. All the people around us were weeping, too, as the pastor attempted in vain to keep the people's attention on his sermon.

As if it had been planned, the closing hymn was, "He Hideth My Soul":

He hideth my soul in the cleft of the rock,
That shadows a dry, thirsty land;
He hideth my life in the depths of His love,
And covers me there with His hand.[1]

After the service, many old friends came over to speak with me. I was surprised that so many were still alive. Again and again, they told me how much my presence meant to them. It was as if they could see I had forgiven Angola for what had happened, and it gave them courage.

The responsibility for rebuilding the hospital now rested on our shoulders. For that task, we looked upward to the place from whence our help had always come. Certainly, the One who had upheld and sustained us as we were sowing with tears would now allow us to rejoice as we worked to gather in the precious harvest.

---

1. Fanny J. Crosby, "He Hideth My Soul," (1890).

▲ We carried all of our earthly possessions across many rivers.

◄ Baby Ferrán spent most of the journey in his basket—his travel accommodations for hundreds of miles.

▼ Our guides, carriers, and armed captors proudly displayed their weapons.